A History of

LUTON

from
Conquerors to Carnival

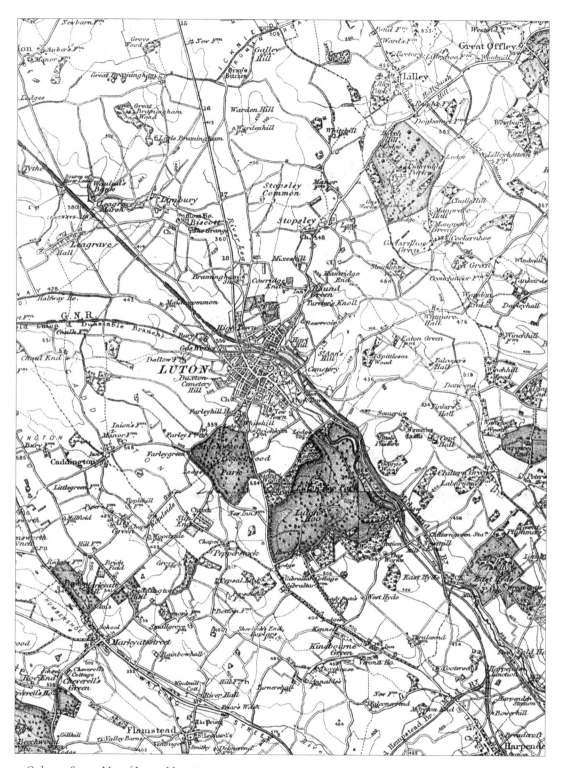

Ordnance Survey Map of Luton, May 1891.

A History of

LUTON

from
Conquerors to Carnival

Anne Allsopp

PHILLIMORE

First published 2010 by Phillimore & Co. Ltd
This revised and updated edition 2018
Reprinted 2019

The History Press
97 St George's Place,
Cheltenham, Gloucestershire, GL50 3QB
www.thehistorypress.co.uk

British Library Cataloguing in Publication Data.
A catalogue record for this book is available from the British
Library.

ISBN 978-0-7509-8598-7

Printed and bound by TJ International Ltd,
Padstow, Cornwall

For my parents

who, very wisely, came to live in Luton

Contents

About the Author

Anne Allsopp was born in Luton and attended Luton High School for Girls. She taught in local schools before gaining an MA and PhD at the London Institute of Education. She published a book on Luton High School and the Technical School to celebrate what would have been the centenary of selective education, and another on the education and employment of girls in the town. Her particular interest is the lives of ordinary people, and her latest research has helped her appreciate Luton's unique character and reputation for being quite unlike anywhere else.

List of Illustrations

Frontispiece: Ordnance Survey Map of Luton, 1891

Illustration Acknowledgements

I would like to offer my sincere thanks to the people who provided pictures for this book.

David Ainsbury, who accessed pictures from the *Luton News* archive.

Barbara Benson for the use of her personal photographs.

The late Roy Bushby, freelance photographer, for his excellent service.

Charlotte Phillips for allowing me to use a picture from the Wernher collection.

Dr James Dyer for many photographs as well as original drawings.

Chris Grabham, photographic officer at Wardown Park Museum, for his meticulous care.

Geoff Cox and the *Luton News* for permission to use photographs from their archive.

Dien Luu at Wardown Park Museum, who is the co-ordinator of the Voices project, and
Nicolas Holzapfel, who designed their logo.

Paul Newman and Owen Allsopp for giving their time to put photographs onto discs.

Mary Rolls for the photograph from her family archive.

Mark Turner for allowing me to use some of his card collection.

Dr Trevor Tween, who sent photographs of the environment.

Michael Wing for the photographs of his family hat factory.

Anthony Woodhouse for his original drawings.

Philip Wright for pictures of hats produced by his company.

Dr Anne Allsopp, 7, 94-6; Barbara Benson, 35, 44, 108-9; Roy Bushby, 70, 73-4; Dr James Dyer, frontispiece, 2, 3, 4, 13, 31-2, 42, 69, 76-7, 79, 80, 99, 117-19, 121-2; James Dyer/ Anderson, 25; James Dyer/Alan Hutchinson, 38; James Dyer/A.C. Jordan, 9, 39, 84, 103, 107, 114; James Dyer/Kurt Lang, 1; James Dyer/*Luton News*, 59, 111; James Dyer/Eric Meadows, 28; Nicholas Holzapfell/Luton Museum *Voices* Project, 71; Luton Museum, 14, 15, 17, 20, 26, 45-6, 48, 58; Luton Museum/A.E. Cox/*Luton News*, 61; Luton Museum/*Luton News*, 41, 47, 57, 62-6, 68, 75, 78, 97, 100-2, 104, 120; *Luton News*, 112, 115; Charlotte Phillips/ Wernher Collection, 40; Mary Rolls, 34; Mark Turner, 21, 24, 27, 33, 37, 49, 60, 98, 81, 110; Mark Turner/A.E. Cox, 19, 22, 30, 43, 82-3, 86, 106, 113; Dr Trevor Tween, 5, 6, 10, 67, 72, 85, 87-92; Michael Wing, 50-4; Anthony Woodhouse, 8, 11-12; Philip Wright, 55-6; 1902 *Yearbook*, 23.

Money and Measurements

One hide = about 120 acres

One acre = 0.404 hectares

One hectare = 2.471 acres

One mile = 1.609 kilometres

One pre-decimal pound = 240 pence (240d.) or 20 shillings (20s.)

One pre-decimal shilling = 12 pence (12d.)

One guinea = £1 1s.

Acknowledgements

I AM COMPLETELY and absolutely indebted to the many researchers who have written about the history of Luton and whose work is listed in the bibliography. In one sense, history does not change but, as new information comes to light, perspectives and interpretations can change. Now is a good time to produce another history of Luton since the town has changed to a very great degree over the last 50 years. Some of the research is based on oral evidence and I am also very grateful to the many people who have willingly given their time when I continued to ask so many questions. I would like them to know that I appreciate their patience, although I have to say that this is what I have come to expect from a friendly town like Luton. Some with specialist knowledge have contributed to the text and their work is suitably acknowledged as it appears.

Dr Elizabeth Adey, curator of Local History, Art and Archives at Wardown Park Museum, has, as ever, been very helpful and supportive. Dr James Dyer is an archaeologist and was one of the authors of *The Story of Luton*. He has been the main contributor to the chapter on the early history of Luton and I could not have written it without his help. Both Dr Adey and Dr Dyer have a bottomless pit of knowledge about Luton. They have also very kindly read my chapters and offered comments. This book owes them both a very great debt of gratitude. I must also thank Dien Luu, from Wardown Park Museum, who has worked so hard on the Voices project, and all the people who contributed to her exhibition and oral archive, which was supported by the Heritage Lottery Fund.

Michael Freedland kindly wrote the Preface and I thank him for his sincere interest.

Some of this research, for example the history of education in the town, has already been published in my book, *The Education and Employment of Girls in Luton 1874-1924*, and, as the copyright for this is shared by the Bedfordshire Historical Record Society, I would like to thank the Society for agreeing to its use.

Staff at the Bedfordshire and Luton Archives and Records Service (BARS) have been consistently helpful to me over the years, as have Mark Stubbs and the staff at Luton Central Library and Alan Bullimore, librarian at the University of Bedfordshire.

Dr Trevor Tween, Environment Manager at Luton Borough Council, spent time discussing the environmental aspect. He also supplied material which is included in the chapter on leisure.

Charlotte Phillips, who is the co-ordinator of the Luton Hoo Walled Garden project, has been very supportive, as have Millie Cooksley, who showed me around the garden, and Zena Dickinson, who gave me a tour of the Luton Hoo Mansion, now an *Elite Hotel*.

I would like to thank Peter Adams and members of Luton Council of Faiths and the Grassroots project as well as the members of the multi-faith community in the town: Gulie Butcher, a member of the Society of Friends; Barbara Felson and Michael Freedland for information about the Jewish community; Dr Fiaz Hussain, chairman of the Council of Mosques; Makham Singh Puar from the Sikh Temple; Syed Rizvi, who talked to me about the growth of Islam in the town; Mary Salvage from the Catholic Church; and Natubhai Solanki for information about the Hindu community and for taking me to meetings of the Council of Faiths.

Thanks are also due to: Barbara Benson for her memories and photographs; Joyce Browne for her memories of the war; Catherine Darlington for details about the Scottish community; Dr Betty Chambers for reading the chapter on education; the UK Centre for Carnival Arts; Dr Margaret Currie, health historian, who allowed me to use her personal archive; Robert Gurney for his poem; Bob Norman for his colourful description of Waller Street and Terry Sell, who is also a mine of information about the area; Mark Turner for his postcards and also his knowledge of the airport and of Luton Town Football Club; Michael Wing and Philip Wright for information and photographs on the hat industry.

There are also official websites that were not available to earlier researchers and a glance at the bibliography will show that local history owes a debt to Paul Bowes at the Book Castle in Dunstable, who has published so many books on Luton in recent years.

Unfortunately, different documents sometimes give contradictory information, for example, differing dates, and I have dealt with each of these situations as I thought best. Thanks are due to everyone who has helped me but, as always, any mistakes are mine.

Preface

Like Elizabeth I and Calais, the name Luton is engraved on my heart.

OK, it's corny and if anyone else said it, I'd probably look for a sick bag, but, quite frankly, it's true.

I think of the place practically every day. Not always affectionately, I have to admit. But now, almost sixty years after leaving the place, I think of it when I think of school, when I remember my first job, when I, often weekly, gather with my closest and dearest friends – all of whom I met in a youth club, in Luton.

It's the town where I spent my formative years, where I learnt about the importance of personal history, just about found out how to add two and two – and where I had my first kiss. You don't forget that sort of thing.

Memories are the part of life that helps make you. I will never forget my first view of Luton as a five-year-old – it was the sign painted in huge letters on the railway bridge in Old Bedford Road, proclaiming 'Thursday Is News Day'. (It took a few years before I realised how relevant that would become in my life.) I can remember that day seeing the conductress in a terrible hat on one of those uncomfortable, browny-red single-deck buses; could she really be doing the same job as the cockney girls on the number 73 London Transport bus at home in Stoke Newington?

I recall Mrs Furlong. She was an elderly lady who saw my parents looking bewilderingly around and plainly needing help. My mum told her we were looking for temporary accommodation. 'Come to my house in High Town,' she said. 'I couldn't let you go back to all that bombing.' She realised without being told that we were refugees escaping from the London Blitz. What a lovely woman she must have been. I am not sure how long we stayed with her, but my parents remembered Mrs Furlong affectionately for the rest of their lives. Now, I wish I had had a chance to say thank you to her myself.

It was at Denbigh Road School that I made my first friends and where I actually learnt facts I have not forgotten even now. Sometimes, I think I picked up more there in a class of fifty-six (yes, fifty-six of us, miraculously kept in order by Mrs Holmes; to say nothing of the headmistress, Mrs Brooks) than I learnt at the Grammar School, which I joined later on, with great pride, care of the 11-plus.

It was from there that my education really began – as a junior reporter on *The Luton News*. I stayed there for nine years in what I later described as a lovely, comfortable rut. I now appreciate how great it was and how wrong I was to call it a rut. Fleet Street, as it then was called, was calling. But the '*LN*' was an education right from my first day. Believe it or not, my mother took me to my job interview with John Sargeant, the editor-in-chief. I should have thought that would have put him off for life, but he, aided by the chief reporter, the kind, brilliant George Smallman, supervised that vital time in what others have called – note, I hate clichés – this university of life. I not only learned the elements of journalism – like, you have to accept this, the sanctity of accuracy – but how to make contacts/friends among people as different as were the various destinations to which I took the bus for stories in Luton (submitting the tickets for expenses).

I can remember the general election when Luton elected its first Labour MP, William Warbey, and later, the inimitable (actually, he was highly imitable) Charlse Hill – the former Radio Doctor who later became head of the BBC, and who gave all us reporters a bottle of whisky at Christmas. We didn't think it was (or, at least, we never admitted it) a form of corruption. We got our stories. As I did from my friend Bill Gowland, the Methodist minister, who came to Luton from Manchester to run a church and industrial mission which he said was 'for people who sweat and swear'.

I am not sure the Reverend Harry Ritvo would have said that about the Luton Synagogue, first in Moor Path and then in Bury Park. Harry was one of my great influences. He died a young man, but spent twenty-nine years in the town, providing Judaism to his followers, most of whom, like my own family, had come from London and needed familiar surroundings in which to say familiar prayers. The stalls in Luton's old indoor market were seemingly almost entirely populated by members of his congregation. He not only helped fellow Jews, but became a fixture in Luton and was responsible for the almost perfect relations between his comparatively tiny flock and the much larger population around.

Maybe that was the secret of the Luton I experienced. Good relations. I like to recall those days every time I pick up a newspaper that describes a very few people who don't seem to have that aim in life. Lutonians, on the whole, always did.

Michael Freedland

Introduction

IT WAS DURING the Depression and there was mass unemployment. A job was advertised in a newspaper for workers at the Vauxhall plant in Luton and Gladys suggested to Charles that he try for it. She gave him money for the early train (which was cheaper back in those days) and packed him a sandwich. He came home at the end of the day, dejected and saddened. He was turned away along with hundreds of others. Gladys asked, 'Exactly what did they say?' He replied that a man came out waving his arms and said to the crowd, 'No more today, no more today.' 'What about tomorrow? Go again early tomorrow.' She gave him some more money for the train fare, another sandwich and her best wishes. He came home jubilant! He had a job at the Vauxhall plant and he could start right away. So Charles moved up from London to Luton to work and stayed with Vauxhall until his retirement in 1967.

Charles was my father and I suppose I owe it to Auntie Gladys that I was born in Luton. My story could be recounted by hundreds of people who came to live here over the years. We may not have roots going back for centuries but we are Lutonians nevertheless and proud to be so. My father grew up in an orphanage in Dover, having been orphaned in 1902, at the age of three weeks, when his father died 'leaving six little children all unprovided for' as a local church magazine described their situation. In comparison, my childhood was so much happier; we were not rich but we always had enough. As children we had the freedom to roam in beautiful countryside around the town and wander over the chalk hills. The river Lea was our river; we fished for frogspawn and sticklebacks, water boatmen and whirligig beetles. How I resented it when 'my' river was built over.

Other books have been written about Luton and several collections of photographs have been published. Many of these books are much more detailed than this one and they are highly recommended. However, the aim of this book is to give an overall feeling of what life in Luton may have been like over the centuries. The first chapters cover its development from a small settlement beside the river Lea to a sizeable market town. The later chapters cover a shorter timespan and it would be too confusing to continue with a chronological approach for these years. Instead there are themes such as education, industry, leisure, local government, migration, transport and the war years. I am thankful for what Luton has given me so I hope you will enjoy the account of this down-to-earth and hard-working town.

I

A Settlement on the River Lea

The archaeological information in this chapter was provided by Dr James Dyer.

Luton owes its very existence to the river Lea. This may come as a surprise to anyone who looks at the tiny little stream that flows through the town now and, in fact, many people are even astonished to learn that Luton has a river, as much of it is channelled under roads and buildings and only re-emerges on the southern side of the Parish Church. But, in the past, it was all very different.

The geological history of Luton began when the underlying Jurassic landscape was flooded by the sea. Over millions of years, the seas became much larger and deeper and chalk was deposited to a thickness of several hundred metres. Generations of Luton children have tapped this abundant supply of chalk to write on pavements or to draw cricket stumps on walls without realising how many thousands of years of history they were holding in their hands.

Chalk is formed mainly from fossilised coccoliths, the shells of dead single-cell plants that lived in the sea in the Upper Cretaceous Period. When the coccoliths died, the shells, which were rich in calcium, sank to the seafloor and compacted to form chalk. These chalk deposits were called the Lower, Middle and Upper Chalk. Below the Lower Chalk was a band of harder chalk known as Totternhoe Stone. Some of this stone was used in the building of many churches in the area, including Luton's Parish Church.

Within the upper deposits of chalk, silica formed into bands of flint. Here again, inhabitants of the area around Luton have, over many thousands of years, used fragments found lying on the surface or dug from the ground to shape tools and weapons for hunting, for making fire, for building and, in medieval times, for decorative work known as flushwork.

Long after the chalk was laid down, there was a series of Ice Ages, known as glaciations, that sometimes reached as far as the south of England. During these periods the land was partially covered by massive sheets of moving ice which flowed out from the ice-sheet to carve deep, wide, U-shaped valleys. When the ice retreated, dry valleys with steep sides and flat bottoms were left behind. We can see such valleys today at nearby Barton Springs and at Pegsdon. From high ground, say at the top of Stockingstone Road, the shape of a wide valley can be made out, bordered by Blow's and Dallow Downs and Warden and Hart Hills. The river Lea flowed through this valley when the last Ice Age ended about ten thousand years ago. In the area of Luton Hoo the valley is around a mile wide and 197 feet deep.

THE STONE AGES

Glaciers pick up all kinds of material from the ground over which they move. This material is then redeposited. The debris is called glacial drift and large rocks that have been brought far from their places of origin are known as erratics. A ridge of glacial gravel, known as a moraine, ran from Warden Hill through Bramingham to Leagrave. Water-borne, glacial and wind-blown deposits accumulated in the Lea valley and on the surrounding hills. Some of this material became the brickearth (clay) that was dug out in the late 19th and early 20th centuries (until 1939) for the local brick making industry. These areas of clay have produced an abundance of artefacts that have given us information about the people who lived in the Luton area. Archaeologists have searched spasmodically for what has been buried in the clay pits at Caddington, Round Green, Ramridge End and Mixes Hill and some of their finds are on display at the Stockwood Discovery Centre. Known as Palaeolithic (or Old Stone Age) people, they may have lived near the marshy ponds or dolines where they hunted deer and maybe

1   *Chalk Escarpment south of Barton-le-Clay, looking south, 1972. This shows the Lower Chalk Escarpment, with the springs emerging at the junction with the gault clay. The Icknield Way ran from left to right (or vice versa) across the middle distance.*

an occasional elephant or rhinoceros and also gathered wild plants, berries and roots. Deep down under the brickearth, hundreds of flint tools known as handaxes, once used by these Palaeolithic people, have been found.

Much later, after the retreat of the glaciers, the climate improved and birch and pinewoods grew, followed by forests of oak, elm and lime. Accumulations of small microlithic flint tools found on the land surface suggest that Mesolithic people may have come to live in natural clearings at various spots and at different seasons, beside the river Lea and its marshes, and also along the hilltops around Blow's Down, Leagrave and Stopsley. There they fished and hunted wild fowl, cattle, boar and deer, collected the eggs of water birds and harvested berries and fungi.

Around 5,500 years ago, Neolithic people who had learnt to cultivate cereal crops and herd domesticated animals for meat and milk arrived in Britain. They settled on open downland, in woodland clearings and by the water meadows. Forest clearances provided timber for building and fuel, and local flint and clay were used for tool and pottery making. In this area, although small farmsteads probably existed, only stone tools and weapons have been found.

About 3000 B.C., Neolithic folk decided to settle beside the springs of the river Lea; the site they chose is near the modern Sundon Park Recreation Ground. It is known today as Waulud's Bank and forms a D-shaped enclosure, about seven hectares in extent, with its curving sides running down from the crest of the moraine to the Lea marshes on the west below. Excavations in 1954 and 1972 showed that a massive bank of gravel, clay and turfs, faced with stout wooden posts, was constructed. The material was obtained from an external ditch, 8 feet 2 inches deep and 16 feet 4 inches wide.

It was clearly built to impress travellers as they passed along the Icknield Way but its purpose remains uncertain. The excavator, James Dyer, sees it as a domestic enclosure, but others have suggested that it may have belonged to a class of public monuments known as henges, which were frequently constructed close to a river and used

2   *Source of the river Lea at Waulud's Bank, Leagrave, 1970.*

3 *Hypothetical construction of the Neolithic settlement at Waulud's Bank, Leagrave.*

for ceremonial purposes, such as feasting, ritual observances and tribal gatherings. As of now, the interior of Waulud's Bank has not been excavated and a recent geophysical survey (2009) has done little to clarify the mystery.

Excavations at the summit of Galley Hill have found the mutilated remains of two young Neolithic men and there is evidence for the existence of long burial mounds (barrows), now destroyed, at the foot of Galley Hill, beside the Icknield Way and at Biscot Mill. The Icknield Way was an ancient track which was in use in Neolithic times. It was probably a wide stretch of open ground rather than a recognised roadway, which travellers could use as and when the vegetation and weather conditions allowed. It connected the east coast (and Europe) to southern central Britain, passing through Leagrave where it crossed the river Lea and following the low ridge of gravel, the glacial moraine, that stretches roughly south-west to north-east across the northern end of the Luton gap between Leagrave and Warden Hill. It is followed today by Bramingham Road and is cut through by Marsh Road opposite the Territorial Army Headquarters.

Over thousands of years, the Icknield Way became an important trackway, constantly in use by traders who moved across the country between the continent, East Anglia and the south of England. The word 'Icknield', derived from the name of the Iron-Age Iceni tribe, is still preserved in the names of modern roads and schools.

THE METAL AGES

After 2000 B.C. metal became widely used and we pass into what is known as the Bronze Age. Tools and weapons from this time have been found in the upper Lea valley but the precise locations of any settlements in our area have not been found. However, we can be sure that mixed farming was practised, with the growing of cereal crops and the rearing of cattle, pigs and sheep. Farmsteads were usually built in sight of ancestral graves or barrows, examples of which have been found between Galley Hill and Lilley Hoo and on the Dunstable Downs.

By the Iron Age, from about 700 B.C., there was much more activity in the area. At intervals along the Icknield Way, formidable boundary dykes acted like toll-gates and separated the countryside into individual territories. At Dray's Ditches, on the northern edge of Luton, dykes were constructed with three deep V-shaped ditches, separated from each other by massive wooden stockades backed with turf and chalk. Each territory was between 2.2 and 3.4 miles wide, and was apparently controlled from a hillfort (perhaps Ravensburgh Castle or Sharpenhoe Clapper) which may have dominated our area. In spite of their names and prestigious defensive appearance these 'forts' were more likely to have been 'townships' or trading centres, with the added capability of protecting the local population if the need arose.

There were many Iron-Age farmsteads on the hills throughout our area, and it is possible that grain or animals were taken to the 'forts' for marketing, storage and redistribution. One farmstead was excavated by Albion Archaeology beneath the University of Bedfordshire

4 *The Iron-Age farmstead of Butterfield, Stopsley, might have looked something like this.*

building at Butterfield, Stopsley, in 2005 and consisted of two circular wooden huts, one 39 feet in diameter, set in a farmyard with watering holes for livestock, and fences, hedges and droveways to keep the farm animals and children in and wild animals out. Numerous fields and paddocks would have stretched towards Bradgers Hill and Lilley, and clearings in the woodland provided pannage for pigs. A more extensive farmstead was excavated at Puddlehill, north of Dunstable, in the 1950s.

During the digging of a quarry on Blow's Down in the 19th century, Worthington Smith found evidence for a group of about two dozen Iron-Age huts overlooking the Icknield Way. Their owners probably grazed their sheep on the adjacent downland. At Leagrave, near Willow Way, huts were built on a clay-covered wooden platform beside the river Lea, high enough to keep them out of the water at times of flood. From there folk could have fished and fowled, and perhaps paddled small canoes downstream for trading purposes.

Today, in the 21st century, we tend to think of Luton's trade and transport links running north-south towards the Midlands and London but, in the early Iron Age, London and the Midland cities did not exist. The movement of people and trade were with southern Britain and the European continent, and were conducted along the edge of the Chilterns, largely along the Icknield Way. A second route ran into central Britain via the Thoidweg or Ede Way, which branched off from the Icknield Way at the foot of Galley Hill and headed through Chalton and Chalgrave towards Oxford and beyond. Initially the first 'Luton' settlements looked east and west for trade; only in the later Iron Age did they begin to turn towards the south and the St Albans area.

As well as the farmsteads and riverside dwellings at Leagrave, there would have been a good deal of movement along the Icknield Way to 'forts' at Maiden Bower (Dunstable) and Ivinghoe Beacon, to Sharpenhoe Clapper, the local territorial capital of Ravensburgh, and further east to Baldock, where there seems to have been a late Iron-Age township (*oppidum*), the regional commercial centre. During the late Iron-Age and early Roman periods, pilgrims would have made visits to a probable cult centre on Pegsdon Common. There, over many years, rich offerings to a water-god have been found near a spring, consisting of gold coins, a bronze mirror, fine-quality imported pottery and a number of cremation burials.

The Romans

By the first century B.C., different tribes had emerged in Britain and the people that lived in the Luton area were called the Catuvellauni. There was plenty to occupy the minds of these people: there was the work of everyday living, growing crops and caring for domestic animals, metal working, potting and weaving but also they had to be constantly on their guard as inter-tribal relationships were not always friendly. Hillforts had to be kept ready so that whole communities could retreat to these places of safety when other tribes became hostile.

Another threat was about to come this way in the form of an army from across the sea. This was a very different kind of challenge, for these soldiers were Romans, very disciplined and organised, and commanded by their famous leader, Julius Caesar. These incursions, in 55 and 54 B.C., were actually reconnaissance visits during which Caesar was gathering information about this island, so very far from Rome. He recorded his findings so we know that, on his second visit to the British Isles in 54 B.C., he attacked the stronghold of Cassivellaunus, leader of the Catuvellauni. This may have been at the place we now know as Ravensburgh Castle, near Hexton, although other possible sites included Colchester or Wheathamstead. If it was Ravensburgh, then it is just possible that Caesar and his men came to the area via the river Lea and the Icknield Way. With a bit of imagination we can picture the colourful Roman legion marching along the wooded river valley that is now Luton.

After Caesar left, the Catuvellauni established a new tribal capital at St Albans under the leadership of Tasciovanus, where from 10 B.C. he was minting his own coins, some of which have been found in the Luton area. It was a good time for the more enterprising native farmers to deal with Roman entrepreneurs and exchange their cattle, dogs, furs and grain in return for fine metalwork, pottery and glassware, wine and olive oil. The more prosperous native farmers and merchants soon flaunted their wealth by rejecting their circular wooden huts in favour of Roman-style houses built in brick and stone.

The Roman army did not return until A.D. 43, but this time they meant business. They were strong and organised, well armed and much to be feared. They taxed the local population and it would have been a foolish person who dared to challenge the power of Rome. Although they dominated the area, there was a positive side to their occupation for they also established a stable and relatively peaceful way of life and it has been said that, under the Romans, the British people enjoyed a more settled and secure life than they were to experience for centuries to come. The Romans believed in a civilised life with a centralised government and an organised lifestyle. The administrative centre for the Luton area would have been at St Albans (*Verulamium*), 12 miles to the south.

They built towns and villas (usually farming estates) and introduced Roman ways. One 'luxury' to be found in the villas was under-floor heating, something which was forgotten when the Romans left our shores and not revived until the 20th century. So far, there is no real evidence for any villa in the Luton area, the nearest known being at Totternhoe and Hitchin. Rather, the people of Luton lived in farmsteads, and artefacts discovered indicate that they were living in the Gooseberry Hill and Round Green areas. Traces of Roman buildings close to St Mary's Church beneath the Arndale Centre (now known as the Mall) were destroyed without record in the late 1970s.

The Romans were famous for their roads that were necessary for maintaining order and for trade. One major road, known as the Watling Street, went from London to Chester, taking a similar route to the modern A5. It passed through Verulamium and Dunstable (*Durocobrivis*), where it crossed the Icknield Way. Although the road did not touch Luton, local people no doubt used it since it was probably regarded as the M1 of the day. However, a lesser Roman road did come our way. It branched off the Watling Street near Flamstead and ran north through the Farley Hill estate and Biscot to Rosslyn Crescent. From there it continued to the Runfold estate, where burnt remains of wooden buildings of the second to fourth centuries A.D. were

6 *Round barrows at moonrise.*

excavated in the 1950s, and then to Streatley, Sharpenhoe and Greenfield and beyond.

In order to pay the Roman taxes in coinage, the population had to learn to trade. Wine and oil were carried in jars called *amphorae* and transported across the Roman Empire. Glass beads were bought and sold. Other commodities traded were: cattle, corn, fish sauces, gold, hides, hunting dogs, iron, silver and slaves. In the Stockwood Discovery Centre in Luton, there are artefacts that demonstrate the kind of buying and selling that went on. Pottery was always in demand and some pieces have been found along the banks of the river Lea between Stockingstone Road and Barnfield College. Roman pottery was made in a kiln and was of a higher standard than that which had been made in the Iron Age. Wares from Gaul have been discovered at Limbury and metal tableware has also been found.

Exhibits at Stockwood also demonstrate what daily life in Roman Luton was like. Writing implements were found at Limbury and there are weights and a door key on display. An interesting story involves the discovery of a pot containing several hundred coins, hastily buried at a time of unrest around A.D. 270, which was found near Luton Hoo. Unfortunately most of these coins were taken by the men who found them, but the offence was discovered and some of the coins traced.

The settled Roman way of life began to be endangered by barbarians from the north and, in A.D. 410, when the threat became too great, the Roman army was ordered to return home.

This they did although, by that time, the ordinary population had in many cases intermarried and the British and Roman identities were by no means so separate or distinct.

Small bands of barbarians had been sacking towns and villages in eastern England for the previous 50 years. An excavation at Galley Hill in 1961 revealed that a massacre had taken place; this suggests that Luton folk also became victims of the marauding tribesmen. The excavation revealed that, soon after A.D. 360, a number of men, women and children were killed and their remains hurriedly buried at the top of Galley Hill. Also, on the Runfold settlement, there is evidence of burning that suggests people there may have been victims. As the Roman legions marched away, life in the Luton area was about to change yet again.

SAXONS

Following the Roman occupation, life became more unsettled as small tribal groups vied with one another for control but, towards the end of the fifth century, new incursions were being made into our land, this time by Teutonic peoples, Angles and Saxons, from across the North Sea. At first some of these were welcomed as allies against the troublesome barbarians but the Saxons did not see their presence as temporary. They stayed, and the Saxon way of life was to define our national identity for many hundreds of years to come, even, in many respects, until the present day.

The Romano-British eventually accepted their new neighbours from the east and, by A.D. 475, a group of Saxons from between the rivers Elbe and the Weser had settled in our area in the region of Alexandra Avenue. During the construction of Argyll Avenue in the 1920s, part of a large Saxon cemetery was found and the burials of more than 40 men and women were exposed. These were among the earliest Saxon burials found in Britain and dated from the early fifth to late sixth centuries. Other, seventh-century, burials at Biscot Mill may have been a later extension of the same cemetery. It is likely that these Anglo-Saxon 'Lutonians' had a settlement on the high ground between Biscot and Limbury, and farmed the land that sloped down to the Lea, and the hillside beyond, perhaps creating the first strip-fields or lynchets along the length of the hills from the People's Park to Bradgers Hill.

The *Anglo-Saxon Chronicle*, which was compiled during the reign of Alfred the Great (A.D. 871-900) refers to a battle fought between the native Britons and the West Saxons in A.D. 571 at a place called Biedcanforda (questionably Bedford), followed by the capture of four towns, one of which was Lygeanbrig, generally assumed to be Limbury. No traces of buildings have been found from this period, and with the area almost fully built up, it is unlikely that much ever will.

By the seventh century, the once-unified Roman way of life had disintegrated into separate tribal groupings that, in turn, became small kingdoms. People living in this area were called Chilternsoeten, but this little group was taken over by Mercia, an area that corresponds roughly to what is now the Midlands. South Bedfordshire (the first reference to Bedfordshire as a county was in 1012) remained under Mercian control for the next two centuries until Alfred the Great, as King of Wessex, unified the country.

However, there was not to be peace: another threat came from the east when the warlike Vikings (Danes and Norsemen) came over the seas in their longships. After considerable harassment and skirmishing between the Saxons and the Vikings, Alfred made a pact with them (c.A.D. 878). Under the terms of the treaty, the country was divided into separate administrative areas, Wessex and the Danelaw. The boundary between the two ran from the river Thames, north along the line of the river Lea to its source and then in a straight line to Bedford.

This agreement was tremendously significant for Luton, which was virtually cut into two. A part of Limbury, Waulud's Bank, Biscot, Warden and Galley Hills, Ravensburgh Castle, Stopsley, half of what is now Luton and East Hyde went to the Danes and became a part of the Danelaw, while the west stayed under Saxon control. However, it is unlikely that there were any serious restrictions on movements at local level and the two sides continued to trade. Contact between the Saxons and Vikings remained sensitive and the power struggle continued. In 1014, the Danish took the upper hand when Canute became king but, in 1042, the Crown was restored to the Saxon Edward the Confessor.

Life in early Saxon times was predominantly agricultural and people lived within small settlements. By the seventh century the field or strip system was being established: fields were cultivated by rotation – grain for food, then barley for beer and, during the third year, the fields would lie fallow and provide grazing for domestic animals. Pigs would forage in the woods, which were also sources of the timber used for building, domestic utensils and firewood. Orchards and individual gardens were planted beside the small thatched homes. Evidence of Saxon agricultural life in Luton can still be seen in the lynchets, or stepped cultivation terraces, which run from Bradger's Hill to People's Park, and at Chaul End. By the late sixth century, there were probably Saxon settlements at Dallow, Leagrave and Limbury (Lygeanburgh). Later settlements followed the line of the river Lea (Lygea) from Leagrave to the Brache and, by the early 10th century, there was a settlement, Lygtun or Ligtun, near the present Park Square.

Roads continued to be important. Apart from the Icknield Way, there was the Pedlar's Way, which followed the route of the present Montrose Avenue from Biscot Mill, via Stockingstone Road and Round Green, to East Hyde. Salt was a vital commodity, carried by pack-horses in their panniers along the route of the old Salt or Ede Way, which ran from Gallows Hill and Dray's Ditches, via Bramingham, Limbury and Leagrave, eventually crossing the Watling Street, about three miles north of Dunstable. This road later linked the ancient universities of Oxford and Cambridge. There is little doubt that a road would have run north to Bedford.

No remains of Saxon houses have been found in Luton but a settlement just north of Dunstable, at Puddlehill, has been excavated by the Manshead Archaeological Society. They found that the Saxons dug down so that the floors of their huts were sunk below ground level and the accumulated chalk was used to build walls. Wooden posts supported the roofs, which were probably covered with turf.

Many items would have been traded with European markets and a considerable number of local Saxon artefacts can be seen today at Stockwood Discovery Centre. There are coins, drinking horns, imported glass, iron weapons and tools, toiletries, jewellery, weaving apparatus with linen and woollen textiles and wooden household goods.

William Austin in his *History of Luton and its Hamlets* has some interesting suggestions about how the Saxons might have spent their free time. For example, they played ball games, honed their hunting skills, enjoyed singing and went swimming and skating in season. Austin also notes that everyday Saxon measurements became a part of English life for generations. They were based on the size of the 'furrows', the allocations of land on which the strip system was based. A furrow was 22 yards wide, which was the length of a cricket pitch. Its length was 220 yards, a standard measurement in athletics before metrication took over.

The river Lea remained central to the life of Luton, one of its most important contributions being the amount of power it generated for the milling of grain. A thousand years ago the water table was higher than it is today and was not being tapped for industrial and domestic use. This would have resulted in a much stronger flow. Water mills came to Europe in the eighth century and, by Saxon times, Luton could boast seven. Six belonged to the King and the seventh to the Church. Owning a mill was an important source of income and mill owners sometimes used their position to hold the country folk to ransom. The first of these mills was near the source of the Lea. The second was close to the place where Neville Road now crosses the river. Mill Street still calls to mind the position of the third mill, North Mill, which was in use until 1859 when it was buried under the new railway embankment. Church Mill was situated to the east of St Mary's Church and the fifth, Brache Mill, was in the area of the present Osborne Road and was in working order until 1890. The sixth, Stapleford Mill, was near the lake at Luton Hoo. At Hyde, on the Bedfordshire/Hertfordshire border, there is still a mill on the site of the seventh Domesday mill.

Across the meadow from this mill, the river still flows and, since the existence of the Luton Hoo Estate has checked the amount of building in the area, there is still a peaceful feel to the area. Yes, the railway line is busy and there is traffic on the roads, but it is just possible to stand at this site and imagine what life beside the Lea would have been like in years gone by.

Luton became a significant Saxon town and by A.D. 975 had been claimed by King Edward the Martyr as a royal manor. Biscot, however, remained a separate hamlet until the 20th century. The church land there became the property of a monastery and, in A.D. 792, the land was given by King Offa of Mercia to the first Abbot of St Albans. A house was built on this land for the Bishop of Mercia, hence the name Bishopscote (Bishop's House) which still survives in the name of the present Bishopscote Road.

When the Romans came to Britain, they were believers in a multitude of gods who, it was thought, had responsibility for the different aspects of human life. However, early in the fourth century, Christianity became the official religion of Rome. When the Saxons first came, they were pagan in their beliefs but, after the arrival of St Augustine in A.D. 596, Christianity began to flourish here. In the following century, the Celtic Christian Church spread throughout the land and by the late seventh century Mercia had been converted to Christianity.

It is thought that the church in Luton was endowed by King Edward the Elder with property of five hides of land and consecrated by his son, Athelston, in A.D. 931. With one exception, this was the largest church endowment in England in Saxon times. The church

7   *The Mill at Hyde, built on the site of one of the Domesday mills.*

was probably built of stone but very little is known about it, although it is likely to have stood not far from the site of the present church. By the time of Edward the Confessor, the priest, Morcar, was the third most important man in Luton. He owned the church lands beside many hectares of woodland and the water-mill which was worth 10s. a year. He also owned land in other parts of the county. The church became the centre of the Saxon settlement of Luton. The surrounding hamlets of Biscot, the Hydes, Leagrave, Limbury and Stopsley originally developed without churches but, by 1933, they had been absorbed into the town.

Luton was now an important Saxon town, owned by the king. England itself was a nation of mixed ancestry, but the Saxons had established an identity that was to endure, for English culture is basically Saxon culture. The Saxons left us our administrative, legal and monetary systems and their language eventually evolved into English. After they were converted to Christianity, they built churches, many of which are still standing.

However, the population was uneasy for, at the time of the Saxon King Harold's coronation in 1066, Halley's comet had appeared. This was seen to be a portent of troubled times to come. And come they did, in the form of William the Norman, who came to claim his right to the English throne.

II

Medieval Luton

THE MIDDLE AGES, or medieval era, between the Norman Conquest and the 16th-century Reformation, were colourful years. King John sealed the famous Magna Carta on which most of our freedoms are based, knights in armour travelled through Europe on Crusades, the 'Hundred Years' War' with France was fought and, in a civil war known as the 'Wars of the Roses', rivals battled to see who had the right to wear the English Crown. Kings had to learn to share their power with a Parliament, English Common Law was established and the jury system instigated. Near to home, uncomfortably so, came the Black Death and the Peasants' Revolt. Then there were significant challenges to the authority of the Church. All these events affected the people of Luton to some extent.

THE NORMANS

William, known as the Conqueror, sailed to England from Normandy, defeated the Saxons at the Battle of Hastings and then set about subduing the country. The devastation he left in his wake was terrible but, as Luton was a royal town and already acknowledged to be the property of the king, it seems to have been spared the type of destruction experienced by most other parts of the country. Biscot, being a separate manor, was not so lucky. It is likely that William visited his Luton manor as he followed his army's march through Bedfordshire and it is intriguing to ponder the fact that this legendary warrior once set foot on local land. King William appointed his compatriot, Ralph Tallebosc (or Talibosc), as sheriff of the royal manor of Luton and, by 1086, Ralph had also claimed the manor of Biscot for Luton. Morcar, the priest, was made to relinquish his post in favour of William the Chamberlain, another Norman.

William wanted to know just how much he owned and what he was worth so, in 1086, he sent commissioners throughout the land to record absolutely everything they could find and all this information was double-checked for accuracy. Details were written in abbreviated Latin and the record is still preserved in our National Archives. The book is unique in historical terms, but it must be remembered that the information also gives us a picture of life as it was before William's invasion. It is an account of Saxon rather than Norman England.

William's men wanted to know how much land there was in every manor and we know from this that Luton, stretching from Streatley to East Hyde, was the largest manor in Bedfordshire. They checked on the number of animals, fisheries, meadows, mills, pasture and ploughs and made a population count of the different social classes. Biscot and Streatley were listed separately, as was the land in Luton which belonged to the Church. Caddington was never one of the Luton hamlets but it is interesting to note that the manor there belonged to the canons of St Paul's Cathedral.

In size Luton, called Loitone, covered 30 hides, which was enough land to keep 82 ploughs busy. Seventy-eight of these were for the village and four worked the king's land. Four plough teams were needed for the meadows and it was noted that the woodland could support 2,000 pigs. There were 80 villagers (villeins) and 47 smallholders (boarders or cottars), and 700 inhabitants all told. Also worth recording was that the village had an annual fair valued at 100 shillings, a weekly market, sheep for wool and eels in the river.

The value of the six working mills on the king's land was 100 shillings. Taxes were 'customary dues' (10s. 8d.) and from tolls and the market 100s. Also it was required that the King's household should be supplied with wheat and honey, enough for half a day. The Queen was to receive four ounces of gold, a packhorse, 70s. and 130s. for her dogs. The Sheriff also demanded taxes: seven pounds of money in weight, 40s. in white silver and one ounce of gold.

At the centre of the town stood the church which had been granted to William the Chamberlain. He held five hides of land which was enough for six ploughs, five for the village and one for the royal land. There were 11 villagers, four smallholders and six slaves. (Slaves were sometimes traded but it was also possible for anyone destitute to offer himself and his labour if there was no alternative.) The church owned woodland enough for 50 pigs, one mill with a value of 10s. and received 20s. a year in tax.

THE MANOR OF LUTON

During the Middle Ages, the people of Luton were living under the manorial system. A manor was an economic unit, an area of land belonging to a landlord who was himself directly or indirectly a tenant of the king. The class system was rigid: clergymen, knights, lords and ladies were very much the aristocracy of the time but the peasant classes had no rights or freedoms and were at the mercy of their lords and masters.

Life was very hard for the peasant classes but they had no legal right to leave the manor to look for a better life. The daughter of a serf or villein could not marry without a licence from the lord. Even in death the system took its toll, for when a peasant died taxes were due to the landlord and also to the church. It has been said that, for someone living in the Middle Ages, the two great certainties of life were, as ever, death and taxation.

8 *Burgess town house, c.1300. The house is timber-framed. The hall is at the front of the ground floor, solar at rear of first floor and there is a cellar. The kitchen is detached from the house because of fire risk. There are outhouses, for example brewhouse, dovecote and woodshed. The outside dirt toilet emptied onto the street.*

The manor of Luton changed hands several times during these years, either as a gift from the king or through inheritance, but by the end of the medieval period the manor had been divided into several smaller manors. The hamlets as we know them had become significant in their own right and smaller farming settlements were appearing. By end of the 15th century there were manor houses at Biscot, Cowridge, Crawley Green, Eaton Green, Farley, Havering, Hyde, Lammers, Leagrave, Limbury, Luton Hoo, Nether Crawley, Ramridge, Stopsley and Whipperley.

At the beginning of the Middle Ages the manor of Luton was owned directly by the Crown. Around 1120, Henry I gave it to his illegitimate son, Robert, Earl of Gloucester. Robert is said to have been of noble character; he was generous and wise and possessed great military skill. One of the first things he did was to set up a new church on or near the site of the existing church. This church, now the Parish Church of St Mary, became the focus of Christian life in Luton.

When Henry I died in 1135 it was expected that his daughter, Matilda, would succeed him but Stephen, Henry's nephew, took the throne. Robert, Earl of Gloucester, supported Matilda's claims, thus putting him out of favour with Stephen who, in revenge, took away all Robert's possessions, including the Luton manor, and assumed the title himself. In 1139 King Stephen gave the manor to one of his foreign mercenaries, Robert de Waudari, who built himself a small wooden castle by the present Matalan site in Castle Street.

King Stephen was not the direct heir of Henry I and one with a stronger claim to the throne came onto the scene. This was Duke Henry of Normandy, son of Matilda and grandson of Henry I. Duke Henry arrived in this country and, in 1153, met King Stephen at Wallingford where a truce was signed. It was agreed that, after Stephen's death, Henry would take the Crown as King Henry II. As part of the agreement, all foreign mercenaries were to leave the country and their castles destroyed. This included Robert de Waudari. He left and his castle was abandoned in 1154 after only 15 years. Excavations in the area in 2005 revealed substantial protective ditches and wooden post holes.

The manor then reverted to William, Earl of Gloucester, son of Earl Robert, but when Henry II became king in 1154 he claimed it back. His son, Richard I, succeeded in 1189 and sold the manor to one of his fellow Crusaders, Baldwin de Bethune, for £80. The manor was to become part of the dowry of Baldwin's daughter, Alice, when she married William Marshall, son of the Marshal of England. Unfortunately Alice died after two years of marriage and for some reason John, who took the throne in 1199, persuaded William to hand the manor to one of John's favourites, a Norman, Falkes de Breauté.

Falkes was a colourful but far from popular character; in fact he has been described as the 'most hated man in England'. He was extremely powerful, was sheriff of seven counties and held several castles, one, of timber with water-filled defence ditches, being in Luton beneath the present University of Bedfordshire, between St Mary's Church and Lea Road. Falkes rampaged through the country taking property and claiming it as his own. To annoy the church at Luton, he dammed the river, flooding the area and preventing the Abbot's mill from grinding corn. Justice caught up with him at last and everything he had was taken from him. He died of poisoning in 1226. Falkes also owned land in Surrey known as Falkes Hall (later Vauxhall). In 1905 the Vauxhall Iron Works moved from that site to a plot of land near Falkes de Breauté's former castle in Luton. So the names Falkes and Vauxhall came full circle. Recent excavations in St Anne's Road have confirmed that a motte and bailey castle did exist on that site and that, in the castle courtyard, there was a timber-framed building.

The manor of Luton reverted to the Crown but in 1225 it was restored to William Marshall, who had meanwhile remarried, his second wife being Countess Eleanor Plantagenet, sister of Henry III. When William Marshall died in 1231, Eleanor became the lady of the manor. Seven years later she, too, remarried. Her new husband, Simon de Montfort, was a very important man who, for a time, controlled a 'Council of Fifteen' that in effect governed the country and is said to have been the beginning of our Parliamentary system. Upon Eleanor's death, the manor passed to the six daughters of Sybil de Ferrers, who were the heirs of William Marshall, and the manor of Luton was divided.

LIFE IN MEDIEVAL LUTON

The most important building in the town was Earl Robert's splendid church, and not far away was the manor house, almost certainly made of wattle daubed with clay and dressed flint. Oak beams supported a great hall and there would have been a cellar, a kitchen and a gallery to accommodate

9 *Moat Farm, photographed by A.C. Jordan.*

10 *The Moat House.*

the sleeping area. Outbuildings would probably have housed a bakery, a brewery and a laundry besides stables, dovecots, pigsties and poultry coops. Some manors may have surrounded themselves with a moat, not so much for protection as a symbol of prestige. At least three moated halls existed beside the Lea in Limbury and Biscot, of which the Moat House (*c*.1370), now much restored, is the last survivor.

The homes of the peasants, however, would have been less substantial, being made of wood and plaster with open shuttered windows. Inside could probably be found a few possessions: a basin, basket, chest, jug and metal pots for cooking and wooden utensils. Beds were straw pallets. There might have been an outside oven and the basic diet would include bacon, bread, cheese, chicken and vegetables with ale to drink.

Unfortunately, many medieval artefacts were destroyed when the Arndale Centre was built and it is to be hoped that, if and when more building is done in the centre of Luton, modern rules and regulations will be observed and archaeologists will be allowed to survey the site, so adding to the limited information now available. However, by looking at road names like Bridge Street, Castle Street and Mill Street, which still exist, it is possible to get some idea of the layout of medieval Luton. Also, at Stockwood Discovery Centre, there

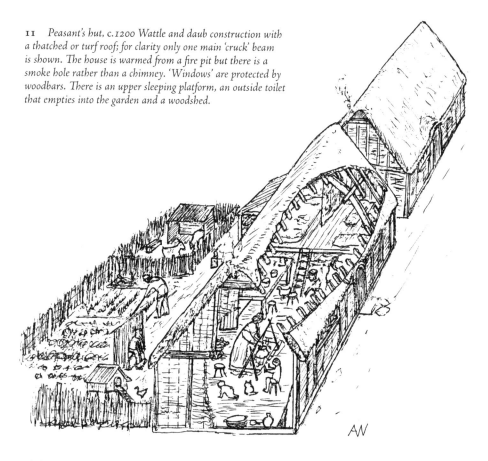

11   *Peasant's hut, c.1200 Wattle and daub construction with a thatched or turf roof; for clarity only one main 'cruck' beam is shown. The house is warmed from a fire pit but there is a smoke hole rather than a chimney. 'Windows' are protected by woodbars. There is an upper sleeping platform, an outside toilet that empties into the garden and a woodshed.*

are lifesize representations of a market stall, a pantry with barley, bread, oats and rolls and a tiler's workshop.

It was important that the market should be controlled so that stallholders could be watched and fraud for the most part averted. Rights to the market, which was held in the centre of the town, were significant because the stallholders paid rent to the holder of those rights, and during Bethune's time as lord of the manor the Abbot of St Albans claimed the right to own some of the stalls. It seems that the stalls were similar in shape and appearance to the mobile lock-up chests, containing scales and weights, and trestles that are found in markets today.

The market had always been held on Sundays but, under Earl Baldwin, it was changed to Monday. This link with medieval Luton lasted until well into the 20th century and many Luton people can still remember visiting the cattle market near Park Square on a Monday morning. A former member of staff at Luton Modern School, which moved into its Park Street building in 1908, wrote: 'the front of the school was very noisy, especially on market day. Then the various stall-holders vied with each other in selling their wares; a china plate would smash; cattle would be driven by; horses' hooves clattered along the road; all very disturbing.'

Fairs were much bigger and involved traders from further afield, some coming from as far away as London. Animals could be bought and sold and entertainers performed in front of the townsfolk. Luton's annual fair was held in the churchyard and started on the evening of 14 August. As the following day was the Feast of the Assumption, a holyday or holiday, everyone from the town and the hamlets (Biscot, Hyde, Leagrave, Limbury and Stopsley) was free to attend. The fair lasted for a week and, if the harvest had been early, harvest celebrations also took place then. Tenants of the manor erected 'booths of the boughs of beech trees' for the fair, a custom that survived until early in the 20th century.

The town's wealth was based on agriculture, and wooded areas surrounded the busy town where pigs could roam. Labourers would be working very hard in the fields and, down by the river, the town's watermills would be grinding corn. On Bradgers Hill and Stopsley Common the strip lynchets used for Saxon 'contour ploughing' were still in use.

The population of Luton was expanding and taxation figures for 1297 tell us that the town, together with the hamlets, could boast two butchers, a cooper, a dyer, seven merchants, a ploughmaker, a tailor, two tanners and two turners. Roads were not maintained as they are today and would have been rutted and muddy; knights might well pass by on horseback. The sheriff's men travelled to and from the town and, from time to time, tournaments probably took place. Traffic which had tended to go from east to west, linking the Great North Road to the Watling Street, began to turn from south to north, so connecting Luton to London and the Midlands.

However, life was not secure and in 1314-15 there was famine. The price of corn shot up, resulting in starvation and death, and in 1317 came an epidemic of animal disease. A serious fire swept through the town in 1336, causing a great deal of destruction to the wooden, thatched houses and barns.

12 *Market and St Mary's Church, c.1320, with west tower under construction.*

There were several levels of justice. The sheriff (shire reeve) had overall responsibility within the county. The manorial court or court leet, presided over by the lord or his steward and, in the case of Luton, sometimes the Abbot of St Albans, dealt with petty offences such as poaching or taking wood. This court was, in theory, held twice a year, in the open air or in the church. Every resident male over the age of 12 was supposed to attend. The court leet decided on the use of the common fields and elected minor officials such as aletasters, constables, haywards, swineherds, woodwards and other minor officials. All decisions were recorded on rolls of parchment. The court leet lasted as one of the few remaining links to the past until 1939 although, by that time, it had only nominal powers. In 2006, the local newspaper, the *Luton News*, reprinted a 20th-century photograph of the court leet with words that were spoken by the Town Crier and Warden of the Pound, Charlie Irons. He said (or cried): 'All persons that do owe suit and services to this Court Leet and Court Baron of Alice, Lady Ludlow, now to be holden in and for this Manor of Luton, draw near and give your attendance and answer your name.'

Then there was the hundred court, Luton being in the Hundred of Flitt, which was an area of administration. Above that came the shire court with the sheriff passing judgement and finally the king's court. Laws could vary from place to place but Henry II changed the system by setting out a 'Common Law' that applied to the whole kingdom, as a result of which travelling judges and the jury system were introduced.

THE CHURCH

In the Middle Ages the Church was all-powerful, claiming its authority from the Pope. It was also wealthy as it owned a great deal of land. Tithing was a tax imposed on everyone through which the Church claimed one tenth of everything a man possessed, and this included a share of his working hours. The Biblical principle behind this was that the tenth should be given to God, but the Church claimed this as their own right. Other taxes were imposed on marriages and funerals.

About twelve miles to the south of Luton was the magnificent and powerful Abbey of St Albans that had been built in A.D. 793 on the spot where Alban, the first Christian martyr in England, died. It was rebuilt and dedicated in 1115. The monks followed the Rule of St Benedict, living as a family under the supervision of the Abbot and taking vows of poverty and chastity. However, they were sometimes extortionate landlords and often led dissolute lives. St Albans Abbey owned manors in Luton, notably Biscot, and by the 14th century they also had the manors of Crawley Green, Dallow, East Hyde and Ramridge End.

The monks at St Albans cast a greedy eye over the five hides of land owned by the church in Luton because the Abbot coveted the income from its rich endowments and, in 1155, William, Earl of Gloucester, agreed to let them have the church lands. The Abbot also built himself a summer residence on St Anne's Hill, a name which is still on our maps, and, in Bethune's time, the monks were given the rights to fishing in the river Lea in the centre of the town. From around 1154, the people of Luton had been required to make an annual pilgrimage to the shrine of St Alban. This was meant to be an act of penitence but could also have been an enjoyable break from the dull routine of life.

13 *St Mary's Church.*

The monks were disliked because they were seen as tyrants; tenants, who were required to work hard, were considered to be church property and the 14th-century Church could not see its way to granting them their freedom. No tenant could sell his land as it belonged to the Abbot, nor could he sell corn or cattle without permission. In 1274 some of the tenants rebelled against the Abbey's demands that their corn should be ground at the Abbey's mill. The matter went to court but was decided in favour of the Abbey. As punishment, the peasants' grinding wheels were confiscated and laid as a patio at the Abbot's residence.

The first church was built, probably by Aethelstan, about A.D. 975 but the newer church, the one we know today, was funded by Robert, Earl of Gloucester, soon after he became lord of the manor. It was not built on the site of the older church but on Robert's own land nearby and was completed in 1137. The church was the focus of life and everyone was required to attend Mass on Sundays. In fact, it probably provided some colour in a hard existence, for the townsfolk could enjoy looking at the religious paintings on the walls and, from time to time, miracle plays may well have been performed outside the west door. The church has been extensively rebuilt and refurnished over the centuries but there are still reminders of Luton's history. The font, *c.*1250, is of Purbeck marble and at the west end of the nave is the baptistry, built *c.*1340, which is made of stone and intricately carved.

The Guild and Local Hospitals

Guilds were groups of like-minded people who formed a religious fraternity or craft organisation. Members paid an annual subscription and would sustain each other in many ways, for example offering help in time of need and supporting one another's religious life. In 1474 a licence was obtained by Sir Thomas Rotherham from Edward IV for permission

Page from Luton Guild Registry.

to found a group in Luton, to be known as the Guild of the Holy Trinity. A beautifully illuminated register, covering the years 1475-1546, survives and lists the names of more than 6,000 members. It demonstrates that the Guild was one of the richest in the land. Details of the Guild have been transcribed and published by the Bedfordshire Historical Record Society.

The Guild built a chantry in the church where priests would sing masses for members' souls, both living and dead, but, on a more worldly level, they also held social gatherings with convivial dinners in a great hall, Brothersed House, which stood at the corner of Castle Street and Market Hill. The Luton Guild's procession and feast were held in May and it seems to have been a very extravagant affair, no doubt causing quite a stir in the town.

Hospitals in the Middle Ages were run by religious communities for the comfort and support of travellers as well as for the care of the poor and the isolation of contagious diseases. There was a hospital at Farley, set up for the poor by French monks. Another, the House of God of the Virgin Mary and St Mary Magdalene, was founded by Thomas Beckett for the care of the sick and was run by Augustinian brothers and sisters. It was on high ground north of Spittlesea Way and near the airport. Leprosy was common in the Middle Ages, although the term probably covered all kinds of skin problems and conditions resulting in maimed or stunted limbs. There was a hospital, St John the Baptist, which cared for these outcasts on Spital Hill, between Leagrave and Limbury.

IMPORTANT LANDOWNERS

Apart from the lords of the manor there were others who held land around the town. In 1115 the manor of Biscot was given by Henry I to St Albans Abbey and it is in Biscot that the Moat House, which is the only genuine remaining medieval building in Luton, apart from St Mary's Church, still stands. It was built by the de Beresford family between A.D. 1370 and 1400. Later the Ackworth family lived there; John Ackworth was one of the founders of the Guild of the Holy Trinity.

Tradition associates the Moat House with a nunnery founded by Roger, Abbot of St Albans, and dedicated to the Holy Trinity. In the 1960s, the architectural historian, A.J. Hales observed a piscina in the interior wall some 16 feet to the right of the front entrance. Sadly it was lost during the conversion to a restaurant. While additions to the outside of the building have been made over the years, much of the original structure, including the roof beams of the original open hall, can still be seen and part of the moat remains. The Moat House is now a popular carvery.

John de Somery became lord of the manor in 1308; the de Somery family had lived in the manor of Someries Then, in 1433, Sir John Wenlock bought the manor, his family, the Wenlocks, having connections in Luton probably dating back to around 1377. Sir John was a great soldier, fighting in France and in the Wars of the Roses. He first fought on the side of the Lancastrians and was wounded at the Battle of St Albans. He then changed his allegiance to the Yorkists but later returned to the Lancastrian fold. Consequently, when he was killed at the Battle of Tewkesbury in 1471, Edward IV confiscated his lands. Both Sir John and his brother, Thomas, became members of Parliament for Bedfordshire in the early 15th century, Sir John becoming Speaker of the House of Commons.

Lord John Wenlock built the late medieval manor house, now known as 'Someries Castle' although it was never actually a castle, soon after 1448. It is an early example of brick building in England and was probably never completed. It has been convincingly argued by Terence Smith that Someries was constructed by Flemish or German craftsmen, probably using bricks made locally. This would represent some of the first brickmaking in England since the Romans left one thousand years previously. The remains of the chapel, gateway and porter's lodge, as well as the garden earthworks, survive today.

The building became a ruin soon after 1740, when it was partially dismantled to provide bricks for the construction of Someries Farm, which was the home of the novelist Joseph Conrad for a short time in the early 20th century. Sir John also built the Wenlock Chapel in the Parish Church, probably in memory of his first wife, Elizabeth, who died around 1461. It is separated from the Chancel by the celebrated 'Wenlock screen'. This chapel contains three tombs, for Lady Rotherham, Sir George Rotherham and William Wenlock.

Recently Luton Museums succeeded in raising enough money from different contributors to purchase the 'Wenlok jug', which is now on display at their site at Stockwood Discovery Centre. It was saved from export on the grounds that it is of outstanding significance for the study of bronze working in medieval England. It is a rare example of metalwork that can be associated with royalty from the 15th century. It is decorated with the English royal arms as generally used between 1340 and 1405 and the East Anglian coat of arms associated with either St Edmund and the See of Bury or St Etheldreda and the See of Ely. The jug is inscribed 'MY LORD WENLOK', which could refer to Sir John or to William Wenlock, who was Canon of the King's Chapel and master of the hospital at Farley. He died in 1391 and is buried in St Mary's Church in Luton. The museum states that:

> Stylistically the jug is similar to ones held at the British Museum and the Victoria and Albert Museum. However, the Wenlok jug is the only one to bear a maker's or merchant's mark cast, possibly the earliest known mark. Research has shown the jug appears to have hinge marks indicating that at one time it had a lid, in line with the other jugs.

After the Battle of Tewkesbury, Sir John Wenlock's lands were given to Thomas Rotherham, Bishop of Lincoln, and the Rotherham name was remembered in the naming of one of the local high schools (though misspelt as 'Rotheram'). The Crawley family bought Someries in 1629 and their connection with Luton continued until well into the 20th century. They were well known in the town as the owners of Stockwood Park.

There were members of the Hoo family living at Luton Hoo as early as 1196 and until the late 15th century. Sir Thomas Hoo inherited the estate in 1410; he fought at Agincourt in 1415 and, in 1429, was made High Sheriff of Bedfordshire and Buckinghamshire. Luton Hoo has changed hands several times and has played a significant part in the life of the town.

15 *The Wenlok Jug.*

A Changing Society

In the 13th and 14th centuries, both the economy and the population of England grew considerably. Consequently there was a need for the clearing of more land for farming. This trend was reversed after the arrival of the dreaded plague, known as the 'Black Death', in 1349, which set in train circumstances that would change life irrevocably. There was no cure for the disease and a monk at St Albans wrote that 'scarcely the half of mankind survived … towns that were formerly very thickly populated were left destitute of inhabitants'. Luton did not escape; upwards of a thousand died, all classes of society being affected. In spite of the vast numbers of dead, no mass burial pits have ever been recovered in the Luton area. When the disease subsided landowners, instead of being able to dictate terms to the peasant classes, found themselves short of labour and at their mercy.

More trouble came in 1380 when a national poll tax of 1s. per person was levied on everyone over the age of fifteen. The peasants had had enough and revolted. Some Luton men joined a march to make demands of the Abbot of St Albans concerning their rights. The spirit of rebellion was also felt in other parts of the land and resulted in the uprising known as the Peasants' Revolt. Some Luton men joined with the protestors from St Albans; they marched on London and met with Wat Tyler, the peasants' leader. At first it looked as though the rebels would succeed in their aims, especially when Tyler spoke face to face with Richard II. But that was not to be: Tyler was murdered and the king later rode to St Albans to restore law and order.

Another significant change came about with the arrival of preachers like John Wycliffe who challenged the power and authority of the Church. Previously, only students of classical languages, Hebrew, Greek and Latin, could read the Bible but Wycliffe and others like him, known as Lollards, were determined to make the Word of God accessible to ordinary people. He made an English translation of the Bible and others, notably Tyndale, followed his example. Attempts were made to suppress the movement but it could not be stifled.

This new challenge to the authority of the church came to be known as the 'Reformation'. The movement grew stronger and, in the course of time, many Luton people accepted the new way of thinking. Later chapters will show that, in the long term, the town favoured these beliefs rather than those of the Established Church and eventually gained a reputation as a nonconformist town.

The Sixteenth Century

Henry VIII ascended the throne in 1509 and is probably best remembered for having six wives. When he decided to divorce his first wife, he came into conflict with the Pope. Henry would not listen and went his own way, declaring that he, not the Pope, was head of the English Church. One of Henry's most far-reaching decisions in this new role was the closing of the monasteries, which had hitherto been a focus of religious and social life. Luton did not have a monastery so was not affected to the same extent as the neighbouring towns of Dunstable or St Albans.

However, some new laws did affect the people of the town. The Injunctions of 1538 stated that registers of baptisms, marriages and burials should be kept in every parish. The cost of such a register was about 1s. 8d. It was also required that an English Bible should be provided in every church: 'one book of the whole Bible of the largest volume in English, and the same set up in some convenient place within the said church … whereas your parishioners may most commodiously resort to the same and read it'. This version came to be known as the Great Bible and each copy was secured with a chain. The cost to the parish is not noted but comparisons with other parish records suggest that it would have been in the region of £1. The book was there for all to read but, although the principle was sound, there remained the question of just how many people had the ability to read. Other laws from 1538 required parish churches to be stripped of any objects or ornaments which could be regarded as superstitious or idolatrous.

Henry was succeeded, in turn, by three of his children, who each had different religious points of view and churchwardens and congregations had to accommodate themselves to each new set of edicts. For example, images, ornaments, screens and vestments were removed by Edward VI but replaced by Mary, while Elizabeth's views were similar to those of her brother.

Edward VI (1547-53) abolished the chantries. This affected Luton as, in 1547, the colourful Guild of the Holy Trinity was dissolved and the property later sold. In 1549 and 1552 books of common prayer (similar throughout the land and in English) were introduced. Also, in 1550, Luton complied with the Act against Superstitious Books and Images that demanded that stone altars had to be destroyed and replaced by wooden communion tables.

After Edward's brief reign, the throne passed to his sister, Mary (1553-8), who was a devout Catholic and favoured the ritual of the earlier church. Back came the Latin Mass, feasts and saints' days. The parish was obliged to spend a considerable amount of money on replacing what had been destroyed and individual donors supplied gifts. For example, Edward Crawley gave a cope and a vestment valued at £5 and also a chalice worth about £7. After Mary's death, Elizabeth I became queen (1558-1603) and she returned the country to the Protestant faith. One Luton vicar, Thomas Rose, was imprisoned and ill-treated for his beliefs during Mary's reign but managed to escape; then, under Elizabeth, he returned to his position.

The parish of Luton in the middle of the 16th century was estimated to be seven miles in circumference and the population about three thousand. Although the basic economy was agricultural, other small industries were being established. Malting was becoming increasingly important and bricks and tiles were being made. Both of these trades were to become significant in Luton life. Sheep were kept for their wool. The nobility were growing wealthier and there were landmarks in the town to which we can still relate today. The *George Hotel* was there and even then was considered old. Barbers Lane, called after a family of that name, still exists, although only as a shadow of its former self and is partially hidden in the basement of the Mall.

And so, at the end of the 16th century, Luton had become a small established town on the river Lea, centred on the church and with some features we might find familiar, but there was still a long way to go before it evolved into the Luton we know today.

III

Seventeenth- to Nineteenth-Century Luton

UNDER THE MEDIEVAL regime, life had been very regulated, but by the 17th and 18th centuries people no longer felt subservient to the same extent and were beginning to reason that they had a right to be treated fairly and as individuals. In the country at large the power of the monarchy had been tested during the Civil Wars and the shocking news of the execution of Charles I in 1649 would no doubt have quickly reached the town. Indeed the 1785 *Directory* for Luton echoed some rebellious thoughts from these times, complaining that 'monopolisers' who were trying to control the straw trade should be driven out, aristocracy crushed and the Commonwealth, set up by Cromwell, restored. The desire for individuality and independence was also demonstrated by the changing religious background.

Luton was a little market town and largely self-contained, but it was affected by national events: Cromwell's men came here as part of their campaign to cleanse the English Church of what they considered to be idolatry. And did the brightness in the sky from the Great Fire of London in 1666 amaze the people of Luton, as did the glow from the London Blitz in 1940-1? World markets began to affect the town: hats were exported as far away as Australia and New Zealand and local trade was threatened when straw plait was imported from China and Japan. Although the world was not 'globalised' in the modern sense of the word, Luton was most certainly not an island and the wider world was not a closed book.

Wars imparted a backcloth to life as they had done in years past and still do today. In the reign of Elizabeth I there had been conflict with Spain and the arrival of the Armada would have been signalled by beacons across the land. During the Civil Wars in the 17th century, the townsfolk were generally supportive of Parliament although the landowners, notably Sir Francis Crawley, were Royalist. There were no large battles in the area although there were minor skirmishes in the town. As the 18th century drew to a close, there were fears of a French invasion and Napoleon became a figure of fear in the land. Then, in the middle of the 19th century, came the Crimean War with Russia.

Apart from the regular army, the country supported a 'militia' whose function it was to provide for home defence while the regular army served overseas. The method of recruiting was for constables to draw up a list of eligible men (the muster rolls) and then the required number would be drawn by lot. If a man was selected, he was not compelled to serve himself but could pay a substitute to join on his behalf or alternatively he could pay a fine. There were therefore two lists: one of men chosen by lot and another of the men who were enrolled, and the burden was naturally borne by the poorer classes. The Bedfordshire muster rolls show that in 1780 the name of John Tuffnall from Luton was drawn but John Piven took his place. As the replacement had a wife, the poor relief may well have been called upon to support her while her husband was away and steps were later taken to divide men into categories, those with fewer responsibilities being preferred.

During the Crimean War, the *Luton Times* (1855) carried information about the progress of the war and also a letter from William Everitt, a Sergeant in the Rifle Brigade, to his mother who lived in Dumfries Street. He says:

> We do not have much time to spare, for our duty here is very hard, as we are in the trenches almost every other night ... The Russian batteries and ours are very close to each other, so that neither party can show their heads above the parapets without getting a dozen shots at them ... I had a very narrow escape on the 19th, for a shell nearly buried me, and in about ten minutes after, a 32lb shot passed between me and the captain on duty as we were talking together. The cholera has broken out here, and we have lost two men by it.

Luton folk may well have been aware of another significant historical movement, namely the slave trade, which was helping to bring wealth into this country from the sugar plantations of America and the West Indies. Robert Hibbert lived at The Hyde, on the border between Hertfordshire and Bedfordshire, and in the early 19th century had taken up a business partnership with his uncle in Kingston, Jamaica. Their sugar plantations were worked by slaves although, unlike many slave owners, Hibbert is said to have been a compassionate master. In 1819, he used some of his wealth to build a row of 12 cottages in Castle Street for 24 poor widows, together with funds to maintain them. In 1881, after a deal with Mrs Frances Ashton's Charity of Dunstable, the cottages were knocked down and new, superior, ones built in Hibbert Street.

Across the Atlantic, the New World beckoned and in 1830 the Marquess of Bute, then the lord of the manor at Luton Hoo, paid for 20 young labourers from Luton to go to America. Mr Thomas Butlin of the *George Hotel* made the travelling arrangements for these young men to reach Liverpool, from where they embarked for New York. They wrote back home to encourage others to follow them, noting that 'living was so cheap that a man could live on one third of his wages'. Towards the end of the 19th century, William Austin, Luton solicitor and historian, managed to secure for one young man's family a large sum of money which the man had left to them in his will in Illinois.

Until 1776, many convicts had been transported to America, but between 1787 and 1868, their destination was Australia. This must have seemed another world to the people of Luton, especially when one considers that the journey of the first fleet of convicts had taken eight months. However, Australia became very real to many Luton people, as the records of Bedford Gaol demonstrate. Most of those convicted were male but Elizabeth Reynolds, aged 57, went there in 1808 and Ann Pitkin, aged 15, in 1851. Ages varied; John Field was just 13 when he was sent but William Scrivener was 53 when sentenced to 14 years for receiving stolen sheep. Very few of them returned to England.

Most of the crimes were for theft. These are some examples: an ass, barley, beef, ducks, a fork, a frying pan, half a crown, horses, jewellery, knives, lead, oats, pigeons, plit (topsoil), sheep, shirts, silk handkerchiefs, straw plait and turkeys. The sentence was usually for seven years but some were for 10 years, 14 years or even life, although it is sometimes difficult to work out the consistency in the sentencing. Arson was supposedly a very serious crime and one of the last in this country to receive a death sentence and yet Thomas Gower, who may have been born in the Luton workhouse, received just 10 years for setting fire to a stack of barley, a stack of clover hay, a stack of straw and four stacks of wheat.

These centuries were also eventful on the home front and were to see the two major changes that came to be known as the Agricultural Revolution and the Industrial Revolution. Landowners in Bedfordshire played an important part in the first of these when they supported experiments to improve the efficiency of agricultural methods, necessary to provide food for a growing population. The Industrial Revolution saw the evolution from an economy that depended on manual labour to one that was driven by machinery. Although Luton was not involved in the social upheaval of the Industrial Revolution, had it not taken place Luton would never have achieved fame as an industrial town.

Against this background Luton was rapidly growing from a small market town to an urbanised society with a population and economy greater than any of its neighbours. Before the end of the 19th century, Luton was to gain considerable independence when, in 1876, it acquired the status of a borough.

RELIGIOUS BELIEF

Serious theological debates had taken place since the time of the Reformation and Christian groups began to separate into two: Catholics and Protestants. Another important aspect of religious life at the time was the appearance of English translations of the Bible; many people chose to read it for themselves and subsequently began to challenge some previously accepted doctrines. In the 17th century, controversies had continued and were frequently focused on the style of worship preferred by the reigning monarch. The atmosphere was succinctly and somewhat amusingly described in the well-known song *The Vicar of Bray*. This fictitious cleric repeatedly changed his religious allegiance to suit the mood of the moment. However, there were many committed believers who refused to conform to the differing decrees and they became known as nonconformists or dissenters. Over the years, many nonconformist groups were established in Luton.

John Bunyan, the famous Bedfordshire preacher who wrote *The Pilgrim's Progress*, was an Independent. There is no record of him visiting Luton but it is very likely that he did so.

Bunyan went to prison for his beliefs but, in 1689, an Act of Toleration gave nonconformists the right to worship according to their consciences and Bedfordshire became very much a nonconformist county. In 1851 a religious census was taken and the figures show that, by that time, Luton had established itself very firmly as a nonconformist town.

In the early 17th century Edward Harrison and later Thomas Hayward led a widely scattered congregation of Baptists, including a number of people from Luton, at Kensworth, a village about six miles from Luton. In 1689-90, a group left to set up a congregation in Luton that was led by Thomas Marsom until his death in 1726. Tradition has it that Marsom was imprisoned with John Bunyan although there is no contemporary evidence to support this. He came from a local family of merchants and shopkeepers who owned considerable property in the town and was said to be an outstanding personality. His sons later became deacons in the Baptist church and Wardown Park Museum holds some of the family's archival material and

an hourglass he used for timing his sermons. It is thought that a group of Baptists met in a house on Dallow Farm that was demolished around 1909. The group then moved to become Park Street Baptists.

The first Baptist Meeting House was built in Park Street around 1698, and in 1785 it was noted that there was a 'numerous meeting of Anabaptists' in the town. The church was enlarged but in 1814 a new one was built that was able to hold 800 people. This was known as the Round Meeting, although it was, in fact, octagonal. In 1870, after the Round Meeting was seriously damaged by a storm, yet another room was erected which survived until 1975. The 1908 Luton *Year Book* described this as 'the oldest nonconformist place of worship in the town' and 'the parent of several others'.

It is part of the pattern of nonconformist groups that they frequently divide and set up separate communities. Sometimes this is to accommodate larger numbers but on other occasions people with different theological interpretations feel the need to move. For example, in 1803, the Particular Baptists moved to Rosemary Lane and in 1832 to the Ebenezer Chapel in Hastings Street, while another group went to Union Street in 1837. Ten years later, the Ceylon Chapel in Wellington Street was opened and in 1938 a Baptist Chapel was opened in Blenheim Crescent.

The Congregationalists, formerly Independents, opened a church at the top of King Street (1865) and there exists a handwritten 'Journal of Home Mission Work 1872' in connection with this church that makes fascinating reading. It describes how pastoral visits were made to private houses and to the Cottage Hospital and Workhouse Infirmary for the purpose of encouraging the sick, while spiritual care was given to the people of Luton who had any particular needs.

The Methodist Revival began in Luton around 1750 when a Mr George Bull, grocer and rush-basket maker, came to live in the town. He had been associated with Methodists and found 'several serious persons, who joined with him in meetings for prayer and praise' in a room in Castle Street. Next they moved to a building called Bull's Barn in Park Street and it was here, in 1766, that John Wesley first preached locally. He described a later visit he made to Luton in January 1772.

The snow lay so deep on the road that it was not without much difficulty, and some danger, we at last reached the town. I was offered the use of the church; the frost was exceeding sharp, and the glass was taken out of the windows. However, for the sake of the people, I accepted the offer though I might just as well have preached in the open air. I suppose four times as many people were present as would have been at the room and about an hundred in the morning. So I did not repent of my journey through the snow.

16   *A Thurston print of the Baptist Meeting House, c.1864.*

In November 1778 he wrote that the Methodists 'had a miserable preaching-house here but Mr Cole has now fitted up a very neat and commodious room, which was thoroughly filled with well-behaved and attentive hearers'. Wesley subsequently made other visits to the town and Methodism became very much a part of Luton life. A plaque with the following inscription, together with Wesley's pulpit and chair, could be seen in the Methodist Church in High Town.

Wesleyan Chapel
Erected by Wm Cole Esq.
and presented in the year 1778, to the
Rev. J. Wesley M.A.
whose last sermon here was preached
November 1st 1785

By 1808 Luton had become head of a Wesleyan circuit with three ministers and 366 adherents. By 1851 membership had grown to more than a thousand. In 1814 a new chapel was built in Chapel Street, then known as Hog Lane, but was demolished in 1879.

The Quakers were part of a national organisation known as the Society of Friends. They were very prominent in business life in Luton and were renowned for their honesty, integrity, philanthropy and thrift and for their commitment to public service. Their presence was felt in many aspects of local life, including the provision of schooling and the temperance movement. The Brown family were leading Quakers and were active as brewers, corn dealers, farmers, maltmen, millers and shopkeepers. The banking families of Marsh, Lucas, Seebohm and

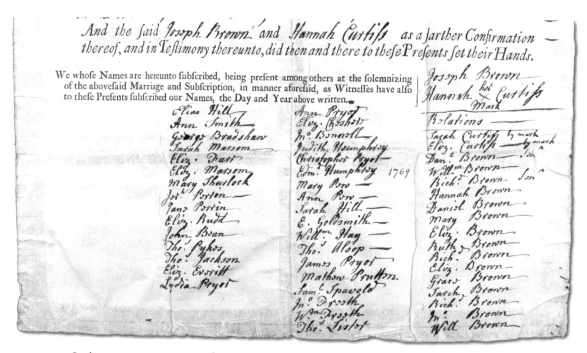

17   *Quaker signatures on a marriage document. Note names such as Brown and Marsom.*

Latchmore were as influential in the business and philanthropic life of the town. The Friends disapproved of the slave trade; they sent money in response to an appeal from American Friends for the support of runaway slaves and some Luton Quakers stopped using sugar.

The Quakers began their connection with the town in 1655. From 1741 they met in houses, but in 1748-9 Daniel Brown fitted up a Meeting House in his premises in Park Square. In 1801 a place of worship was set up in Castle Street on land bought from Dr Chase. The 1851 census noted that there were 70 people attending the Luton Meeting in the morning and 49 in the afternoon. The room was enlarged in 1866, and in 1963, when Luton town centre was redeveloped, the Quakers moved to a new Meeting House in Crawley Green Road.

Between 1685 and 1850 the Roman Catholic Church had no dioceses in this country and was governed from abroad. Members of the Catholic faith were disadvantaged in many ways but, over time, the restrictions were removed, culminating in the Catholic Emancipation Act (1829). In September 1850, the English Hierarchy was restored and the Northampton diocese, which administers Luton, came into being. Between 1780 and 1800 there was just one Catholic priest in Bedfordshire. In 1884 the first resident priest Joseph O'Connor said Mass in his house in Rothesay Road and, two years later, an iron church, Our Lady Help of Christians, was set up in Castle Street. By the 1880s there were 160 Catholics in the town. The iron church in Castle Street was replaced by a new church in November 1910 and enlarged in 1959. Since then, other Roman Catholic churches have been opened.

Travel, Transport and Inns

In 1785 Luton was described as an 'irregular built town, and situated on low ground, but enlivened with a few good houses, and distinguished by good corn markets'. In 1800 it was a 'small, dirty, old-fashioned town of only five streets'. Thirty years later it was said to be a 'flourishing and respectable market town' and in 1847 'an improving market town'. A visitor in 1800 would have been aware of the river Lea flowing into the town from Leagrave and Limbury and out again through Luton Hoo Park on its way to join the river Thames. Entering the town along South Street or Sheep Street (Park Street), he would have passed Blackwater Lane (Lea Road) and Church Street on his right and London Road on his left. Blackwater Lane was not a pretty sight for there lay an open ditch full of rubbish and decaying animal and vegetable refuse; this was, of course, before a clean sewage system was built. A newspaper reporter noted in 1876 that:

> There was nothing beyond Windsor Street and Napier Road ... beyond the Gas Works there was nothing in Dunstable Road except Bury Farm and a few cottages. This farm was regarded as a long way out of town ... In Old Bedford Road, the town practically ended at North Street, the roads beyond having since been cut out of what was at that time Burr's Field ... Around the Parish Church ... were fields known as Lane's Meadows, where an agricultural show was held.

The centre of the town was Market Hill, once known as Middle Row. Hog Lane (Chapel Street) ran to the left towards Caddington. Beyond Market Hill was George Street, also known

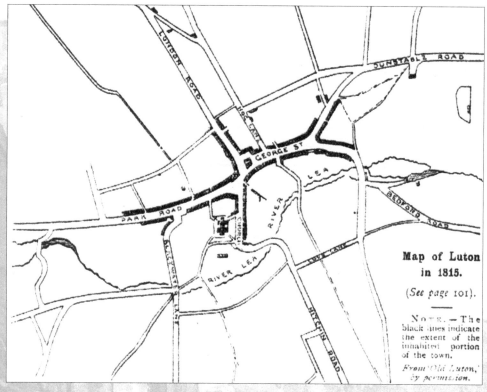

Map of Luton
in 1815.

(*See page* 101).

N o t e. — The black lines indicate the extent of the inhabited portion of the town.

From 'Old Luton,' by permission.

18   *Map of Luton in 1815 from the* 1904 Year Book.

19   *New Mill End Road at Hyde.*

20 *Painting by George Shepherd of Park Street, 1811-19.*

21 *Wy-Ax-Ye?, in Park Road.*

as North Street or High Street, where the gardens on one side ran down to the river; this went as far as a fork in the road where the town hall now stands. One branch was Dunstable Lane (Upper George Street) and the other Tower Hill (Manchester Street). This is a description of the town as it was in 1800:

> In some parts of the centre of the town houses projected so far into the roads that carts could not pass each other; there were also banks on each side of the streets, with grass on almost every part; the houses were in general very low-built with stud walls, and

22 *A bit of old Luton: Davis Shop, Park Square, 1906.*

23 *Market Hill, c.1860, from the 1902* Year Book.

24 *A bit of old Luton: corner of Chapel Street.*

25 *Old Chapel Street, photographed by Anderson.*

26 *Tower Hill almshouses, c.1862.*

the upper floors overhanging in front two feet. The buildings were chiefly public houses, farm houses, maltings and old thatched cottages, the few shops had small low windows.

During the 19th century, the extensive garden between George Street and the river which belonged to the Waller family was developed. Cheapside was extended and John Street, Melson Street, Silver Street and Waller Street were laid out. There were also four farms in George Street until the 1890s but this interesting landscape has now been destroyed by development.

George Street was the site of the weekly straw plait market but, in 1869, this was moved into the new Plait Halls and later a number of hat factories were established along the road. By the mid-19th century there were a number of lanes and courtyards running off the main road, some of which had been reduced to slums. The worst of these was Adelaide Terrace where, in 1853, there was a serious cholera outbreak. On a more positive note, George Street was paved in the mid-19th century. Wellington Street, begun in the 1840s, was home to many of Luton's middle classes and was also for a time the main shopping area in the town. King Street and George Street West boasted better-class houses.

27 *Wellington Street, Luton, postmarked 1903.*

28 *Plait merchant's houses, from 1850. 3-5 George Street West with Harold Cooke. Photograph by Eric Meadows.*

E.V. Lucas reminisced about his childhood here in the 1870s: he remembered a town which was small enough for the bell on a local hat factory to be heard all over the town; the bonfire on 5 November; spending his pocket-money on a sausage-roll or on penny conjuring tricks and how he and his friends used to lean over a railway bridge to see the Scottish express roar by. He also remembered stealing apples from the store-house in his grandfather's old house in Park Street and the time when there was a 'Spring Heeled Jack' scare, which is said to have been a ploy used to frighten children into behaving. As a consequence everyone was too scared to use the path that led to the church at night in case 'Jack' jumped out on them.

The old main road was from St Albans, via Harpenden, to Bedford and Rushton. Originally it had followed the course of the Lea and entered Luton at the southern end of Park Street. After the Hoo Park was enlarged in 1623, travellers had to go via Chapel Street (Hog Lane) instead. Thomas Jefferys' map of 1765 shows the road running along the western edge of the Hoo estate, down Chapel Street, through the centre of Luton, and along the Old Bedford Road to Streatley.

In 1727, the road came under the control of a Turnpike Trust. A turnpike was a road authorised by a private Act of Parliament; it had a toll gate at each end where the tolls which paid for and maintained the roads were collected. These were graded according to the size of the cart or carriage and the number of horses. Charges were also made for animals to be driven along the road. The first toll-gate recorded (1736) was at the end of the Moor. Later, toll gates were positioned at Gibraltar Farm on the London Road and by the ford in Bridge Street, north of the town.

Beyond Bridge Street, the road to Bedford was one to be avoided if possible because it took a difficult route over Barton Hills. In 1797 the ford crossing was improved by a bridge, hence the name, and in 1832 the Turnpike Trust was able to offer a much superior road to the north when Barton Cutting was dug out and the New Bedford Road opened. Until 1784 the road to Dunstable followed Dunstable Lane (Upper George Street) and along a track through Skimpot but then it was redirected along the road as it is today. In 1799 a bridge was built over the river Lea at the eastern end of Church Street to assist traffic travelling to Hitchin.

Until the coming of the railway, travel was on foot or horseback and by coach or wagon. There were regular services which increased considerably over the years and it is easy to plot all the comings and goings from details given in the local *Directories*. The *Henington Directory* for 1785 noted that a wagon went to London on Mondays and Thursdays. The timetable for coaches in 1836, advertised in *The Times*, noted that it took four hours to travel the 31 miles between London, Barnet, St Albans and Luton, leaving from London at 5 p.m. and from Luton the following morning at 8 a.m. The *Peveril of the Peak* service (1836) left London at 7.45 a.m. and took 21 hours to travel to Manchester via Luton and Derby.

There were also carriers which took goods and a few passengers, but in less style. These left from various inns in the town, on set days, and delivered to Ampthill, Bedford, Cambridge, Dunstable, Hitchin and Royston, Kettering, Leighton Buzzard, St Albans and Wellingborough.

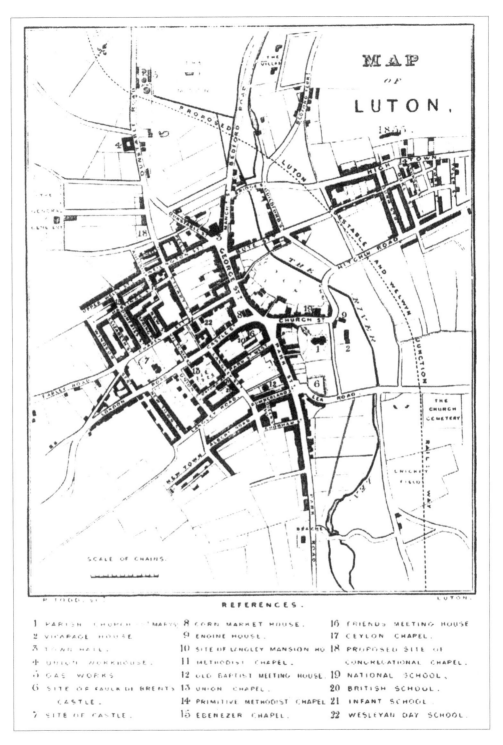

REFERENCES.

1 PARISH CHURCH ST MARYS 8 CORN MARKET HOUSE. 16 FRIENDS MEETING HOUSE
2 VICARAGE HOUSE 9 ENGINE HOUSE. 17 CEYLON CHAPEL.
3 TOWN HALL. 10 SITE OF LANGLEY MANSION HO 18 PROPOSED SITE OF
4 UNION WORKHOUSE. 11 METHODIST CHAPEL. CONGREGATIONAL CHAPEL.
5 GAS WORKS 12 OLD BAPTIST MEETING HOUSE 19 NATIONAL SCHOOL,
6 SITE OF FAULK DE BRENTS 13 UNION CHAPEL. 20 BRITISH SCHOOL.
  CASTLE. 14 PRIMITIVE METHODIST CHAPEL 21 INFANT SCHOOL.
7 SITE OF CASTLE. 15 EBENEZER CHAPEL. 22 WESLEYAN DAY SCHOOL.

29 *Map of Luton, 1855.*

From Leighton Buzzard, goods could be transferred to the Grand Junction Canal or the London and Birmingham railway. There were omnibuses which went to Hitchin railway station and others which travelled to Dunstable, Hatfield and Watford. In 1853 there was an office for the London and North-Western Railway in Langley Street, so apparently journeys could be booked ahead. It was also possible to hire horses for independent travel from John Brown in Park Street, Elizabeth Butlin in George Street, John Ireland in Dunstable Road, George Powell in Manchester Street and Peter Wilson in George Street.

30   *Rolling at Eaton Green, Luton.*

31-2   *Luton Midland Road Station, opened 1868.*

By 1848 nearby Dunstable had a railway line, but Luton had to wait another 10 years for the Great Northern Railway Company line to be extended as far as the town and then another two years before a link was made to Hatfield and the line to King's Cross. In 1868 the Midland Railway Company opened a line through Luton that linked the town to London and the Midlands. Luton then had three stations: one in Midland Road, one in Bute Street and another at Leagrave.

During these years the postal service grew in size and efficiency. The Royal Mail had been created by James I in 1609 and by the middle of the century towns across the land were connected by a postal service. Letters were carried by horses that were changed at regular 'posts'. By the end of the 18th century mail coaches were being used, and soon afterwards letters went by rail. In 1840 the famous 'Penny Black' stamp was introduced.

In 1785 there was a post office located at the *George*. In 1830, when Hannah Griffiths was the postmistress, letters arrived from Dunstable at 8 a.m. and were dispatched at 8 p.m. Nine years later Eliza Griffiths was in charge and letters were coming from London 'and all parts' to Leighton Buzzard station. Mail was sent to Leighton Buzzard at 7.30 every evening and letters were received in Luton every morning at about 9 a.m. In 1847, some letters were coming on horseback from Tring and others, via a foot post, from Hitchin.

In 1862 Mr John Jordan was postmaster, still in George Street. Now that there was a rail link, the mail arrived from London at 5.50 a.m. and 11 a.m. and was dispatched at 8.10 a.m., 1 p.m., and 6.55 p.m. By 1890 the mail was big business; there was a parcel post and telegraph service and the people were able to use pillar boxes sited around the town. Luton's first telephone directory (1896-7) contained 22 numbers. Mr Wing, from a local hat manufacturing family, noted that his grandfather's number was Luton 9. This gentleman was also the first customer at Barclays Bank in Luton.

There was a direct link between roads, travelling and inns. Travellers would stop overnight at the inns and horses could be rested. Inns were clearly regarded as reference points in the town, just as they often are today, and Luton certainly had its share. The 1785 *Directory* gives the names of two: the *George* and the *Red Lion*. An inn called the *George* existed as early as 1509 and was probably there well before that. It was still an important part of Luton life in the 1960s when it was destroyed and the site taken over by Littlewoods. Behind the *George* were meadows and farmland, stretching down to the river. In 1781, Dr Samuel Johnson paid a visit to the *George* and 'dined and drank his majesty's health' with his friend James Boswell. In 1785 the innkeeper was John Smith. The *George* was involved in a riot between townsfolk and a recruiting party in 1800 and some damage was done.

Then, in 1837, Victoria was officially proclaimed Queen in front of the inn. Soon afterwards, in 1841, a very important meeting to discuss the possible building of a railway line from London, via Luton, to Manchester was held at the *George* and one of those attending was George Stephenson, inventor of the first successful steam engine. Unfortunately, when it transpired that there was considerable opposition to the scheme, Stephenson took umbrage and vowed that no railway would come here as long as he lived. The *George* has certainly been witness to much Luton life over the centuries.

The other inn listed in the 1785 *Directory* was the *Red Lion* on Market Hill, site of the former Luton Guild of the Holy Trinity; the innkeeper was William Green and he also provided a base for the tax office. The *Red Lion* was near the sheep fair in Castle Street and in front of it stood the town stocks. It was on the road to London and became a busy coaching inn and a stopping off point for commercial travellers. Another interesting part of the *Red Lion*'s history was that, in 1650 when copper coinage was in short supply, the landlord, Richard Hopkins, together with some other traders in the town, issued his own tokens which could be used instead. Tokens were not valid after 1672.

In George Street, above the present Waterstone's bookshop, the name of *The Bell* can still be seen high up on the building. In the 18th century the Ampthill coach stopped here. There were other inns with long histories, some of them coaching inns, and many of them have had name changes over the years. For example, the *Two Brewers* became the *Duke of Clarence*. In 1870 there were 226 inns and it may not be a coincidence that when some of the licences were withdrawn, the number of commitments to gaol fell from 257 to 73 individuals.

The existence of so many inns was a temptation to Luton folk, many of whom were pleased to take advantage of the amenities. Members of churches in the town, notably Methodists, attempted to counteract the evils of drink by encouraging people to avoid alcohol altogether. Nothing but complete abstinence would do and it was important to pass this message on to children before they were tempted. Around the middle of the 19th century, Bands of Hope were set up for this purpose; they provided a good social life for children but also required them to 'sign the pledge' which committed them to an alcohol-free life. By 1890 there were nine such Bands in Luton, each having its own coloured banner, and members wore an enamel brooch in the shape of a white ribbon bow. Sometimes, on a Bank Holiday Monday, Bands would gather on Park Square and walk through the town to Scarborough Meadow, Dallow Lane, where they would enjoy games and take tea.

There were alternative beverages on offer: in the 1860s, Benjamin Holdstock had a Temperance Hotel and coffee and dining rooms at 3 Upper Bute Street, and the Burgess factory manufactured ginger beer, lemonade and soda water at their premises in Langley Street. An interesting story involves a Sunday school anniversary celebration. When the collection plate was passed around, someone put in a note to say that he 'could not conscientiously give anything to the collection because some of the money would be spent on beer to give to the children and teachers at the annual treat'. Apparently no beer was supplied after that. The story is not as strange as it seems when one considers that weak beer was the staple drink for previous generations and was more likely to be pure than some local water supplies. T.G. Hobbs had another way of promoting the temperance message. In the 1880s he helped to run a Lantern Mission which gave popular shows with a moral message using hand-painted glass magic lantern slides. His particular version of the *Rake's Progress* traced the story of a Luton man as he declined under the influence of the demon drink.

Life in the Town

Life was basic but punctuated by markets and fairs. Monday was the day for the regular trading of corn and straw plait, the first Mondays in April and October were cattle market days, and in September came the annual Statute Fair. Country people for miles around and the lower classes in the town looked forward to the 'Statty' as the great holiday of the year but it was regarded by many inhabitants and nearly all tradesmen in the town as 'an indecent Saturnalia and an intolerable nuisance'. E.V. Lucas remembered that there were 'stalls and booths and naphtha lamps and in one of these booths was a Fat Lady'.

In 1840 there was a report that people going to the corn market were harassed by 'the noise and contention of persons assembled in the corn market for the purpose of selling harness, books, drapery, pottery etc. who invaded the space allotted to the buyers and sellers of corn'. Then again, there were complaints about the moveable butchers' shops, carts and wagons that were left standing in the High Street and in Beggars' Lane on Sundays 'to the great nuisance of the inhabitants'. Owners were ordered to remove them every Saturday night by 11 p.m. and not to bring them back before Monday morning. The markets were tidied up in 1869 when corn trading was moved to the new Corn Exchange and the straw plait market took up residence in the Plait Halls.

Market tolls were to be paid to the lord of the manor until 1911 when Sir Julius Wernher relinquished the role with a 'deed of conveyance transferring to the Corporation these ancient and interesting franchises which had been for centuries exercised by kings of England and by a long succession of lords of the manor of Luton'. The town purchased the rights of the lord of the manor for £8,000.

33   *Corn Exchange and Market, postmarked 1905.*

34   *Mr H.C. Squires, coachbuilder from Chobham Street, Luton, with his wife and daughter, Mabel.*

The little town of Luton would have had its share of typical tradesmen who kept the place functioning. Most of the manual work would have been done by labourers, many of whom were hired on an annual basis at the Statty fair. Skilled workers would probably have served an apprenticeship, commonly for seven years, under the eye of a master craftsman. If they completed the apprenticeship they would become tradesmen in their own right or even masters of their own workshop. Experienced workmen could hire themselves out as journeymen who lived in the home of their employers or as day-labourers. Then there were the professional classes and the gentry.

From various records we can build up a picture of the social make-up of the town. There were bakers, blacksmiths, brewers, brickmakers, butchers, carters, coopers, farmers, gentry, innkeepers, maltmen, manufacturers of all types of clothing, printers, shoemakers, shopkeepers, surgeons, workers in wood and horn, and yeomen (hard to define but generally small landowners). Boys were recorded as apprentices to blacksmiths, builders, candle-makers, clothing manufacturers, gun-makers, haberdashers, iron-mongers, leather-workers and printers. Girls and women in the town had been busy straw plaiting and bonnet making since the 17th century.

In 1785 professionals listed were: 'Samuel Chase and Sons', apothecaries, men-midwives and surgeons and there was another surgeon, Robert Kirby. Hampson and Son and John Jackson were attorneys at law. Trades not already noted were: auctioneer, brazier, builder, carpenter, currier, draper, fellmonger, flax-dealer, glazier, grocer, ironmonger, manufacturer of hats, miller, plumber, sack-maker, watch-maker and woolstapler.

***

An *apothecary* like Samuel Chase would attend the sick and prepare medicines, either of his own making or according to the prescription of the physician. Apprentices had to be good scholars and know Latin.

The *blacksmith* would make and repair metal goods. Blacksmiths once also shoed horses but this became a specialist trade; farriers, as they were called, needed to understand the anatomy and the needs of different kinds of horses. This trade was crucial when transport depended on horses.

Brewing was important to Luton, becoming one of its main industries. Beer was the staple drink in this country when the purity of water could not be guaranteed. It was made from hops, malt, water and a little yeast; experience and skill were required to find the proper proportions of each ingredient, the correct temperature to heat the mixture and how it should be worked afterwards. Stages in the production were mashing, boiling, cooling and fermenting. The hops might well have been bought at the important hop market that was held on Stourbridge Common in Cambridge.

A *cordwainer* was a shoemaker. Shoes were often made-to-measure on special lasts. The master usually cut the leather while his apprentices sewed the parts together. A related trade was that of patten making; pattens could be fixed to a lady's shoe to keep her out of the mud and were apparently uncomfortable to wear; they were on sale in Luton in 1839.

Dyers needed specialist training in how to prepare different materials for dyeing. This became important to Luton when the hat trade began to flourish.

Gunmakers would start with a bar of iron and had to be skilled in boring, filing, forging the locks, making and fixing the breech and then polishing. The ownership of guns in Luton was probably limited to those who worked the land, especially on the big estates.

Haberdashers sold beads, caps, gloves, ribbons, purses, pins and toys, but in 1502 were joined by the hat makers' fraternity. From then on, there were two kinds of haberdashers: merchants of small goods and also dealers in hat materials. This is particularly significant because Luton was to become famous as a hat-making town.

Leatherworkers included fellmongers, furriers and skinners. A currier was the last in the line of leatherworkers; he tanned hides and prepared them for the use of book-binders, coachmakers, harness-makers, saddlers and shoemakers.

Malting, linked to brewing, was never a cottage industry as a lot of space was needed for the preparation. Maltmen bought barley from the farmers and soaked it in water for about 60 hours for it to soften and swell. Then the grains were spread on a floor where they began to germinate. Heat was generated and the germinating seeds had to be turned with

35   *The house of Thomas Waller, surgeon, b.1833 (no relation to the hat-making family), on Market Hill.*

a wooden shovel to control the temperature and humidity. When ready, the grain was taken to a kiln where it was dried and became tasty malt. Pale malt was heated to a low temperature but dark malt was exposed to higher temperatures.

Printers had a laborious job. The type had to be selected piece by piece and then set by a compositor who needed to be good at English. The rest of the work was done by pressmen who used ink made from oil and lamp-black. Local newspapers included the *Luton Reporter* and the *Luton Times*.

Tallow chandlers were candle-makers. Candles were made from equal parts of bullock's or sheep's fat (tallow) and the wicks from loosely twisted cotton. Tallow was melted in a large copper, and after it was well skimmed and refined it was put into a mould. The wicks were dipped again and again until the candles were the right size. Special candles could also be made, for example candles with wicks made of split rushes or thin cotton that would burn during the night. Lucy Luck, a straw hat sewer in Luton, tells how working until late by rushlight damaged her eyes. This was probably true of many local girls.

***

As has been noted, there were apothecaries, midwives and surgeons in the town but NHS style care was certainly not available and cost was probably the most important problem for ordinary people. Two names that appeared in subsequent listings were Peter Wootton, chemist, and Edward Woakes, surgeon, men who were significant in the history of the town. However, Mrs Drewett, a Quaker lady, was probably typical of the kind of care that many people provided. Her grandson, recalling the 1870s, wrote that:

> There must be many left in Luton to remember Mrs Drewett's treatment and cures. She was celebrated there and in the neighbourhood as an unqualified doctor, and three of her remedies were famous: her cough medicine, her rhubarb mixture (exceedingly unpleasant) and, above all, her ointment – 'Grandma's Ointment' we called it … I remember clearly my grandmother in her black dress and white shawl and her quiet, unhastening, efficient way: always doing something, baking her wonderful brown bread, making a pork pie … mixing with secret rites her ointment, or retiring with a patient to the little room known as the surgery. But she never hurried or forgot her dignity.

Smallpox was a very contagious and much-feared disease and any who had contracted it needed to be isolated in pest houses. In Luton there was a common pest house on the Great Moor (New Bedford Road) and a private one at Cowridge End (Stockingstone Road). One method of immunisation was to introduce body fluid from a contaminated person into the skin of the person to be inoculated. This was a much less safe method than that discovered by Edward Jenner in the 1790s.

In 1782 Ann Ransom (Brown) from Ampthill took her three sons to Dr Robert Kirby in Stopsley to be inoculated by the first method, as this was considered to be safer than catching the disease in the normal way. The boys became ill but recovered and convalesced at the home of their uncle, John Brown in Luton. Apparently Dr Kirby was paid six guineas for his services. Two years later, Dr Kirby performed a similar operation on three more of Ann's children.

POLITICS

Professionals like Dr Kirby would no doubt have been male, over 21 and a '40 shilling freeholder' (that is to say, an owner of land to the value of 40s. a year) and was therefore permitted to vote. Names of Bedfordshire's property owners (1685 to 1735) can be found in James Collett-White's books *How Bedfordshire Voted*. Luton did not have its own Member of Parliament until 1885, when the constituency of South Bedfordshire was created, but was represented by Members for the County of Bedford. As far as Luton was concerned, the gentry certainly had the vote but so did independent farmers, innkeepers, shopkeepers, stonemasons and tradesmen. Those anxious to record their vote would have had to travel to Bedford to do so but would have been well rewarded by being entertained, at the candidate's expense, at the *Swan* (if a Whig) or the *Bell* (if Tory).

Some of the Luton voters were out-voters, which means that they owned property in the town but did not live here. It is not clear just what property they held or where it was; it could have been land or commercial or residential property. Studies have shown out-voters living in Buckinghamshire, Hertfordshire, Northamptonshire and Wiltshire and many from London.

From 1696 lists of men eligible to serve on juries (with age and property qualifications) were published. They give us an idea of the gentry, professionals and tradesmen who were active in the town, for example, John Crawley Esq. and Daniel and Richard Brown, who were Quakers, and Thomas Godfrey Burr, a brewer. Occupations mentioned include brickmaker, draper, farmer, grocer, maltster and miller. It is an interesting exercise to look at a street map of Luton and see some of these people from the past recorded in the names of local streets, for example, Burr Street, Bute Street, Chase Street, Coupees Path and Napier Road.

LOCAL GOVERNMENT

During the 16th and 17th centuries, local government was in the hands of the Vestry. Churchwardens would call rate-payers to Vestry meetings which dealt with the civil side of parish life. Little by little, over the 19th century, more formal arrangements were established.

Since Elizabethan times, the Poor Law had insisted that it was the responsibility of every parish to support those born there if they were in need. The Vestry therefore appointed overseers whose job it was to care for the aged, infirm, orphaned and unemployed, finance being supplied through the parish rate. As part of this provision, there was a small workhouse near Park Square. In the 19th century, T.G. Hobbs became an overseer and noted that his responsibilities included signing cheques and helping to value properties.

It also has to be remembered that there were individual commitments to philanthropy by people with money and a social conscience. For example, land or property could be given over to the care of trustees and the rents used for charitable purposes. In 1602, Edward Vaughan gave three properties and an orchard and garden on Tower Hill (Manchester Street) for the 'only proper use of the poor people of this town'. In 1610 Thomas Yeoman made a similar bequest to the value of £2 for 'old, aged, lame, blind or impotent men or women of this town or parish for ever', and in 1660 Elizabeth Winch gave seven acres, the rents and profits of which were to be distributed to the poor on St Thomas's Day. The almshouses provided by Robert Hibbert have already been mentioned and, in 1715, another member of the gentry, Sir Theophilus Napier, gave £5 in 'bread for the poor of the parish belonging to the Church of England'. These were just a few of the charitable trusts in the town.

In 1834 the new Poor Law Amendment Act attempted to make the system more efficient by combining parishes into a Poor Law Union. Those linked with Luton were Barton, Caddington, Dunstable, Houghton Regis, Hyde, Kensworth, Leagrave, Limbury, Stopsley, Streatley, Studham, Sundon, Totternhoe and Whipsnade. In 1836, a new workhouse was built on the edge of the town, at the junction of Dunstable Road with Dallow Road. This was run by a Board of Guardians together with a governor and a matron who were usually husband and wife. Workhouses became notorious after Dickens wrote *Oliver Twist* and Luton's health historian, Dr Margaret Currie, has explained that life in Luton's workhouse was not very different. The building had stone flagged corridors, poor lighting and dark paintwork. Those admitted included the aged, the chronically and incurably sick and the mentally infirm as well as those who were unable to support themselves financially. All were dressed in drab clothing.

At the beginning of the 19th century, the town was in a sorry state. Roads were often muddy and made uneven by horse-drawn traffic and improvements were needed to cope with the increase in personal and commercial traffic. Another enormous problem was the abysmal standard of some of the local housing; some areas, notably Tower Hill, were overcrowded, badly ventilated and unsanitary slums. In 1850 a report to the General Board of Health summarised the problems and the remedies that were needed and this did not make for happy reading. Its recommendations were that there should be a public sewage system to which all houses would be connected. A powered pumping station must be built to provide clean water for every household. House building should be controlled and houses ventilated. Roads needed to be improved with flint from the chalk hills and footpaths with York paving and pebbles. The provision of a public slaughterhouse was absolutely necessary. All these improvements would prove to be expensive and as a result, and not without some bickering between leading residents, a Board of Health was set up in 1850. In 1864 the Board of Health took over the Fire Brigade and, until Luton became a Borough in 1876, the local Board of Health was in effect an unofficial town council.

Local utility services were set up to improve the quality of life. The Gas and Coke Company was founded in 1834 and the Luton Water Company in 1865. By 1870 this company had bored deep wells to reach a pure water supply and had laid a system of water mains throughout the town. Cemetery companies were established in 1854, one in Crawley Green Road for Church of England burials and another in Rothesay Road for the rest of the community. An Electricity Station was built in 1900.

The Vestry had the power to appoint constables. The office of constable had once carried considerable status, but by the 19th century this had diminished and constables were subordinate to the magistrates who were from the ranks of the aristocracy, clergy or landed gentry. The post was certainly not sought after: constables were chosen by ballot and served for one year; they were not paid and their many responsibilities meant that they could not take up any other full-time employment for the year. In 1830 Luton had one constable for day duty and two night watchmen, and prisoners were kept in a 'cage' by the pond on Park Square. Stray animals were kept in the 'pound' on the corner of Lea Road and Windmill Road.

To address the rising crime rate in the country, legislation was passed to formalise the situation, and in 1840 a Rural Police Force was set up, funded by county rates. Then, in 1876, Luton became a Borough and was able to appoint its own police force. The first police station was built in 1849 at the junction of Peel Street and Dunstable Place and nine years later it was replaced by a new one on the corner of Stuart Street and Dunstable Place.

Luton did not particularly enjoy a reputation for being a law-abiding place. From time to time there were riots and Michael Wing is still wondering what became of the man who attacked members of his family in 1865. A very detailed description of the perpetrator was circulated: he was 'an ugly man with sabre wounds, and a gruff voice, calling himself Ellis or Smith'. In spite of all the publicity, the attacker was never found.

Another aspect of life which became the subject of legislation was the education of children. This had been the responsibility of the churches and the focus of attention from local benefactors. Little private schools, some of a reasonable standard and others of very little value at all, came and went. In 1870, the Forster Education Act was passed, which required that, where insufficient school places were available, towns should elect a School Board. This met with a great deal of bad feeling in Luton but, in 1874, the town had to bow to the inevitable and elected a Board which worked well on behalf of local children until 1902.

The aspirations of the town, however, depended on securing the status of a Borough, especially since neighbouring Dunstable had gained theirs in 1864. A public meeting was held in December 1874 to consider applying for a Charter of Incorporation. As with the formation of the other local committees, differences of opinion were expressed but most people were in favour, and on 26 February 1876 Luton became a Municipal Borough. At the ceremony the town clerk is reported to have dropped the seal, which consequently broke. The following May there were elections. The three wards, North, East and West returned six councillors each and there were six aldermen (elected by their fellows), making a total of 24 members on the Borough Council.

The editor of *Luton Reporter*, Alfred Robbins, who was just 19 at the time, said that much of Luton's success was due to the very striking and strong body of public men of both parties Luton then possessed, for example William Bigg, John Cumberland, Alfred Welch, Henry Blundell and ardent religious ministers of various denominations. They 'brought out the fire which turned Luton from rather a slow-going town in many ways into what it has now become'. William Bigg (1814-78), who became the first mayor of the town, was a retired

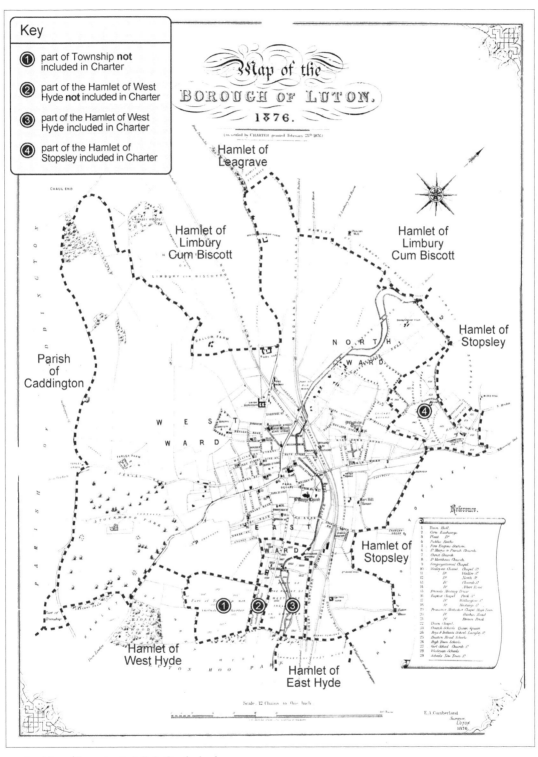

Key

① part of Township **not** included in Charter

② part of the Hamlet of West Hyde **not** included in Charter

③ part of the Hamlet of West Hyde included in Charter

④ part of the Hamlet of Stopsley included in Charter

Map of the
BOROUGH OF LUTON.
1876.

(as settled by CHARTER granted February 25th 1876.)

Hamlet of
Leagrave

Hamlet of
Limbury
Cum Biscott

Hamlet of
Limbury
Cum Biscott

Hamlet of
Stopsley

Parish
of
Caddington

NORTH WARD

Hamlet of
Stopsley

WEST WARD

EAST WARD

Hamlet of
West Hyde

Hamlet of
East Hyde

Scale 12 Chains to One Inch

E.A. Cumberland
Surveyor
LUTON
1876

36   *Map of Luton in 1876, E.A. Cumberland.*

37 *George Street and town hall, Luton, postmarked 1906.*

bank manager, promoter of the local gas and water companies, chairman of the School Board, a leading Quaker and a supporter of the Adult School, the Literary Institute and the Mechanics Institute.

Luton began to change almost beyond recognition. Land for building became available and a thriving property market developed. As a result many small businessmen and tradesmen could afford to buy houses, sometimes several, and become landlords. There was still a professional class of bankers, doctors and solicitors, and a middle class began to emerge that consisted of people who had prospered in the hat industry. They made good money but also responded by serving the community in many capacities. The Established Church was still represented but the nonconformist values of hard work, honesty, temperance and thrift were very apparent. It would not be possible to name everyone who contributed to the modern Luton but some can be acknowledged.

Thomas E. Austin was a solicitor and clerk to the Board of Guardians, a member of the Literary Institute and a supporter of the railways. His son, William, also a solicitor, and a clerk to the Justices and the Board of Guardians, was steward of the manor of Luton and in that capacity was able to study the local archives. He compiled the definitive *History of Luton and its Hamlets*. Joseph K. Blundell, a Wesleyan Methodist, was a hat manufacturer. His son, Henry, also a Wesleyan Methodist, opened the leading draper's shop that became an established part of the town for many years. He became mayor in 1886.

The Carruthers family came from Scotland and set up as hat manufacturers in George Street West and King Street. George Carruthers looked after bleaching and dyeing while his brother, Colonel Andrew Carruthers, VD JP, was head of manufacturing. Andrew Carruthers became Chairman of the Bleachers and Dyers in the local Chamber of Commerce. His wife Emily, a local girl, became active in educational circles, becoming the only woman to serve on the School Board. She was manager of several local schools and, when appointed to the Bedfordshire Education Committee, was described as having 'special experience in local education matters'.

The Higgins family were well known in the town. John, a painter and plumber, was on the first Town Council, the Board of Health, the Board of Guardians and the first School Board. William Hiram, his brother, was a hat manufacturer. He had five children: Walter, Hiram, Dorcas, Rebecca and Catherine. The ladies deserve a mention. Dorcas gave a lecture to the Scientific Literary and Artistic Club after which a book, *Old Luton*, based on her talk, was produced. The book was illustrated by Emily and Catherine Higgins. Rebecca, who was at one time governess in the home of Salusbury G. Payne, JP for Bedfordshire, was involved with education in Luton and was on the Education Committee of the Bedfordshire County Council.

T.G. Hobbs began work in the hat industry at an early age. He had plenty of initiative and was able to invent some machinery to facilitate the work. As a commercial traveller in the hat trade, he travelled to many parts of this country and abroad and also opened a business in Cheapside, selling cotton and other hat accessories. Hobbs was a delegate for the Luton Chamber of Commerce and attended the seventh Congress of the Chambers of Commerce of the Empire in Sydney, Australia, in 1909. He was also a photographer and produced illustrated books: *Luton and Neighbourhood, Illustrated*; *Wardown (Luton) Illustrated* and another about the Parish Church. One of his most popular projects was the printing of the local 'Hobbs timetable' which was in circulation until well into the 20th century. Hobbs was also a pioneer travel agent.

The Reverend James O'Neill, vicar at St Mary's, was a staunch supporter of the Established Church. He was a belligerent man who fought for his principles. This meant that those who agreed with his ideas warmed to him but, to put it mildly, many other people had a somewhat different opinion. However, he did restore the fabric of the church and brought improvements to the standard of its music. He supported the educational provision of the Church in the town and was a nominal member of the School Board. The pulpit beside the Wenlock Chapel in St Mary's Church was presented to him in 1882 to mark his 20th anniversary as vicar.

As Luton developed, some fine buildings were erected. However, preserving the past does not seem to be one of the town's priorities and none of the ones mentioned here have survived. The Corn Exchange stood on Market Hill on the site of the ancient market house. It was built in 1868 in the Gothic style at a cost of about £3,000 and was opened on 18 January 1869. Underneath the corn exchange area was a meat market and in front of it was a drinking fountain, erected in 1875 and funded by public subscription. It was in memory of Colonel Lionel Ames, who had lived at The Hyde and was commonly known as the Pepperpot.

The Plait Halls in Cheapside and Waller Street were built in 1868 and opened on 18 January 1869 to take the plait market away from the main street. They were set up on land which had once been the house and garden of John Waller. A post office was opened in Cheapside in 1881 and a free library was established on the corner of Williamson Street. A town hall was erected in 1847 at the north end of George Street. It was designed by John Williams and Son and was the property of the Town Hall Company. The clock on the town hall was funded by public subscription to celebrate the end of the Crimean War.

By the end of the 19th century Luton had become a substantial town with a thriving hat industry and an industrial future. Its inhabitants were hard-working and deserving of the prosperity that the future offered.

IV

Country Houses

THE LARGE COUNTRY houses to be found in and around Luton once reflected the 'Upstairs Downstairs' style of life but have all taken on new roles. Luton Hoo is now an *Elite Hotel*, Putteridge Bury is a Conference Centre, the grounds at Stockwood have been opened as a Discovery Centre and Wardown is a Museum.

LUTON HOO

Towards the end of the 12th century, the manor of Luton was divided, one of the new manors being Luton Hoo. In 1245, this new manor was held by Robert de Hoo as the King's 'Tenant-in-Chief'. The men of the family all seem to have been called either Robert or Thomas; Robert's grandson, another Robert, became a knight of the shire, while Thomas II entered Parliament. Thomas III fought in France and was made Baron Hoo and Hastings in 1447. When he died, there was no male heir and the four heiresses sold the manor in 1523.

Subsequently, the house belonged to the Rotherham family. Then, *c.*1601, it was sold to Sir Robert Napier, who had made a fortune as a Turkey merchant and grocer and was a member of the Grocers' Company of London. The Napiers, sometimes known by the name Sandy, came from a Scottish family. Later, *c.*1611, Sir Robert bought the manor and, in 1611, he was created 1st Baronet of Luton Hoo by James I who was visiting the house at the time. In the same year, he was High Sheriff in Bedfordshire. When he died in 1637, he left four houses on Tower Hill in Luton as homes for the poor.

These were troubled times, with loyalty in the country being divided between allegiance to the King and support for Parliament and Cromwell in particular. The Napier family were supporters of the Crown. In 1623, Robert's son, also Sir Robert, was given permission to take over 300 acres of land as parkland. Sir Theophilus Napier (1672-1719) married Elizabeth Rotherham, so uniting two old Luton families. The Napier family remained lords of the manor until 1762 and their name is still commemorated in Napier Road in Luton.

The last male Napier had died in 1742 and, *c.*1762, the estate was bought by John Stuart, 3rd Earl of Bute (1713-92). The Earl of Bute was a prominent Tory; he was a friend of Frederick, Prince of Wales, and mentor to his son, King George III. He was Prime Minister, though an unpopular one, between 1762-3. One of his claims to fame was the introduction of a much-hated tax on cider. His wife, Mary Wortley Montagu, inherited from her father an interest in his fortune made from production in the coalfields. Bute was passionately interested in botany and was one of the brains behind the setting up of the Royal Botanic Gardens at Kew. His portrait, by Sir Joshua Reynolds, can be seen in the National Portrait Gallery in London.

The house at Luton Hoo was in a poor condition when the Earl bought the estate so Robert Adam, who was a favourite architect of the upper classes at the time, was commissioned to refashion the interior. Details of his plans can still be seen at Sir John Soane's Museum in London. Another famous designer, Lancelot (Capability) Brown was called upon to landscape the gardens that eventually covered 1,500 acres. A five-acre octagonal walled garden was also planted; this provided flowers, fruit and vegetables for the house for almost two centuries. Bute's interest in horticulture involved the cultivation of precious and expensive plants, many of them imported and, in this, he no doubt competed with the owners of other large gardens, as was the fashion at the time.

It was possible to apply to view large country houses and there are reports that were written by visitors to Luton Hoo. One of these was Mrs Mary Delany, a famous letter-writer and artist, who compiled a description of society life. When she visited Luton Hoo in 1774, she found Lady Bute to be agreeable with good principles and sense while Lord Bute was polite, obliging and entertaining. The grounds, she said, were fine and there was a view of the river. The interior of the house was also impressive: the library was magnificent, 'extremely well lighted and nobly furnished'. Every room was filled with pictures and there was a great variety of fine vases, both foreign and English, and marble tables. The beds were damask and rich satin in blue, crimson, green and white.

In the same year, Lady Mary Coke visited the Hoo. She was very impressed with the house and the 'very fine flower garden ... with stoves [tropical glasshouses] etc. for exotic plants'. Mrs Boscawen came in 1776, her main aim being to see the 'delightful conservatory in particular and the garden in general'. The porter at the gate allowed her to enter, asking her to be sure to keep to the gravel paths. She had spent over an hour there, being entertained very civilly by the gardener, when a servant came from Lady Bute inviting her to dine with the family. She accepted most gladly and was afterwards shown around the house by Lady Bute.

Other visitors, this time in 1781, were Dr Samuel Johnson and his friend James Boswell, who had obtained tickets. They described Lord Bute's 'magnificent seat', remarking that 'it is a very stately place, indeed; in the house magnificence is not sacrificed to convenience, nor convenience to magnificence'.

There was a fire in the house in 1771 and another in 1843. The housekeeper, Mrs Partridge, earned herself a mention in the *London Illustrated News* (November 1843) when she was commended for supervising the removal of paintings and furniture after the fire broke out, causing great damage to the structure of the house. The furniture was moved to Mt Stewart on the Isle of Bute. Lord Bute moved to Hampshire, where he died in 1792.

The 4th Earl of Bute (created the Second Marquess in 1796) had, by marriage, acquired property in Cardiff and the family interests came to be focused on the building of Cardiff Docks. In 1847, the house and estate at Luton Hoo were sold to a Liverpool solicitor, John Shaw Leigh, who, though not a member of the aristocracy, had made a fortune from his interest in brewing, the Liverpool Docks and speculating in property. He paid for the house to be restored. His son, J. Gerard Leigh, inherited it in 1871 and, the following year, married a widow, Mrs Dudley Ward, who was a close friend of the Prince of Wales. Gerard Leigh died in 1875 and left the Hoo to his wife for her lifetime. In 1883, she married Christian de Falbe, a Danish diplomat. Madame de Falbe died in 1899 and the estate passed to her former husband's nephew, Henry Leigh, who died very soon afterwards, and the house was left empty.

Madame de Falbe, as she was known, took an interest in the people of Luton. In wintertime, they were allowed to skate on the lake in the park for a small admission fee, the money being donated to the poor. One of her visitors, in 1881, was Sir Arthur Sullivan, the well-known composer who wrote that Mrs Leigh (as she then was) had opened a bazaar. Sullivan had donated £5 and had also accompanied a lady in the *Lost Chord*.

During the 19th century, the gardens at Luton Hoo became famous. Fifty or more gardeners worked there at any one time and it was said that the gardens were so well respected that anyone who had worked at Luton Hoo could be sure to find work elsewhere. There was a hierarchy of

38   *The Mansion at Luton Hoo; photo by Alan Hutchinson.*

39   *The Lodge Gates at Luton Hoo; photo by A.C. Jordan.*

gardeners – who were encouraged to be teetotal. Head gardeners enjoyed considerable status. In the Hoo gardens there were decorative trees and many thousands of bedding plants were set out around the mansion. The walled garden was very productive and heated glasshouses were maintained for the production of more tender crops such as cucumbers and melons and flowers for the decoration of the house. It is said that, at one time, there were 5,000 pots just for growing strawberries. The estate was self-sufficient, coal for heating being brought by way of the local railway station.

It became fashionable for society people to visit at the weekends. They would take the meandering path from the house to the gardens, men probably walking and women perhaps in their carriages, to take tea at the beautiful little tea house. This, together with the dairy, was constructed for Madame de Falbe and the two were linked by a covered walkway. They were built of knap flint and were originally thatched in the tradition of the *'cottage ornée'*, that is to say a rustic retreat. The walls of the dairy, which had a dovecote on the roof, were decorated with beautiful Italian tiles and there was once a fountain in the middle to keep the air cool.

In 1899, Luton Hoo was let to and, in 1903, bought by Julius Wernher. Sir Julius, as he later became, was from Germany and his wife, Alice, was the daughter of a Polish immigrant. Their considerable fortune was made from the diamond industry and anyone visiting the 'Big Hole' at Kimberley in South Africa can still see a map of 'claims' that includes one in the name of Julius Wernher. He formed a syndicate, Wernher, Beit and Co. and became a life governor of the diamond monopoly DeBeers. He was also a fine art collector and a philanthropist, one of his important contributions to education being support for the establishment of the Imperial College of Science in Kensington.

Lady Wernher loved her garden and it continued to flourish. Beatrice Webb, on a visit in 1908, said:

> Sir Julius Wernher has bought a great country mansion with an historic name … The family spend some Sundays at Luton Hoo and a few months in the autumn, but all the rest of the 365 days the big machine goes grinding on, with its 54 gardeners, 10 electricians, 20 or 30 house servants and endless labourers … the only noise the perpetual whirring and calling of the thousands of pheasants, ducks and other game that were fattening ready for the autumn slaughter.

At the time there was a huge glasshouse with miles of pipes for heating, and ornate Edwardian gardens. 'Malmaison' carnations were a speciality and flower arrangements were said to have been changed up to four times a day. After the death of Sir Julius, Lady Wernher remarried and was well known in the town as Lady Ludlow.

Sir Julius Wernher's son, Alex, was killed during the First World War and his mother gave the Memorial Park, at the top of Tennyson Road, to the town in his memory. Their second son, Sir Harold, married Countess Anastasia (Zia) Mikhailovna de Torby, elder daughter of the Grand Duke Michael Mikhailovich Romanov, grandson of Tsar Nicholas I of Russia, and a relative of Pushkin, who brought valuable Russian artefacts to Luton Hoo, where they were for many years on show to the public.

During the Second World War, Luton Hoo hosted Eastern Command. It was also used as a training farm for land girls between July 1941 and March 1946. The girls learnt dairy and glasshouse work and specialised in growing tomatoes and many kinds of fruit. Some were accommodated at The Bothy which had previously housed students from the Royal Horticultural Society. After the war, Sir Winston Churchill, a friend of Sir Harold, visited the Hoo and copies of some of his paintings are still on show.

The family were close friends of the Royal Family, and Queen Elizabeth and Prince Philip spent some of their honeymoon at the estate. Every year, at the time of their anniversary, they would visit and attend Sunday morning service at the Parish Church. Sir Harold and Lady Zia were very supportive of Luton life. During this time the gardens were, for a while, open to the public and there was also a garden centre. However, there was no longer a need for large estate gardens to be showpieces and labour was not so easy to come by, so the gardens were no longer maintained to the same standards.

After the death of Lady Zia, her grandson, Nicholas Phillips, and his family lived in the mansion. Between 1991 and 1997, the chapel that had been built by John Shaw Leigh was commissioned for monthly Russian Orthodox services, a fitting reminder of Lady Zia's ancestry. The chapel is no longer in use but the beautiful paintings of martyrs, such as St Catherine and St Lucy, are still to be seen on the walls.

Large estates, always expensive to run, need to seek funding from other sources and Luton Hoo became popular with film and television companies which hired the mansion as a

40   *Luton Hoo Gardens, c.1911 from the Wernher Collection.*

background for their productions. Famously, the film *Four Weddings and a Funeral* was shot at the Hoo and the most profitable leasing was the three-month shoot of *Eyes Wide Shut* with Tom Cruise and Nicole Kidman. Advertisements for Walkers Crisps were also filmed there. Unfortunately, Nicholas Phillips died at an early age and the changing financial situation required that the mansion be sold.

The remarkable Wernher collection, including valuable old masters, Lady Ludlow's collection of Chelsea, Bow, Derby and Worcester porcelain, Sir Julius's medieval ivories and Renaissance jewellery, needed to be rehoused. Much of this can now be seen at the Ranger's House in Greenwich but the ivory 'Wernher Triptych' of the Virgin and Child surrounded by angels and saints was given to the government and is on display in the Medieval Gallery at the British Museum and three pictures are in the National Gallery.

The estate has now been divided. The arable farmland is still run by Mr Edward Phillips, great-great-grandson of Sir Julius, who has launched Hoo's Food as a 'regional food hub'. The aim is to supply large stores with food such as bacon, beer and cider, eggs, sausages and yoghurt from local suppliers. They will be retailed in shops

across neighbouring counties and will have travelled an average distance of just 26 miles. Some of the old farm buildings are rented out as small industrial units or offices and Miss Charlotte Phillips, his sister, is the project manager for a delightful scheme to open up the old walled garden.

This plan is being supported by an enthusiastic group of volunteers but funding is needed so that the whole site and the buildings can be restored. In particular, it is hoped that the old Edwardian greenhouses comprising 'six fingers, a conservatory and connecting passages' can be restored to their former glory. This time it is not being run for a small élite but for the local community and as a social amenity. Once the estate was separated from the town and the people of Luton were invited to the Hoo just for special occasions such as the 1919 Peace Celebrations, but now they can come on a different basis. There are study tours and excellent talks with a horticultural theme. School parties and other groups are welcomed to find out about the past and to watch the garden come back to life.

The Grade-I listed mansion is now a 5-star *Elite Hotel*. It has had the benefit of a £60m refurbishment and offers 144 bedrooms, with some suites aptly named after Fabergé, Pushkin and Romanov. There is an 18-hole golf course and a spa. The gardens are being refurbished and the restoration has attempted to follow Capability Brown's original designs. One project involves the Victorian grass tennis court together with its novel pavilion that can be rotated to follow the sun. A new building, known as Warren Weir, is a luxury meeting and wedding venue with views over the lake.

The Luton Hoo Estate has seen many changes since the owners were lords of the manor but both the house and grounds are still a considerable asset to the town. Not least, the existence of the estate has prevented the growth of the town to the south and gives a rural feel to that part of the county, especially on the road to Hyde and on past the water meadows.

SOMERIES

Someries Castle is not a castle, rather a ruined medieval manor house. The remains of the chapel, gateway, porter's lodge and earthworks, associated with Sir William de Someries, survive and the place is designated a Heritage site. Just a few years ago, the surrounding area was a precious taste of the past even though, incongruously, the runway at Luton Airport could be seen (and heard) just a field away, but now the nearby farm buildings are used as workshops, hedges

41 *Someries, 1934.*

have been felled and earth is being excavated all around. The area could also be at risk if permission is granted to build another runway at the airport.

The Crawley family bought Someries in 1629. They lived there until 1712 and the estate was sold to Sir John Napier in 1724, after which it fell into disrepair. Soon after 1740, much of the manor house was pulled down and the bricks used in the building of Someries Farm as well as of the adjoining buildings and cottages. By 1787 Someries looked much as it did at the end of the 20th century.

In 1907 the novelist Joseph Conrad, who lived at the farm for a short time, wrote to Henry James and also to R.B. Cunninghame, Graham describing Someries as 'less than 40 minutes from London with many trains a day' and 'very accessible from London and only two and half miles from Luton. It is a farmhouse on the Luton Hoo Estate belonging to that knight-errant, Sir Julius Wernher. A flavour of South Africa and Palestine hangs about our old walled garden.'

STOCKWOOD PARK

The Crawley family is Luton's oldest recorded family. There is a reference in a document from 1332 to Thomas de Crawley and the family tree can be traced from 1445. Between the mid-16th century and the late 19th century, they were buying large areas of agricultural land on three sides of Luton. Many of the family served the community, for example as Members of Parliament, magistrates or Justices of the Peace. One important family member was Sir Francis Crawley (1584-1649), who was a lawyer, a judge and Registrar of the House of Lords.

In 1708 Richard Crawley bought the Stockwood estate and, during the time of John Crawley, the house was built, being finally completed in 1740. It was a large two-storeyed building with a grand staircase and a fine marble fireplace. There was a stable yard, an icehouse and small houses for estate workers. As was usual with all these large houses, there was a walled garden supplying fruit and vegetables for the house, as well as wonderful roses. During the 1800s the walled garden was extended and apricots, grapevines, nectarines and peaches were planted. The main drive was lined with chestnut trees and there was a right of way across the park for villagers who came into Luton to work.

The last of the family to live at Stockwood House was Miss Joan Crawley and her husband, Captain Harry Ross-Skinner. They involved themselves in local life and supported fund raising activities such as fêtes and bazaars. Around 1920, Miss Joan Crawley gave a lovely stretch of hills off Dallow Road to the town. The family left Stockwood House in the 1930s. Though smaller than Luton Hoo, Stockwood was an impressive country estate.

During the Second World War, Stockwood House became the home of the Alexandra Hospital for Crippled Children and, for the next 18 years, children with polio, TB and other orthopaedic complaints were treated there, some of them staying for 10 years or more. It was a very happy place, run as a family unit. As well as receiving medical care, the children were educated at the hospital and help and entertainment were provided by volunteers from Luton.

In 1945, Stockwood House was sold to Luton Town Council. There was a petition to keep the hospital open but the costs of modernisation were perceived to be too high and it was closed in 1958. Then, sadly in 1964, the Council decided that it could not afford to repair and restore the house and it was demolished, only the stable block and walled garden remaining. They were opened as Stockwood Park Museum in 1986. The parkland around remains open to the public and for a variety of sporting activities. The Bagshawe collection of rural crafts and trades, one of the finest in the country, was moved from Wardown to the stable block and the bees, known to generations of visitors to Wardown Museum, also came to Stockwood.

George Mossman, who was born in Caddington in 1906, became a butcher's delivery boy when he left school and this started his lifelong interest in horse-drawn vehicles. He was involved in several successful enterprises, one being a leasing company providing horse-drawn carriages for special occasions. He drove his carriages in London's Lord Mayor's Show for many years and even became involved in the Coronation procession in 1953. Mossman gathered together an impressive collection of horse-drawn vehicles: an 18th-century landau, a 19th-century barouche and a charabanc from the 1890s, to name but a few. There are trade and working vehicles as well as much grander conveyances and the exhibition also displays replica vehicles that were used by the film industry. The collection is of national importance. It was given to Luton Museums in 1991 and housed in Stockwood Park in a special building, paid for by a Mossman legacy.

Another exhibit is the last Luton tram. The tram service in Luton operated between 1908 and 1932, after which the trams were sold and served a variety of strange purposes including offices, greenhouses or even chicken sheds. However, this one (No. 6) was found in a field in Oxfordshire and is being restored.

In July 2008 Stockwood Park Museum was reopened as Stockwood Discovery Centre after a transformation costing over £6m and a great deal of work by staff from Luton Museums. It is, remarkably, still free to the public. Money for the revamp included donations from the Heritage Lottery Fund, the European Union and from individual supporters. The new building work is environmentally friendly and has received a 'highly commended' award from the Royal Institution of Chartered Surveyors (the property Oscars). Interestingly, car parking has had to be re-sited to accommodate rules concerning the flight path into Luton Airport.

Some of the exhibits are housed in the old stable block. They include information about the geology of the area and archaeological digs, interactive displays, scenes from different eras in history as well as oral history and the important rural crafts exhibition created by Thomas Bagshawe. The Mossman carriages remain, together with a collection of early steam and motor transport. There is a room devoted to textiles and changing displays are put on in the Discovery Hall. The beautiful 'world gardens' contain plants from different climates across the world and the medicinal garden demonstrates how plants can be useful to mankind. The old walled garden has become a series of 'period gardens' and a special part of the park is devoted to six sculptures by Ian Hamilton Finlay, an internationally respected artist.

However, the 'jewel in the crown' is probably the medieval Wenlok Jug that was saved from export in 2005 (see p.24). It is hoped that future research will be able to explain more about the jug's history and its possible links with Luton.

PUTTERIDGE BURY

Putteridge Bury is just over the border into Hertfordshire and, while there were of necessity strong links between the house and neighbouring Hertfordshire villages, it also had connections with Luton and the hamlet of Stopsley in particular. In 1525 Richard Lyster sold the estate to John Docwra, after which it changed hands several times. In 1808, when it was owned by John Sowerby, the mansion was destroyed by fire. It was rebuilt on a nearby site and the grounds were designed by the well-known horticulturist and landscape designer J.C. Loudon. It seems to have been very much the fashion of the day for large estates to compete with one another over the excellence of their gardens.

John Sowerby's grandson, Colonel George Sowerby, inherited the estate in 1868 and took a real interest in Luton. He supported the Luton Cottage Hospital and was president of the Luton Choral Society. He was also a keen naturalist and kept a small private zoo in the grounds. Children from Stopsley School were invited to the park for treats and to watch agricultural demonstrations. Unfortunately, on 2 August 1888, Colonel Sowerby was killed in an unexpected attack by a stag from his collection. After his death, Putteridge Bury was rented by Mr George Herring, who also had a friendly relationship with people in Stopsley, and in 1908 the estate was sold to Captain Thomas Clutterbuck whose family lived there until 1919.

The house was rebuilt between 1909 and 1911 to a design based on Chequers, now the country home of the Prime Minister, where the Clutterbucks had previously lived. In 1919 it was let again until it was bought by Sir Felix Cassel KC in 1922. Edward Lutyens and Gertrude Jekyll were involved in designing the gardens. King George V and Queen Mary sometimes visited and, in 1926, the King planted an oak tree on the south lawn. In 1953 Sir Francis's son, who was a talented pianist, inherited the estate. He died in 1967.

During the Second World War, the house was requisitioned and prisoners of war were housed in Nissen huts. After Sir Francis died, it was bought as a base for research by British Celanese. Then, in 1964, the mansion and 40 acres were acquired by Luton County Borough for use as a non-residential Teachers' Training College. It originally focused on mature students who wished to qualify as teachers and up to 300 students were trained in any one year. The College did not last, however, as Luton lost its County Borough status in 1974. Four years later, Putteridge Bury and Luton College of Further Education were amalgamated and became the Department of Business and Management Studies of Luton and then, in July 1993, part of the University of Luton, now the University of Bedfordshire.

Putteridge Bury is still owned by the University of Bedfordshire and is a postgraduate business school. Departments represented include the medical school, midwifery, law and travel and tourism. The ground floor is a conference centre that offers facilities for civil weddings and corporate and social events.

WARDOWN

The house that is home to Wardown Park Museum is smaller than Luton Hoo, Putteridge Bury and Stockwood but is a good example of an upper-middle-class family home. Many Luton children will remember watching the bees flying in and out of their hive set into an upstairs window and seeing the life size hedger and ditcher and the shepherd. These have been moved to the Discovery Centre at Stockwood. Members of staff at the Museum have been able to research its history and have published much of this information in one of their education packs.

In 1868 Mr Frank Scargill bought the old farmhouse and estate known as Bramingham Villa and then accessed more land until the property covered 50 acres. He was a solicitor in Luton; the 1890 *Directory* records that he was a partner in Scargill and Latham, solicitors, in King Street. Also in 1868 he married Elizabeth Kennedy, a widow, whose first husband came from an iron ore mining family in Lancashire and had left her a considerable fortune.

Between 1875 and 1877, Frank Scargill demolished Bramingham Villa and replaced it with a new house to be known as Bramingham Shott. (This may possibly refer to an old word 'Shot', a cultivated strip of land in a ridge and furrow field.) The date 1877 can still be seen carved into the archway that led to the stables. The house was built of bricks known as 'Luton greys'. In 1897, an inventory noted that there were 16 bedrooms, a billiard room, boudoir, dining room, four dressing rooms, drawing room, two kitchens and a smoking room. Besides these, there were cellars, a dairy, a laundry and a schoolroom. Then there was an apple room, a boot room, conservatory, game larder, three bathrooms, four lavatories and also the servants' quarters. Outside were a cricket ground, lodges and a park. Other reminders of the time are two small stones that are still on the lawn opposite the main entrance to the house; these were the gravestones of family dogs. The information pack also details the hierarchy of servants that would have been employed at the house.

The Scargills moved away from Luton in 1894, first to live at Hove and then Ireland. The house was rented to B.J.H. Forder, the owner of a Bedfordshire brickmaking firm. He changed the name to Wardown as a reminder of his former home in Hampshire, although to the people of Luton it was generally known as 'Scargills'. The next tenant was Halley Stewart, who became chairman of the London Brick Company. In 1903 Luton Town Council dithered when they had the opportunity to buy Wardown as a local amenity. However, Asher Hucklesby and Edwin Oakley, both Luton town councillors, were more far-seeing and stepped in to buy the property. In the sale description, the grounds were said to:

43   *Wardown House.*

Comprise three tennis lawns, croquet and bowling green overlooked by a prettily-built rustic summer house, and surrounded by numerous winding and secluded walks, fringed by old English borders and shaded by well-grown ornamental trees and plantations; and an extensive kitchen and fruit garden, all in perfect order and condition; also a conservatory and four other glasshouses and several useful farm buildings, together with two detached freehold cottages and gardens.

There was also an osier bed. Osiers were thin branches harvested from willow trees that grew along river banks and were used in the making of baskets. The river Lea ran through the park, as it still does, and perhaps the osiers were a marketable crop to add to the family income.

The following year, Hucklesby and Oakley sold Wardown to the town. It was opened to the public in 1905/6 and, more than one hundred years later, the people of the town are still able to enjoy the facilities. It was hoped at the time that a museum would be established, and in 1931, that hope was fulfilled when a collection that had been housed in the Carnegie Library since 1927 was transferred to Wardown. The Council extended and marked off a part of the lake to make a swimming pool and provided pleasure boats for hire. A suspension bridge was built by the boathouse. There was a bowling green and tennis courts. Fêtes were held in the park and bands regularly played at the bandstand. The walk from the town to the park and back was an accepted evening activity indulged in by a large proportion of the town's population and became known as the monkey parade. Today, the grounds are the focus of the magnificent multicultural Luton Carnival.

Over the years, Wardown Park has been witness to a variety of activities. The house was used as a hospital in the First World War and, afterwards, became a tearoom. During the Second World War 'Holidays at Home' were necessary and the grass grew long enough for children to play hide and seek. Thurston's Fair came for a month every summer. Civil Defence personnel used the buildings near the cricket ground as a base and the schoolchildren of the town sat on the steps around the lower ground to join together in the well-remembered patriotic singing.

The first curator, and later director (1927-47), of Luton museum was Thomas Wyatt Bagshawe (1901-76). He had a love of history and began a small private museum in Dunstable in 1925 and another in a room at the Carnegie Library in Luton. He was afraid, and rightly so, that traditional crafts and trades would disappear so he undertook a search of Bedfordshire villages to find people who had grown up with those skills. He interviewed them, collected old tools or items of interest and samples of work. He made notes, and collected photographs and illustrations, all of which he catalogued meticulously. These all came to the museum, together with his books on relevant subjects. The collection is particularly important as it is relates specifically to Luton and neighbouring counties. It was first displayed, in 1930, in one room at Wardown but eventually took over most of the building. It has now been moved to Stockwood Discovery Centre.

Charles Freeman (1906-65) became assistant curator in 1930 and succeeded Thomas Bagshawe as curator in 1936. Together they built up one of the finest local history collections in the country, and in 1938 a rural industries gallery was opened, designed on principles based in Scandinavian countries that were at the forefront of folklife museums in Europe. In 1939 the Dunstable collection was taken to Wardown. Charles Freeman was also chairman of the South Bedfordshire Archaeological Society (1952) which was very much the brainchild of Dr James Dyer, who is an authority on archaeology and has also been a lifelong supporter of the museum.

Another person who deserves recognition in the story of Wardown Park Museum is Dr John Dony (1899-1991), whose interests included botany and local history. In 1936 he became Honorary Keeper of Botany at the Museum. He wrote several definitive books on natural history in the area, besides being a member of the Linnean Society and also a member, and later president, of the Botanical Society of the British Isles. His PhD thesis (1941) was on the Luton hat industry and the book based on his research is still the standard work on the subject.

A recent imaginative Heritage Lottery funded redevelopment of Wardown House Museum and Gallery brings to life the Victorian mansion now surrounded by Wardown Park. The imposing entrance hall leads to the billiard room, library, morning room and drawing room, all furnished with items from the museum collection, which give a taste of life in Victorian times, as well as exploring the history of the town and the museum itself, while the dining room is the café. A grand staircase leads to the first floor, with a lady's bedroom showing jewellery and lace as well as interactive displays on the daily life of a maid. The dressing room displays clothing and accessories from the costume collection, while the bathroom has objects connected with health, medicine and the use of the building as a military hospital during the First World War. The Bedfordshire and Hertfordshire Regiment museum and the Luton Life Gallery are also here.

Wardown House and Park continue to play a lively and important part of life in the town.

V

Education

EDUCATION HAS TRADITIONALLY been regarded as the prerogative of the Church and was usually reserved for the privileged few. However, since the Reformation, there were moves, especially by nonconformists, to introduce schooling for everyone. It may seem strange to our generation to find that there was considerable resistance to this, one argument being that the labouring classes would get ideas above their station and another that people would read seditious pamphlets and develop rebellious and revolutionary thoughts. Fortunately, those who believed in universal literacy won the day, although it was not until the early 19th century that the government of this country took on any responsibility for providing schooling.

As schooling was not supported by taxation, funding had to come from elsewhere: bequests, the Church, endowments or trusts, parents and subscriptions. Examples are given below of the types of schools which were to be found in Luton. This is by no means a definitive list.

ENDOWMENTS

Cornelius Bigland was a Luton barber-surgeon who left £6 a year in trust in his will, dated *c.*1673, 'for clothing, maintaining, schooling and educating six poor children of the town for ever'. In 1695 Roger Gillingham bequeathed £10 a year from his manor at Shillington for a schoolmaster to teach, without charge, poor children from the parish of Luton, who had to be nominated by the owners of Luton Hoo. John Richards, a Luton tin plate worker, left property in trust in 1731 to pay for three years' schooling at the Church School for five poor boys from Luton whose parents belonged to the Parish Church. Another trust was financed by Thomas Long, who in 1736 left £1,000 to the churchwardens of Luton 'for the use of the masters and boys of the free school of that town'. £15 was to be paid to the master of the school and the rest was to be used for boys' apprenticeships. However, over the years, most Luton families aspiring to educate their children to a high standard would probably have had to send them away, for example to Bedford where the much richer Harpur Trust supported excellent schools.

Such trusts were scrutinised by the Charity Commissioners, who in 1822 reported that the total income from the Bigland, Gillingham and Long bequests amounted to £14 18s. 4d. a year, out of which £10 was devoted to apprenticeships in accordance with the Long bequest. The remainder was given in part-payment of the salary of the master at the Church School, which amounted to £52 10s. a year. In 1915 these three trusts were combined to offer grants and maintenance for 'necessitous boys and girls' from Luton and, the following year, provided seven free scholarships at Luton Modern School. The trust 'ceased to exist' and was removed from the Charity Commissioners' Register in June 1998.

Private Enterprise

Over the years, there were private establishments where one person, maybe a clergyman, would open a school that offered a suitable curriculum. This type of school was frequently short-lived. Standards would, of course, vary according to the ability of the master or mistress. There were the 'dame schools', held in private houses by a woman who needed some kind of income and who would take in children to give them a basic schooling. Basic it certainly was and, while some of them may have been of a reasonable standard, most were not. A list of dame schools open in 1874 was compiled by Joyce Roberts and can be found in the local archives.

Schools (otherwise sometimes known as academies or private adventure schools) were advertised in local directories or year books. The entries for 1853 list a day school in Wellington Street run by Hannah Beeby and a boarding school in Park Street run by Lucy Elizabeth

44 *Norton House School (1865-81).*

Beeby. Susan Harradine held a day school in Park Street West and Mary and Sarah Hinson (maybe sisters, maybe mother and daughter) kept a day school in Stuart Street. Ann Housden had a day school in Wellington Street. Robert Henry Newland ran a day and boarding school in Church Street while Edward Parsons kept a similar school in New Road. There is no way of knowing the level of achievement reached in any of these schools.

However, some of the private schools must have provided a good education. One of these was Luton Collegiate School, run by the Reverend C.B. Harris, where a number of prominent townsmen were educated. Among these was William Austin, who became a solicitor and compiled the respected *History of Luton and its Hamlets*, and a photograph taken in 1865 shows some of the boys, all wearing mortar-boards. There was also Norton House School (or College) for boarding and day scholars, which was opened in 1865, first in premises in George Street and then in Upper George Street. In 1881 the school moved to a new building on the corner of Havelock Road and North Street but closed in 1893.

Girls were not ignored and a cluster of independent day and boarding schools was concentrated on the area around Cardiff Road. They aimed to attract girls from outside the town and offered, for example, a 'sound education' with 'qualified and experienced teachers'. St Dominic's Convent and Brathay Lodge were two such schools.

Another school, for children from less wealthy families, was York House. A former pupil, Greta Kent, wrote in 1976 that the school was a happy one and she paid tribute to 'the kind and patient women who well earned our love and respect'. Most of the private schools closed as state education increased.

Church and Charity Schools

In 1698 the Society for Promoting Christian Knowledge (SPCK) was founded and, the following year, began to open charity schools to promote schooling for poor children. They were supported by fees and endowments and were linked to the parishes. Children who attended had to be members of the Established Church and were obliged to learn the church catechism. They were also taught 'habits of industry' such as gardening, knitting, ploughing, spinning and sewing.

In 1717 and 1720 the Bishop of Lincoln sought information about the number of children in Luton who were being schooled. It was noted that there was one public school, endowed with £15 (possibly from the Long trust), at which about 70 children were 'well taught' and also 'well informed in the principles of religion and duly attend the services of the Church of England'. This school was probably held in the church and seems to have survived throughout the 18th century.

The 1818 Select Committee on the Education of the Poor noted that, in Luton, there was 'one school on a charitable foundation instituted in 1809 in which at present 135 boys are educated and the same number of girls, the former during the day and the latter in the evening'. The master was paid £52 10s. a year for instructing 60 boys plus 10s. for every boy in addition to that number. His wife was paid £31 10s. for superintending the girls' school (par for the course when women were consistently paid less than men). The school was financed by bequests (£40) and voluntary contributions.

PLAIT SCHOOLS

In south Bedfordshire there were the famous plait schools. Parents paid for a place for their children to learn the simpler patterns of straw plaiting while, at the same time, receiving basic instruction. Most of these were, in fact, little straw plaiting workshops where children were expected to complete a certain amount of plait each day. The plait was then sold to dealers or hat makers.

The 1818 Report noted that there were a number of such schools where children were sent 'for the exclusive purpose of learning straw-plaiting'. Then, in 1843, a *Report on Child Employment in Bedfordshire*, including Luton, stated that 'plaiting is a complete bar to anything like education, for as soon as children can use their fingers they are put to it'. In the Church School Inquiry 1846/7, there were still concerns over the plait schools; there was a school in Luton for 130 day and 85 Sunday schoolboys but girls only came on Sundays. There had been attempts to start a girls' day school but it was not successful owing to 'the nature of the business of this place, viz: straw bonnet making'.

Fortunately straw plaiting had died out in Luton by the mid-19th century, although it was still to be found in neighbouring hamlets and villages. However, the demands of the hat industry still affected attendance in Luton schools even after schooling became compulsory.

SUNDAY SCHOOLS

One of the most important providers of schooling for the labouring classes was the Sunday school movement that flourished from around 1780. Robert Raikes is generally given the credit for these schools, although he was not the only pioneer. He was prominent because, as a publisher, he was able to spread information about the schools throughout the country. He lived in Gloucester and had been perturbed to see factory children running wild on Sundays, their only day of freedom. He reasoned that, if they were given schooling on Sundays, they could be taught not only to read but also to follow a better way of life. The idea went even further: the children would then take these values home and introduce them to their families. Some saw this as a method of social control but, whatever the motivation might have been, the Sunday school movement became hugely successful and helped to introduce the culture of respectability and self-help that became the hallmark of the emerging working classes.

Sunday schools were much favoured by nonconformist denominations and, as Luton was largely a nonconformist town, the schools flourished. They were cheap to run and did not interfere with the work commitments of either the children or their teachers. The Wesleyans in Luton were so proud of their schools that they claimed them to be 'the harbingers not only of the fine schools that are now our pride ... but also a great stimulus to the educational movement in general'. Children continued to learn on Sundays but when, in 1874, day schooling

45 *Limbury Baptist Church Sunday School, 13 June 1918.*

became compulsory in Luton, Joseph Hawkes, a Wesleyan, remarked that this 'had relieved Sunday school teachers of the drudgery of secular teaching which was absolutely necessary a while ago'.

The teachers were almost all amateurs, sustained by their commitment and dedication. Children were not always well behaved and one Luton teacher felt the need to offer this prayer: 'Lord, Thou knowest we have need of patience, for, O Lord, Thou knowest the scholars are often very contrary'. Instruction was very simple and reading texts were based on a strict moral code. Here is a sample:

> The child that lies no one will trust,
> Though he should speak the word that's true;
> And he that tells one lie at first,
> And lies to hide it, makes it two.

At first schools were opened wherever a space could be found, but eventually fine purpose-built schools were established. In 1833 there were six schools, all supported by voluntary contributions. Three belonged to the Baptists and taught 223 males and 311 females and these had libraries. The others were Wesleyan with altogether 165 male and 148 female scholars.

The 1851 *Ecclesiastical Census* lists the number of children attending schools in Luton. They were from all denominations: Baptists, Primitive Methodists, Wesleyan Methodists, the Parish Church and the Union Chapel. The highest attendance was recorded at the Union Chapel in Castle Street where 450 children attended in the morning and 400 in the afternoon. In 1884 there were 1,972 scholars in Wesleyan Sunday schools looked after by 331 officers and teachers. By 1913 many schools had joined the Sunday School Union that recorded 14 Free Church Sunday schools in Luton and seven in nearby villages, with 5,905 scholars and 671 teachers. Of these, 2,116 were enrolled in the Band of Hope which encouraged children to sign the pledge and become teetotal.

Sunday schools changed in character over the years. They began to be more fiercely denominational and also became the hub of much of the social life in the town. Important occasions were the anniversary celebrations, when significant amounts of money were collected, and annual outings, popular venues being Scarborough's Meadow, Ashridge, Totternhoe and Wheathampstead. The Sunday schools became so important to the town that they even challenged the authority of the School Board, which was obliged to close the board schools on the days of the outings.

MONITORIAL SCHOOLS

In the early 19th century came the monitorial schools, which provided popular education on a large scale. The concept behind these was that one teacher could instruct several older children, known as 'monitors', and they in turn would repeat the lesson to their own little group. In this way, one teacher could easily teach 100 or more children. Joseph Lancaster, a Quaker, was one of the initiators of the scheme and his work was supported by the British and Foreign School Society (1814), which was nonconformist. At much the same time, Andrew Bell introduced a similar scheme, but he was backed by the Established Church and the National Society

46 *The National School, Church Street.*

47 *The school at Swift's Green, Stopsley, was opened as a National School in 1858 and taken over by the School Board in 1879. It closed in 1912 and was demolished in 1956.*

(1811). There were, therefore, two types of monitorial schools, British Schools and National Schools, with similar methods but different ideologies.

In 1833 the government paid grants to the British and National Societies to help with the cost of building new schools. Questionnaires were sent out to assess the provision in Luton and it was decided that, as there were not enough children in Luton to justify giving grants to both societies, money should be allocated to the National Society. This amounted, in 1834, to £144. The nonconformists were not best pleased and, as Dr Dony remarked, 'the die was cast for a dispute that was to disturb the peace of Luton for seventy years', a dispute as to whether education should be controlled by the Established Church or be non-denominational.

Church Street National School was built in 1835 on land given by the Marquess of Bute. It cost in the region of £600 and was paid for by the grants, subscriptions and money from the National Society. It was closed in 1857 and the building used by the Society of Friends. In that year Queen Square National School was opened and used until 1965. The Iron School in Church Street, also National, was open between 1864 and 1885. Several more Church Schools were built, with a flurry around 1874 when the town was threatened with a School Board that

48 *Langley Street School, built in 1836.*

supported secular education.

The nonconformists also built schools. Between 1809 and 1835 there was a Lancasterian School in Park Square, and in 1833 it was noted that there were two Day and Sunday Lancasterian schools, endowed with £36 a year. A Lancasterian School was opened in Langley Street in 1836 at a cost of £400. It was supported 'chiefly by dissenters for the education of the children of those poor persons who have a conscientious objection to the catechisms' that were taught in Church schools. The school fees were two pence a week. The Langley Street School was added to in 1837 when an evening school for girls was opened. They paid one penny a week and were taught English and how to make their own clothes. Daniel Brown, a leading Quaker, endowed an Infants school next door; this was supported by donations, voluntary contributions and weekly pence. Langley Street School closed in 1964.

In 1854 a British School was begun in High Town in the Primitive Methodist Church. It was so popular that a school for younger children had to be opened in a lower room of the same building and more teachers had to be found. Children had to pay 3d. a week and were taught the Bible and moral education. This school was demolished in 1878.

State Provision

During the 19th century the state became more and more involved with the provision of education. In 1807 Bedfordshire's Samuel Whitbread tried to introduce a Parochial Schools Bill in Parliament, in the hope that rate-aided schools could be built in the parishes. Then, in 1833, came the introduction of building grants to the National and British Societies. In 1839 the momentum increased with the setting up of a Committee 'for the consideration of all matters affecting the education of the people' and 'to superintend the application of any sums voted by Parliament for the purpose of promoting public education'. The first secretary of the Committee of Council for Education was Sir James Kay-Shuttleworth, one of the most significant people in the history of education in this country. One of his observations was that teachers needed to be trained and this was to result, from 1846, in the end of the monitorial system and the introduction of pupil-teachers.

Pupil-teachers were former elementary school scholars with acknowledged ability who were given the opportunity to improve their own education while at the same time acquiring teaching skills under the guidance of a headteacher; they were, in a sense, apprentices. The subject is too complicated to be addressed here, but the logbooks of Luton schools are full of details concerning the progress of local girls and boys who took up teaching through this scheme. From 1892, the headteachers were relieved of some of this burden when the Luton School Board offered classes at a Pupil-Teacher Centre in Waller Street.

Money from the state was not awarded without strings attached, and inspectors were sent in to assess the standard of work in each school. From the 1860s, 'payment by results' was introduced and the detailed annual reports of Her Majesty's Inspectors can also be read in Luton school logbooks. A visit from an inspector filled both children and teachers with dread. One outcome of this scheme was the limitation of the school curriculum to the subjects to be examined. Another inevitable consequence was that good schools got better because they received more grants while the less successful schools became poorer. Eventually, in 1900, block grants replaced payment by results.

The Adult School

Adult Schools, also known as First Day Schools, reflected the ideals of the Sunday schools as their aim was to teach the labouring poor to read. They were established by leading Quaker families but later became non-denominational. Luton Friends' Adult School opened in 1862 in the old National School building at the lower end of Church Street and seems to have been extremely popular. The initial membership was 32 men and 42 women but, by 1883, 1,968 men and 1,504 women had been admitted, and by 1892 3,260 men and 2,041 women had been enrolled.

Classes were held between 9 a.m and 10.15 a.m. on Sundays. The 'First Half Hour' was devoted to the teaching of reading and the rest to the 'instruction of young men and women of the more neglected class in reading writing and the Holy Scriptures'. No one under the age of 16 was allowed to attend. As time went on, and especially after schooling had been made compulsory, the Adult School provided a broader education covering historical, political and literary themes as well as religious topics. Dressmaking and knitting classes were also set up. Later, activities were offered on other days besides Sundays and branch schools appeared in Bury Park, Castle Street Meeting House, Waller Street School and at Leagrave, Slip End and Stopsley. A social life became associated with the classes and clubs were formed, for example an excursion fund, a savings club and a temperance society.

GOVERNMENT CONTROL

The schooling of children had therefore been somewhat random with private enterprise, Sunday schools and limited government support. With this in mind, the government decided to step in and introduced the Forster Education Act (1870) which required local authorities to assess the position in their locality and, if there was a shortfall in the number of places available, to remedy the situation by electing a School Board. Many Luton people were far from impressed by this and violent disagreements ensued.

In this context, the Reverend James O'Neill should be mentioned. He was the extremely forceful incumbent of the Parish Church who was loved by a few for his support of the Church but hated by many for his aggressive attitude towards other people and other causes. He was, and remained a determined opponent of the School Board. The supporters of the Church promised to build enough new schools and to provide a sufficient number of places, thereby warding off government interference. The nonconformists, however, wanted a School Board and demanded that the matter should be put to the vote.

Arguments against were that, once you had a Board, you would not be able to get rid of it and that the necessary taxation would become a burden. It was also feared that, if you educated children with public money, this would lead to feeding and clothing them as well. Those in favour welcomed a release from denominational instruction and also believed that children would receive a fairer start in life. Another important issue, as far as Luton was concerned, involved the traditional employment of children in the hat industry. Children sewed, fetched and carried to and from the markets and looked after siblings so that their mothers were free to work. If the children were obliged to go to school, all this would have to change.

A poll was held on 7 February 1871. The Church party won but that was by no means the end of the story and the arguments continued. In January 1874 the Education Department in Westminster ordered that there should be a School Board in Luton and another election took place on 17 February. The Church party, known as the Prayer Book Five, had more votes, but the nonconformists, the Bible Five, had more members on the Board. The Reverend O'Neill was elected but remained opposed to the idea and made his feelings known over the years by his absences and frequent unwillingness to vote. One of the Board's first actions was to make school attendance compulsory for children between the ages of five and thirteen.

Elections were held every three years. Members had no professional expertise in educational matters but they had enthusiasm and served the town well. It was important to find out how many new school places were needed so a census was taken. This found that 694 children (just over a sixth) were receiving no instruction so more schools had to be provided. The Church wished to maintain as much control as possible so built St Matthews (1874), Christ Church (1874) and New Town Street (1875) Schools. The School Board took over Hyde, Langley Street, the Primitive Methodist and Stopsley School, and built new schools in Leagrave and Limbury (1875), Waller Street (1876), Chapel Street (1880), Old Bedford Road (1883), Surrey Street (1891) and Dunstable Road (1898). In 1890, Waller Street became a Higher Grade School for Boys that provided a higher standard of teaching than was, strictly speaking, allowed under the terms of the 1870 Act. The religious debate continued but gradually mellowed and the schools eventually began to work together.

School fees were a real difficulty and parents in Luton had to bear a double burden because their children were no longer able to earn money during school time. The financial dilemma was partly resolved in September 1891 when elementary schooling became free. Even so, non-attendance remained a real problem and the figure of the Attendance Officer loomed large. Parents were threatened with legal proceedings and could be fined; in extreme cases children were sent to an industrial school. However, the emphasis began to change and children were given rewards for good attendance, the ultimate being a gold medal, inscribed by the Luton School Board, for fulfilling all the conditions for four years.

Until the 1890s, some Luton children were allowed to work half-time after consultation with the Visiting Officer and the Factory Inspector. Another way of shortening school life was to obtain a Labour Certificate, in which case children could leave after the age of ten. There were two ways to do this: either children could qualify by passing an examination set by a school inspector or they could become eligible for what was called the Dunce's Certificate by attending for at least 250 school sessions each year for the previous five years. In 1893 the minimum leaving age under this scheme was raised to eleven.

The next significant date for the schooling of children in Luton was 1902 when the Balfour Education Act was passed. School Boards were to be abolished and County Councils, which had been set up under the terms of the Local Government Act (1888), were to take over responsibility for education. According to this Act, however, Luton was large enough to become what was known as a 'Part III authority' and was therefore permitted to keep control of elementary education within the borough. The upshot of this was that Luton Education Committee took responsibility for the town's elementary schools while the Bedfordshire Education Committee controlled secondary education in the town and all education in rural schools. This took effect from 1903. Between 1908 and 1922 more new schools were built: Stopsley (1908), Beech Hill (1910), Norton Road (1913), Tennyson Road (1915), Denbigh Road (1921) and a special school, The Briars (1922).

The 1902 Act also allowed local authorities to establish secondary schools. The Bedfordshire and Luton Education Committees worked together and immediately set about making plans to open such a school in Luton. In September 1904 a combined Day Secondary School and Technical Institution for Luton and South Bedfordshire was opened in an old hat factory on Park Square. This was to provide secondary education for boys and girls during the day and technical classes for older students in the evening. Scholarship examinations were held for

49 *The Modern School building in Park Square, built in 1908.*

the day school and there were fees to be paid, although the Board of Education required that 25 per cent of places should be free.

A new building was opened on Park Square in 1908 and was known as Luton Modern School. However, there was always a shortage of space and, in 1919, the girls moved to temporary accommodation in Alexandra Avenue where a fine new school, renamed Luton High School for Girls, was opened in 1930. In 1938 the boys moved to their excellent new building at Bradgers Hill which, from 1944, became Luton Grammar School for Boys. The first two formidable headteachers, Thomas A.E. Sanderson and Helen K. Sheldon, were recalled with fear and trepidation for years but it is fair to say that generations of Luton boys and girls were educated to a high standard in these two schools. Books to celebrate the lives of these schools, and also the local Technical School, were published in 2004 which would have been their centenary had comprehensive education not brought about their closure.

Attitudes were changing and education began to be based on wider concepts. Children were no longer receiving mere instruction but enjoyed a wider curriculum which aimed to stimulate them as individuals with physical and mental needs. Medical examinations were introduced and children were taught hygiene and how to care for their teeth. Spectacles could be provided. At first these had to be kept at the school but later children were allowed to take them home. Swimming lessons could be taken at the Waller Street Baths.

There had always been concern about children who came to school hungry and, in 1890, the Hitchin Road logbooks record that Mrs Toyer, the wife of the mayor, had brought in a hot dinner for the poorest children and more food was provided from private funds. The

Education (Provision of Meals) Act (1906) allowed local authorities to become involved if necessary but Luton seems to have relied on philanthropy, although during the First World War a large number of meals, as well as cocoa and biscuits were given to children. Another difficulty concerned the teaching of children with special needs. This was addressed and 'The Briars', a house in Osborne Road, was bought and approved by the Board of Education. This school served the children of the town until 1960.

This example from a girls' arithmetic book (1909) would no doubt bewilder some of today's schoolchildren, and maybe adults too.

The <u>Least Common Multiple</u> of two
or more numbers is the <u>smallest number</u>
which <u>contains</u> them exactly.
In fractions, we often call it the
Least Common <u>Denominator</u>
Mem: cf Measure Factor or Diviser   }
with Multiple Product or Dividend   }
e.g. 24 is the L.C.M. or 3,4,6,8,12

<u>Ex</u>:- Find the L.C.M. of 6,10.15.16 & 25
6 = 2 x 3
10 = 2 x 5
15 = 3 x 5
16 = 2 x 2 x 2 x 2
25 = 5 x 5
L.C.M. = 2 x 2 x 2 x 2 x 3 x 5 x 5
= <u>1200</u>

Children in the early 20th century inherited an Age of Empire and every year, from 1908, Luton schools celebrated Empire Day on 24 May, the anniversary of Queen Victoria's birthday. Geography lessons helped children to learn about the countries of the Empire and communications with the colonies were encouraged. It would appear that the 'mother country' took the responsibility for lands across the sea very seriously and school logbooks indicate that children were taught to have feelings of duty and service towards the family of countries upon which, it was said, 'the sun never set'. For Empire Day in 1909, the Luton Education Committee stipulated that lessons on citizenship should be given. These included principles like these:

Love and fear God
Honour the king
Obey the laws
Regard the rights of others
Consider duties rather than rights
Seek knowledge
Work for others
Consider the poor, suffering and aged.

In 1932, the elementary schools were reorganised. Infant schools remained but a break was added at 11; schools for children below that age were to be known as junior schools and those for older children became senior schools. New schools continued to be opened: Maidenhall (1932), Hart Hill (1937), Beechwood (1938) and Sundon Park (1939).

EDUCATION FROM 1944

Significant changes came about with the passing of the Butler Education Act (1944). It is worth pondering that, when this Act was passed, the country was at war and yet it was considered equally important to direct resources into educational reform. Primary and secondary schools were to take the place of elementary schools and the 11+ examination was introduced. This gave all children the right to a free secondary education that suited their 'age, aptitude and ability'. Under the terms of this Act, Luton lost control of its schools to Bedfordshire County Council.

The story of education was, and still is, one of continuing change. In 1964, Luton became a County Borough, winning back control of its schools, and significant plans for the reorganisation of secondary education were under consideration. The question of selecting children for grammar school education at the age of 11 was a contentious one and many people saw the 11+ system as flawed. At first it was planned to introduce a scheme devised by Dr J.A. Corbett, the town's Education Officer, but, in 1965, the Luton Education Committee decided that schools should become fully comprehensive. The 11+ examination was scrapped and all Luton children were to be transferred to 'High Schools' (the old senior schools) until the age of sixteen. After that, they could move to the new Sixth Form College in Bradgers Hill, the first of its kind in the country.

By 1970 this transformation was complete and the scheme is still in place. In 2004 the Sixth Form College achieved 'Beacon Status', which acknowledges the very best providers in the field of further education. Similarly, the Ofsted Report (December 2008) rated the college as having one of the highest performances by a Sixth Form College in the country.

TECHNICAL EDUCATION

From the late 19th century, Luton was a flourishing centre of industry and was therefore reliant to a certain extent on the amount of technical education available in the town. This was of national importance too if the country was going to maintain its status in the world of industry. In 1889 the Technical Instruction Act gave County Councils the power to establish Technical Instruction Committees which were able to teach 'the principles of a trade'. As a result, the Luton Technical Instruction Committee was set up. It offered classes connected with the straw hat trade, such as applied mechanics, chemistry and the principles of advanced straw plaiting. Other classes, no doubt for women, were cookery, laundry work, needlework and basic health care.

The Luton Technical Instruction Committee was replaced in 1904 when the new Secondary School and Technical Institution opened on Park Square; evening classes were held in art, building, commerce, domestic knowledge, engineering, language and literature and science for young people over the age of sixteen. In 1937 the name was changed to Luton Technical College, and a Junior Technical School, established as a part of the College, was opened in the same building. The following year, when the Modern School for Boys moved to Bradgers Hill, the Technical School took over the premises in Park Square. The school remained there until 1958 when a purpose-built school was opened for them at Barnfield. By this time the school had acquired a similar status to the other two selective schools in the town.

The opening of this building was a dream come true, as technical education had always been the 'poor relation' when it came to accommodation. Throughout its life the school had been short of space and all kinds of available buildings were called upon to provide a refuge. Some of these temporary homes were: the Baptist Chapel, the Central Mission Hall, the Crypt at the Methodist Chapel in Guildford Street, the old Fire Station in Church Street, former hat factories in Guildford Street, Luton Boys' Club, the Masonic Hall, rooms above the British Home Stores, St Mary's Hall and wooden huts on the site. It is true to say that, in spite of all the difficulties, the 'Tech' was an extremely happy and successful school, as generations of former students are happy to confirm.

From 'Institution' to 'University' (1904 to 1993)

Further education continued to be offered at the Park Street site and, indeed, it still is, although huge changes have occurred over the years; for example, it is difficult to keep up with all the different name changes. As has been noted, it began its life in 1904 as the Technical Institution and then, in 1937, became Luton Technical College.

The College has had various name changes over the years and it has not been possible to date these accurately. However, the Technical College became Luton and South Bedfordshire College of Further Education and later the Luton College of Technology. In 1976, the Teacher Training College at Putteridge Bury merged with the Luton College and together they became Luton College of Higher Education. More mergers took place in 1991 when the College linked with the Bedfordshire School of Nursing and the Bedfordshire Colleges of Midwifery. The changes reflect different educational ideas. More were to come!

Accommodation was still a problem. In 1959 the old Modern School on Park Square was demolished and a new building, started in 1954, was ready for occupation by Easter 1957. Stage IV was completed in 1968 on a much-enlarged site, thanks to the compulsory purchase of many of the old familiar buildings in that area of the town.

The College was being run by Bedfordshire County Council when, in 1988, the government passed an Education Reform Act which allowed colleges to assume responsibility for their own finances. The County Education Authority, as the controlling body, was far from pleased about this and actively sought to maintain the status quo. However, in April 1989 Luton College became independent. The Governors had hoped to gain polytechnic status but were unsuccessful. However, better prospects lay ahead for, after much hard work by the College Governors and the Director, Dr A.J. Wood, the Privy Council allowed the establishment of the new University of Luton from 14 July 1993. Sir David Plastow was appointed the first Chancellor and Dr Wood was appointed the first Vice Chancellor.

Higher education in Luton had come a long way but that was not the end of the story, for in August 2006 the University of Bedfordshire was created by order of the Privy Council, following a merger between the University of Luton and De Montfort University's Bedford Campus. Putteridge Bury Campus houses the Postgraduate Business School and University Conference Centre. There is also a new Campus (2008) at Butterfield Park where students based at the Luton, Dunstable and Bedford hospitals enjoy teaching facilities. An interesting development is the plan to establish a foundation course in Carnival Arts from 2010 in conjunction with the UK Centre for Carnival Arts housed in Luton.

The story continues and there are plans to invest millions of pounds in the Luton campus and halls of residence. The university's website lists many successes from the past and ambitious plans for the future. One of many proud achievements was the award of runner-up for University of the Year (2007) by *The Times Higher Education Supplement*. According to *The Times Good University Guide*, the university is the 'highest-climbing institution in the UK'.

There are now (2010) in the region of 1,000 members of staff and 17,000 students, including postgraduates. Of these, 64 per cent are female, 45 per cent are over the age of 24 and 29 per cent are from overseas, many from Eastern Europe. The breadth of the subjects offered has grown beyond recognition from the time when technical education in Luton was focused on the hat industry, the main departments now being Creative Arts, Technologies and Science, Education and Sport, and Health and Social Science. The number of students living in Luton has had a significant effect on the housing market as well as on retailing and leisure in the town.

VI

Industry

L UTON CAN BE described, in the most general of terms, as a small market town that became a busy centre for the hat industry and then a thriving industrial town with Vauxhall Motors Ltd as the dominant employer. Subsequently, industry declined in favour of smaller firms and service providers and the local council is now promoting new regeneration schemes.

Luton did not prosper on account of rich natural resources. Apart from pockets of brickearth for brick making, fresh, clean water from under the chalk hills that supported brewing, and straw from local fields that supplied the hat industry, there were few raw materials. There was no navigable river nearby and the railway did not arrive until 1858. The main road route in the area had for centuries been the Watling Street, but that ran through Dunstable, not Luton. It appears, therefore, that credit for Luton's position as one of the leading industrial centres in the south of England should be attributed to the 'enterprise and foresight of its citizens'.

BREWING

One of the earliest trades to bring prosperity to the town and which was to last until the end of the 20th century was brewing, and between the 15th and 17th centuries Luton monopolised the brewing industry in Bedfordshire. In 1655 it was recorded that *The Wheelplough*, an inn in Park Street with its own brewing and malting premises, was bought by James Wilkins, who later took on Robert Parrot as a partner. The brewery remained in the possession of the Wilkins family until 1820 when it was sold to Solomon Burr, who already had a brewery in Park Street.

In 1857 Burr's Brewery, together with all their hotels and inns, was sold to Thomas Sworder. He expanded his business extensively and later combined with two other breweries, Anstee and Bennett. At about this time, J.W. Green set up his Phoenix Brewery, also in the Park Street area. In 1869, he took over Pearman's Brewery and in 1897 purchased Sworder's considerable assets for £139,000. J.W. Green eventually became one of the leading breweries in the country, winning awards, nationally and internationally, for ale, bitter, mild and stout. Famous brands of bottled beer included Dragon's Blood, Brewmaster and Poacher. Green's Brewery merged with Flower and Sons Ltd (famous for bitters) in 1954 and the new company became known as Flower's Breweries Ltd. In 1961 Flower's Brewery merged with Whitbread and Co.

The Whitbread family is a long-established Bedfordshire family which has served, and still serves, the county well in different capacities. The company was set up by Samuel Whitbread (1720-96), who established a partnership with Thomas Shewell in 1742. Their brewery was on the corner of Old Street and Brick Lane in London but in 1750 moved to Chiswell Street. The company was renamed Whitbread and Co. Ltd in 1799 and became a highly successful commercial business, the first purpose-built mass-production brewery in Britain. Beer was last brewed at Chiswell Street in 1976.

In 1969 Whitbread opened a new brewery in Leagrave but this closed in 1984. In 2000, after more than 300 years of brewing, Whitbread sold its brewing interests to Interbrew, which was renamed Interbrew UK. This became InBev UK Ltd and continues to have its head office at Capability Green in Luton. Whitbread has moved into hospitality; it has head offices in Porz Avenue in Dunstable, just across the Luton town boundary, and also in Oakley Road in Luton.

Coopering, or barrel making, was a related trade. Ken Kilby, whose family was connected with the trade for generations and who was himself apprenticed to J.W. Green for seven years, has described coopering as 'the second hardest trade next to mining'. 'Making a barrel was a precision craft and much of the work was judged by eye.' If a cooper worked really hard, he could make two barrels in a day. Nowadays, oak is still used for wines and spirits but beer is kept in barrels made of cheaper materials such as aluminium.

Daniel Brown was the first member of the family to come to Luton and he arrived from north Bedfordshire some time around 1700. He bought a house and orchard on the west side of Park Street, began a malting business and prospered. He was also a member of the Quakers or Society of Friends, a community renowned for honesty, integrity, philanthropy and thrift. Quakers were committed to public service and the Brown family's influence was seen in many aspects of local life, including the provision of schooling and the temperance movement. They branched out into other trades such as brewers, corn dealers, farmers, millers and shopkeepers. Henry Brown and Sons Timber Ltd, founded in 1817, traded at the corner of George Street and Chapel Street before moving to Dunstable Road in 1898. The company imported wood and supplied the building trade.

Frederick Brown opened an ironmonger's on Market Hill in 1837. He manufactured kitchen stoves and in 1840 went into partnership with his cousin Joseph Green. So the firm, Brown and Green Engineering, was established with expertise as braziers, coppersmiths, ironmongers and tinplate workers. The iron foundry moved to George Street and supplied a large variety of ironwork including gates, girders and fencing. They were able to exhibit at the famous 1851 Exhibition in Hyde Park and in 1860 developed a Velociped bicycle, which sold for £7 10s.

Brickmaking

Wind-blown sediment collected in hollows (dolines) in the Upper Chalk during the ice ages and was buried beneath layers of clay-with-flints and plateau drift. Some of this material became the brickearth (clay) that has been dug out since the middle of the 16th century and was important to Luton until the early 20th century. Pockets of brickearth were to be found in areas around the town such as Bailey Hill, Caddington, Round Green and Stopsley. Someries Castle, dating from around 1448 and now just across the field from the airport runway, is said to be one of the earliest brick buildings in the country and it is likely that the bricks were made from clay dug nearby.

A former Luton brickmaker, George Souster, explained to Dr James Dyer in a taped interview how local bricks were made. Between December and April the clay was dug by hand, while still wet, using picks and spades and then left in piles to be broken down by rain and frost. After Easter, the clay was puddled, that is softened by the addition of water and by being stirred and trampled, and then stored in barrels. The next stage was the moulding of the bricks, which were then left to dry for three or four weeks before being placed in a coal-fired kiln. The colour and quality of the bricks were determined by the chemical content. The shade of 'Luton greys', which gave the town its characteristic appearance, was due to the high levels of iron oxide in the brickearth and a silvery grey tone was produced by lime.

Hat Making

Straw hats were made at least as early as the 17th century. Although straw plait was produced in much of south Bedfordshire and neighbouring Hertfordshire, Luton gradually became the main centre of the straw industry. Just why it became dominant is open to debate. Whatever the reason, hat making was important throughout the 19th century and during the first decades of the 20th century and was partly responsible for the fact that, while other towns suffered badly in the Depression of the 1930s, unemployment levels in Luton were significantly lower. The town became almost synonymous with the industry and the local football team is even now proud to be known as The Hatters.

The earliest hats were made of local wheat straw that was plaited into various patterns, and a thriving cottage industry grew up. Women and girls plaited all their lives, day in and day out, and it was apparently unusual to see one without a bundle of straw on her arm rapidly being turned into plait. Plaiting became a way of life. Boys also plaited and so, apparently, did the men when circumstances required. Plaiting schools appeared which were schools in theory but in practice most were little straw plait factories where children were expected to complete a certain amount of plait every day.

Sometimes dealers travelled around to buy the plait but at other times the plaiters brought their work to the plait market to be sold, and on Mondays George Street in Luton would be full of women anxious to sell their work. New ideas were introduced and tools were invented to improve the quality and quantity of the work. One important innovation was the straw splitter

50-4 *Photographs of the hat factory of Wing, Arnold and Wing: dyeing, stiffening, blocking, machining and trimming.*

that made it possible to produce a finer type of plait. Another major change was that Luton women began to concentrate on sewing hats, while plaiting became mainly a village activity. Sewing the straw plait into bonnet shapes was a skill that took several years to master.

For many years, all the sewing was done by hand. The invention of sewing machines in the 1860s was very important for the women of Luton. In many industries, for example the cotton and wool trades, the arrival of machinery forced domestic and small work units out of business, but in Luton this did not happen. Homeworkers were able to buy or hire sewing machines and housewives throughout the town would machine, particularly in the busy season from February to May.

In the second half of the 19th century hat making could be found in three types of production units: homes, small businesses and large factories. There was the old cottage industry scene where, in the busy season, hats could be seen 'drying in front of the fire and on the sitting-room tables and chairs' while the lady of the house was busy sewing or machining. Then there were the family businesses set up for very little outlay where it was possible for makers to become quite prosperous, especially if they were fortunate enough to produce a successful design. Often, behind what appeared to be an ordinary house, there would be a two-storeyed extension. The lower floor would take the blocking machinery (blocking was the

STIFFENING

BLOCKING

shaping of hats) with the heavy work being done by men, and the sewers would work upstairs. Hat making was a predominantly female occupation but, as well as blocking, men and boys would help with transporting the hats.

In the early 19th century, large hat factories came to Luton. Just why they came here is not at all clear, but Luton's prosperity grew as they marketed their hats, not only in this country but also to Europe, Australia, Canada and New Zealand. In 1826 the London firm of Vyse and Sons moved to Luton. Sir Herbert Janes recalled their 'grim, begrimed, red brick' factory on Park Square. The Wallers were another London family that became established in Luton in the first quarter of the 19th century. In 1832, Luton had 13 hat manufacturers and four of these belonged to Wallers.

Asher John Hucklesby, who came to be known as 'Luton's Hat King', was born in Stopsley; his father was a blocker and his mother a plaiter. At the age of 13 he went to work for C.J. Rosson, a Luton manufacturer, and was able to acquire a wide understanding of every aspect of the trade. Then, at the age of 28, he went into business himself. He had hundreds of employees but, rather than establishing a factory of his own, he relied on smaller firms to produce hats to his designs. He had warehouses in George Street, Bond Street, Guildford Street and also access to the railway and was able to develop an export market with houses in Paris and New York and agencies in Australia, Canada, Europe and New Zealand.

Asher Hucklesby served the town in several capacities; he became a town councillor and was elected mayor five times. He was a member of the Chamber of Commerce and instrumental in the founding of a secondary school in 1904. As a member of the

Congregational Church, he worked tirelessly for the Sunday school and was a staunch supporter of the temperance movement.

With such a choice, it was possible for Luton women to change their place of employment freely or work at home. This flexibility resulted in the hat workers having a very relaxed attitude to punctuality and time-keeping which became something of a problem when, in the 20th century, new employers on the scene expected a more regulated attitude to life.

The hat industry was supported by other trades that became part of the Luton scene. These were bleaching, block-making, cardboard-box making (for carrying the hats), dyeing, gelatine for stiffening and ribbon manufacturing. Examples of such firms include Clay & Sons Ltd, which made ribbons and velvets and, in the 20th century, branched out into the manufacturing of a much wider range of goods. Lye & Sons Ltd were important as bleachers and dyers; they too increased their productivity in the 20th century with the making of fur and woollen felt hoods. Westly & Co. Ltd made braiding, petersham and ribbons.

By the early 20th century the local straw plait industry had more or less died out because of competition from the Far East. From the 1920s, felt hats, made from sheep wool or rabbit fur, became very popular and hoods made from hemp, sisal, ramie and other fibres were imported. Trimming hats became important. Much of the trimming was done in homes and it was common to see women or members of their families taking the large boxes of trimmed

TRIMMING

hats back to the manufacturers and bringing home more boxes filled with untrimmed hats, together with a 'sample' and a collection of bows, elastic, feathers, labels, lining, ribbons, wire and veiling, according to the fashion of the day.

One of the more memorable days in the history of hat making in the town was 25 February 1930 when an employee at Vyse's factory in Bute Street started a serious fire while heating beeswax. Unfortunately, eight workers died in the blaze. Another occupational hazard to be addressed involved the fumes from the glue used to stick ribbons and trims onto hats.

Luton remained an important centre for the making of hats until the middle of the 20th century, but from then onwards there was a steady decline. One significant reason for this was that people no longer routinely wear hats. Rationing and austerity during and after the Second World War played a part, but changing lifestyles have made a difference. Nowadays the kind of headgear worn by the younger generation is a far cry from the straw boaters of yesteryear.

Hat making has not completely disappeared but there are very few firms and these aim at particular markets. Whiteley Hat Company, with its premises at Bramingham Business Park, is one firm still in business. It has been associated with ladies' fashionable hats for more than sixty years and uses imported hoods. The Whiteley label advertises a 'designer collection of modern classic hats, contemporary headpieces and essential casual wear', each hat being 'individually handmade from the finest materials using traditional skills'. They also sell an 'affordable range of ready to wear fashion and occasion hats'. Now, in a vastly different world from the one where the straw plait trade began, hats can be bought online.

Olney Headware was set up by Albert E. Olney in 1910 and is run by the fourth generation of the family. They make 'fine English Headwear', from top hats to trilbies, which are available in the best shops all over the world. W. Fischer and Sons have been trading for over 75 years, through three generations, and now import

55-6 *Designer hats from Walter Wright Ltd.*

hats, including baseball caps. However, flamboyant hats, like those worn at Ascot, can still be supplied.

Walter Wright Ltd was formed in 1889 when Walter and Minnie-Susan Wright married. Walter came from a felt-hat-producing family (involved in the making of hats for over 300 years) and Minnie-Susan from a family established in the local straw hat industry. The firm became successful and is now run by Philip Wright, who was trained at the London College of Fashion. Nowadays hats and trimmings are made from materials sourced from around the world. The firm will make individually styled hats for special occasions such as Ascot and weddings and also supplies hats for films, theatres and television besides boutiques and chain stores. In November 2009 Philip Wright welcomed the Princess Royal at his factory in Albion Road, Luton, to celebrate the 120th anniversary of the business. Another designer to visit if you want to go to the races is Marie-Louise Millinery.

A related skill was block making. Hats were placed on the specially shaped blocks and pressed or steamed into shape. Luton can now boast the only block-making firm in the country and that is Boon & Lane Ltd, which was established in 1966 and still supplies hat manufacturers across the world. Metal blocks are preferred for mass production, but wooden blocks are more suitable for smaller quantities. The firm claims to have produced more than 7,000 different shapes for clients.

New Industries

In 1877 a Chamber of Commerce was set up; this served as a forum for local leaders of industry to meet in order to discuss any difficulties. One of the major problems was that, by the end of the 19th century, Luton had become too dependent on the hat industry, which employed a large proportion of women. It was decided that future prosperity involved inviting a wider range of industries into the town and a New Industries Committee was formed to make the necessary plans. Advertisements appeared in newspapers and trade journals. Luton, it was claimed, had an effective rail system, a clean water supply, plenty of cheap and accessible land, good local government, cheap gas and electricity, good housing, good health and education facilities and the opportunity for happy relaxation. It was also a town 'relatively free from the restrictions of trade union organisation' and could offer 'well-paid occupation for female operatives'.

The sales pitch worked and many firms came to the town. In the early years of the 20th century, Luton was transformed from a hat town to a manufacturing town as different firms moved in. Most notable were: Hayward Tyler's (1871), Laporte Chemicals (1898), Co-operative Wholesale Society (CWS) Cocoa and Chocolate Factory (1902), British Gelatine Works (1903), Vauxhall Motors (1905), Commercial Cars (1906), Davis Gas Stove (1907), Kent's (1908) and Skefko (1910).

One effect of this transformation was that Luton ceased to be described as a town where 'the men were kept by the women'. Another change came about because some of the firms brought workers with them. For example, the Davis Gas Stove Co. brought employees from Falkirk in Scotland. This new employment scene was more disciplined as punctuality and timekeeping became more important.

The New Industries Committee worked hard to relieve the town from dependence on one trade. They were successful in ensuring that Luton did not remain just a 'hat town', but by the middle of the 20th century Luton was once again dominated by a single industry for it had become, in effect, a 'Vauxhall town'. Vauxhall Motors Ltd was far and away the main employer and its influence was such that even school summer holidays were set to match the weeks of the factory's closure.

Vauxhall Iron Works Co. Ltd was a small company based near Vauxhall Bridge in London which had amalgamated with West Hydraulic Company and moved to Luton in 1905. In 1907 the company became known as Vauxhall Motors. By 1925 the business was struggling and was rescued by the American car-making firm General Motors. From then on it prospered, making a range of popular cars as well as trucks and vans. The sturdy 'Bedford' trucks were known across the world.

Vauxhall Motors was vital to the war effort during the Second World War. Then, in the early 1950s, the manufacturing of motor vehicles increased considerably and much of the output was exported. More production space was needed and a factory was built in nearby Dunstable (1955-9) and another in Ellesmere Port (1963). The years between 1950 and 1970 were the boom years and Vauxhall workers were able to enjoy good wages.

From the 1970s the motor industry was in decline. Len Holden, in his book *Vauxhall Motors and the Luton Economy 1900-2002*, has examined the possible reasons for this. One

57 *Vauxhall Factory, 1914.*

important factor was that decisions were often not made locally but by the parent company in Detroit. Then there were the problems that affected all the car-producing factories in the country: challenge from imports, notably Japanese, economic recessions, industrial unrest and the rising cost of oil and petroleum. Motoring became more expensive and demand slumped. The Luton factory had low productivity and much of the designing for new Vauxhall models was based at Opel, the General Motors plant in Germany.

The production of Bedford trucks in Dunstable ended in 1987 and the plant was sold to AWD. In the same year, Vauxhall and Izuzu combined, under the name IBM, to produce vans on the Luton site. Then, in 2002, came the shock news which no one in the town had ever expected to hear, namely that car production at Luton was to end. The firm's headquarters remained at Griffin House in Osborne Road, a parts warehouse is based on the outskirts of the town and vans are manufactured at the Luton site. The situation remains precarious although GM is committed to continuing production for the immediate future.

Industrial Luton in the Mid-20th Century

In 1951, to mark the Festival of Britain and also 75 years since Luton became a borough, an Industrial and Trade Exhibition was held 'to celebrate a half-century of unparalleled progress'. It was said that, at the time, there were 'two Lutons': around the centre could be seen the many large and small hat factories and the piles of cardboard boxes being loaded, while on the outskirts were great factories manufacturing, for example, aeroplanes, ball bearings, cars, cookers, refrigerators, trucks and vacuum cleaners.

The old industries that had come at the invitation of the New Industries Committee were still employing thousands of people but, during and after the war, even newer ones had arrived. These included the manufacturers of women's coats and dresses, stockings and underwear, two well-known names being Ballito Hosiery (1951) and Ellis and Goldstein (Luton) Ltd (1940).

The British Gelatine Works was producing photographic and technical gelatine. Commercial Cars (Commer's) had become part of the Rootes Group in 1928 and manufactured commercial vehicles. The Davis Gas Stove Co., then Jackson Industries, made New World cookers at the Diamond Foundry. In 1959 Jacksons entered the refrigerator market but by 1965 there was talk of the firm's possible closure. Electrolux were making vacuum cleaners and refrigerators. The English and Scottish Joint Co-Operative Wholesale Society Ltd still operated. Hayward Tyler & Co. Ltd made bottling machinery, pumps and turbines. Kent's specialised in making instruments and meters. Laporte Chemicals Ltd had its main works at Luton where hydrogen peroxide and related products were manufactured. Skefko was said to be still 'helping the country's production drive'.

Fifty years later, in the early 21st century, most of these firms have ceased production or have merged with other companies. Many have moved away from Luton, some to cheaper areas overseas. Others, for example SKF (Skefko), remain, although the Leagrave Road site was closed in 1977 and production is now based at Sundon Park while there are also other branches across the world. SKF celebrates its anniversary in the town in 2010. Hayward

58 *Band rehearsing for the opening ceremony at the CWS Cocoa Works, 1902.*

Tyler still produces electric motors and pumps after nearly 200 years and claims that this is because of the superior quality of their products, their outstanding customer service and the commitment and skill of their workforce. The Luton scene has changed beyond recognition and the main employers now are the airport, the Town Council and the university.

LONDON LUTON AIRPORT

The airport site was not the first to see the manufacture of planes in Luton. At the beginning of the 20th century, Mrs Hewlett and Gustav Blondeau were making planes at Oak (later Oakley) Road on the site that later became the home of Electrolux. In 1936, the Town Council bought land from Eaton Green Farm and Davis Estates for an airport to the south of the town. This was officially opened on 16 July 1938 by the Right Honourable Kingsley Wood, Secretary of State for Air. A celebratory display was held and one of the pilots taking part on the day was Miss Amy Johnson, who in 1930 had become the first woman to fly solo from England to Australia. While the old farmhouse became the headquarters of the airport, the stables were to become the home of the Luton Flying Club.

Percival Aircraft moved to the site in 1936/7 and subsequently built many hundreds of small aircraft, notably the Proctor. In 1944 the company was taken over by the Hunting Group. Civilian and RAF training aircraft were designed and built there until the early 1960s, when the company became part of the British Aircraft Corporation. The BAC ceased to operate from the airport in 1966. Another firm to arrive was Napier and Son Ltd, which used the airport as a Flight Test Establishment for 22 years from 1940 and carried out thousands of test flights. In the 1950s, the English Electric Co. Ltd, electrical and mechanical engineers, carried out guided missile work at the airport.

During the war, Luton Airport became a base for B flight of 264 Fighter Squadron. Together with all the important buildings in the town, the airport was camouflaged but that did not safeguard it from enemy attacks. Bombs damaged the runway on 27 August 1940 and more bombs fell on 30 August. On 24 September a parachute mine became wedged in the roof of the Percival factory but did not explode and was defused the following day by the Mines Disposal Section.

In 1952 the airport once again became a base for civilian flights and a new control tower was built. Seven years later, a concrete runway was laid and radar was installed. Then, in 1960, the airport gained international status and 24-hour customs facilities. By this time it was becoming an important provider in the increasingly popular package holiday market.

During the 1960s it was possible for people to take a trip to the airport to watch planes coming and going, although flights were not very frequent. The family car could be parked on the grass nearby and the few spectators were able to stand beside a wooden fence, so close to the planes that the prop wash from the propeller engines could be felt. A hundred yards or so away were the administration buildings, or rather huts. Nowadays, it is quite a different scene and security is a major issue. Plane spotters are still ever-present but their lives are much more controlled.

By 1969 a fifth of all holiday flights from the UK departed from Luton and the airport was becoming very profitable. During the following years, some airlines, for example Clarksons and Court Line, went into liquidation but the airport continued to expand and in 1985 a new international terminal building was opened by HRH The Prince of Wales. The following year, Monarch Crown Service inaugurated scheduled flights to Spain and Ryanair opened routes from Luton to Ireland. In 1990, the airport was renamed London Luton Airport to mark its position as part of the London airport network.

Since then, facilities have been upgraded: there is a new access road, new air traffic control tower, new cargo centre and a larger passenger terminal. Luton Airport has prospered with the introduction of low-cost flying, with EasyJet in particular making Luton its main base. In 1999 an £80m development was completed. There are now 60 check-in desks, modern flight information systems and a wide range of shops and restaurants. This new complex was

59 *Luton Airport, July 1968.*

opened by HM Queen Elizabeth and HRH the Duke of Edinburgh. A new station, Luton Parkway, was opened nearby and this can be accessed by shuttle bus. This station links with the Midlands and with the splendid new St Pancras International station in London.

In 2001 Luton Airport was rated as the UK's seventh largest airport, with over six million passengers passing through. Four years later the numbers had risen to over nine million. Flights leave for more than 90 destinations in Europe, Africa and the Middle East. Names of carriers include Aer Arann, EasyJet, Flybe, Monarch, Ryanair, SkyEurope, Thomsonfly, Wizz Air and there are many charter flights. The airport is run by London Luton Airport Operations Ltd. The year 2008 saw the 70th anniversary of the opening of Luton Airport. It employs around 8,500 people and is one of the largest private sector employers in the area. Thousands more are employed indirectly through the airport supply chain. Luton has lost almost all of its hat trade and the car industry is in serious decline, but Luton Airport has taken on the role of major employer in the town.

OTHER SIGNIFICANT EMPLOYERS

Service industries are now probably some of the largest employers in the area. The University of Bedfordshire, which was created by the merger of the University of Luton with the Bedford campus of de Montfort University in August 2006, now employs in the region of one thousand staff. One of the main departments in the university is the Business School;

this is certainly in keeping with the commercial history of the town and the university has 'an excellent reputation for preparing students for employment'. The Town Council, which is responsible for all administration in the town, now employs around ten thousand people; Luton National Health Service, formerly Luton Primary Care Trust, and Luton Community Services employ approximately six hundred, while the Luton and Dunstable Hospital at the end of 2009 employed 3,299 staff.

Figures for the years 2007 and 2008 from Office for National Statistics indicate the range of employment in the town.

	2007	%	2008	%
Manufacturing	11,000	12.9	11,000	12.8
Construction	3,000	3.5	3,000	3.5
Distribution, hotels and restaurants	18,000	21.2	17,000	19.8
Transport and communication	11,000	12.9	11,000	12.8
Banking, finance and insurance	18,000	21.2	19,000	22.1
Public admin, education, health	20,000	23.5	21,000	24.4
Other services	4,000	4.7	4,000	4.7

TWENTY-FIRST-CENTURY INITIATIVES

It is interesting to compare the modern initiative with the incentives offered by the New Industries Committee more than 100 years ago. Luton claims now to be a key area for business and commerce in the south east of the country. More than £4bn has already been invested in the town and the Town Council promises that advice and support will be given to existing businesses 'to enable them to develop, expand and explore ways of exceeding their expectations'. Support is also given to 'find premises, provide research and statistics' and to help with networking, funding and grants. Plans should provide a mix of urban buildings and open spaces. There should be a multi-lingual, highly skilled local workforce and educational opportunities should be provided.

Access is one of the main considerations. The town 'lies just off the M1, minutes from the M25 and a short distance from the A1'. New roads (the East Luton Corridor) link the M1 to the airport. There are three train stations and a guided bus route is planned. Regeneration projects are underway in the town and small business parks are attracting well-known companies.

Capability Green was built on land which was previously part of Luton Hoo, and lies between the airport and the M1. Interestingly, the name Capability Green was chosen to connect with the landscape designer Capability Brown, who designed Luton Hoo Park. Companies include Astra, Zeneca, Selex, Ernst & Young, Tui (Thomson Holidays), EasyJet, Monarch and Inbev (Interbrew).

Butterfield Business Park is a new development on the A505 road to Hitchin. It is said to be an 'award winning Innovation Centre and Business Base' operated by Basepoint and provides more than one hundred affordable small business units for offices, studios or workshops. Occupiers include the *Hilton Garden Inn*, the Royal Bank of Scotland and the University of Bedfordshire.

Plans to develop Napier Park on the old Vauxhall site and near to Parkway station are on hold at the moment but it is hoped that the area will include conference and hospitality facilities, commercial, residential and retail units as well as a casino. The park will be landscaped with a water feature.

Century Park, near the airport, has offices and warehouses. A landscaped 'urban village', mainly residential, is being built at High Town. Between High Town and the town centre there will be an improved station and transport facilities as well as residential properties, a hotel and parking, which will be known as Station Gateway. In the centre of the town the Mall is set to attract 'prestigious retailers' and work at St George's Square should improve the appearance of the town and provide café and bar space. Power Court, off St Mary's Road, will bring leisure and retail facilities.

At the end of the 19th century there were plans to introduce new industry into the town. These plans were successful, but Luton probably became too dependent on the motor trade. Now, once again, the Town Council has decisions to make and it remains to be seen in what way the town will prosper in the years to come.

VII

Luton at War

ARS HAVE AFFECTED the town in many ways. Invasions by conquering nations such as the Romans, Saxons, Vikings and Normans touched life in very tangible ways and the Civil War of the 17th century was also felt locally. But probably the most significant effect of war has been the call to arms and Luton men were not exempt. Some joined the army voluntarily but others under duress, for example when their names appeared on the muster rolls. William Everitt wrote to his mother from the trenches during the Crimean War (1853-6) and Luton was well represented on the African veldt during the Boer War (1899-1902).

One of the most memorable events of the Boer War was the Relief of Mafeking, which was under siege between October 1899 and May 1900. Sir Herbert Janes recalled: 'I remember very well Mafeking Night in Luton. Everyone went mad … The streets were thronged with people shouting and singing.' When the war ended, a memorial service was held on 2 June 1902 at 7 p.m. in front of the Luton town hall to celebrate the declaration of peace. A large platform was erected and the leading men of the town, including the mayor, Alderman Giddings, and the vicar, the Reverend E.R. Mason, 'irrespective of class or creed', met to give thanks to God. Included in the service was a third verse of our National Anthem, not often heard today.

Not on this land alone,
But be Thy mercy shewn
From shore to shore
Oh, may the nations see,
That men should brothers be
And form one family
The wide world o'er.

THE FIRST WORLD WAR

On 4 August 1914, Britain declared war on Germany and so began over four years of austerity, heartbreak and privation. The regular army was placed on a war footing and the Territorial

Army was mobilised, but many more troops were needed. Mass meetings were held in Luton at which eager young men were encouraged to volunteer for what many believed would be a short and successful war. By 1915, more than 4,000 men had enlisted. Little did these enthusiastic recruits realise what troubles lay ahead. Later in the war, the Military Service Act (1916) introduced conscription, initially for single and then for married men. It was possible for certain categories of people to go before a tribunal to claim exemption from military service; those able to apply were men who would suffer economically, for example the self-employed, any involved with essential war work, those in poor health and also people who had a conscientious objection to war. However, it was by no means certain that the tribunal would approve the request.

A pupil from Luton Modern School, Doris Garside, wrote a poem which was printed in the school magazine. It helps to explain the pressures put on young men to enlist.

> O'er England's shores is cast again
> A cloud of strife and war:
> Yet not of war for greed, for gain,
> But justice to restore.
> Your duty and your country call:
> Why tarry then, I pray?
> Why let your comrades for you fall
> Whilst you at home do stay?

One of the first effects on the town was the arrival of a large number of troops sent to Luton for training. Camps were set up on open sites such as Luton Hoo, the Moor, Round Green and Stockwood Park. At first there was such a demand for accommodation that schools were requisitioned as billets, much to the distress of the staff, for their premises were not treated with respect. Leagrave, Limbury, the Modern School on Park Square, Norton Road and Stopsley Schools all recorded that their buildings were left damaged or dirty, and Hitchin Road School, which was occupied for two weeks, noted that cupboards were opened and articles, particularly the children's exercise books, were missing. Children were offered alternative accommodation, as in the case of New Town Street School which shared the Surrey Street Infants' School. The schools also closed for two days, one in September and another in October so that children could watch military reviews. Later, a permanent army camp was constructed at Biscot.

Before the Bedfordshire Regiment (1st/5th Bedfords) embarked for service overseas in July 1915, they marched around the county and then gathered in front of the town hall in Luton where they were welcomed by the mayor, Walter Primett. This Regiment was destined to fight at Gallipoli and later in Egypt and the Middle East.

Many Luton men were never to return, one of these being 2nd Lt Alex Pigott Wernher, son of Sir Julius and Lady Alice Wernher from Luton Hoo, who served with the 1st Welsh Guards and was killed on 10 September 1916. Lady Wernher gave the Memorial Park to the town in his memory. In 1916, the Reverend and Mrs Mahon lost their only son, Arthur, who was killed

60 *Limbury Road, near
Luton, 1916.*

on 1 July 1916 while serving with the London regiment. The Luton Memorial list contains
1,284 names. Lieutenant Ernest Barrow (2nd East Lancashire Regiment), who had been on
the staff of the Modern School, was killed on 23 October 1916 at the Battle of the Somme. In
this letter to the school, he described some of his army training.

> We have learnt very thoroughly, and some of us at our cost, that the old adage – 'an army fights on its
> stomach' – is true in more senses than one. To be running and then fall flat, with lightning celerity,
> while burdened with rifle and pack, needs practice if it is to be done without a severe shaking up.
>
> One unhappy sight, after a shower of rain, was to be seen scampering madly up a hillside, with
> a rifle in one hand and a greatcoat in the other. On the word of command to drop, the coat went
> down first, then the rifle, and lastly the man on top of the coat.
>
> We know (some of us) what it is to be on night guard, with the rain coming down in sheets,
> wet through to the skin, with mud over the boot tops, and three quarters of a mile of delightfully
> slippery mud, traversed by deep trenches, to plough through on the way to and from the
> guard-hut.

The departure of so many men caused problems on the employment scene but the
replacement of skilled labour by semi-skilled and unskilled labour (dilution) often caused
bad feelings, both during and after the war. Women were traditionally paid less than men,
but in Luton workers from the seasonal hat industry seem to have been tempted by regular,
better-paid, work in the factories and there is evidence that higher wages in industry also lured
teachers away from the schools. The matter of relative pay for men and women remained a
cause of concern and the conflict of opinion resulted in strike action, not something familiar

to the people of Luton. In 1916 women from Vauxhall Motors Ltd went on strike for higher wages, the dispute being used as a test case by the National Federation of Women Workers. Their pay was raised from £1 to £1 50s. a week. The following year, the national Munition Strike received so much local support that the strikers needed to use the Luton football ground for their 10 days of mass meetings.

All the resources of Luton's industrial strength were directed towards the war effort. George Kent Ltd is an interesting example: they opened up a new factory at Chaul End as a filling factory for detonators, fuses and gaines (tubes attached to fuses), where both men and women kept continuous day and night shifts operating. This was dangerous work and girls who worked with TNT became known as 'Canary Girls' because handling the explosive caused their skin

to turn yellow. As in busy times in the hat industry, girls from the surrounding districts came into Luton to work and accommodation was at a premium. Violet Golding, aged 16, was working at Kent's in 1916, putting caps on detonators, when one exploded in her hand. She lost the tips of one finger and thumb and suffered severe burns to her left arm. Violet returned to work after three months and was given £50 by her employers, part of which she spent on a bicycle, which saved her the daily walk she had previously made to and from her home in Dunstable. She was also honoured as one of the first people to receive an MBE.

Hilda Hewlett, mentioned in *The 100 Greatest Women in Aviation* by Liz Moscrop, was born in 1864 and was the first British woman to get her pilot's licence. Together with her business partner, Gustave Blondeau, she opened the Omnia Works in Leagrave, Luton for the manufacture of aircraft under licence. At its peak during the First World War the factory supplied more than 800 military aircraft for the war effort, employing 700 people, before the site was sold to Electrolux in 1926.

Clerical posts needed to be filled and the Home Office put pressure on the local education authority to provide adequate training for women. Vauxhall Motors Ltd took on women in their General, Drawing, Cost and Works Offices and George Kent Ltd employed female office staff, as did the Munitions Office.

61   *Tank on Market Hill, July 1918.*

Another 'gap to be filled' may not have been quite so popular: women were desperately needed to work on the land to replace conscripted farm labourers. If this caused problems, official permission was given for older daughters to be absent from school to take over childcare. These girls were to be recorded as 'employed in agriculture'. The rules were also bent during the war years to allow boys to leave school before the statutory leaving age so that they could help on the land, as happened at Norton Road School.

Food production was of paramount importance. Any suitable land, including parkland, was to be dug and planted. For example, two roods (one fifth of a hectare) of playground at Hyde School were given as an allotment for the duration. School gardens were popular and

medicinal herbs were to be grown as well as vegetables. Centres were opened for instructing teachers, male and female, in gardening. One of these centres was at Leagrave and was well supported while another course of lectures was held at Hyde. Children were also allowed to undertake the cultivation of cottage gardens if the occupants had enlisted. In 1916 the Summer Time Act was introduced in order to make the best use of daylight. A consequence of this was that children in Luton schools were said to be coming to school still sleepy, no doubt having stayed up late the night before.

Children were also involved in campaigns to collect food from the countryside, some to be sent to the troops and some to hospitals. One request seems rather strange; this was an appeal for horse chestnuts, the reason being that the starch could be converted into acetone, used in the manufacture of the explosive cordite. In February 1918 it was reported that Luton children had collected three tons of them. Fruit stones were also gathered, as they were 'required for an urgent war purpose'.

In 1915 and 1916, local teachers gave a series of lectures and demonstrations at Charles Street, Dunstable Road and Langley Street Schools on how to economise on food and a handbook on the subject was given out at the end of the course. The kind of information that the Board of Education wanted to promote involved cutting back on meat in favour of other nutritious foodstuffs and the prevention of waste. In 1917 groups of schoolgirls were taken to an exhibition on the subject held at the town hall.

As the war went on, there were complaints because so many children from local schools were either absent or late as a result of being sent to stand in the morning food queues. One response to this was a request for butchers to open their shops in the afternoon instead. Local schools were also told to minimise on the use of gas, not to make up fires late in the afternoon and to economise on stationery and other materials.

The war was very much a part of people's lives. Luton schools were advised that, if there was an air raid, children were to be kept at school and parents were asked not to visit until the situation was safe. There were sandbags to be filled, garments to be made, paper to be collected and canteen work to be undertaken. Each year the Bedfordshire County Council allocated £100 to provide materials so that children in the schools could make garments for soldiers.

Funding was needed for a variety of projects. There was a Serbian Relief Fund and the celebration of Kosovo Day. Belgian refugee children were admitted to local schools; Norton Road School received sixteen. Also a Belgian Self Help Society (Société Belge de Luton) was set up in the town. A War Savings Association was formed and people were asked to contribute to a Children's Empire Fund. Alexandra roses (to support army nurses) were sold. Some schools received special praise because the money that had been allocated for prizes was invested in war savings instead, apparently with the approval of the children. Money was sent to the Jack Cornwell Memorial Ward at the Star and Garter Home at Richmond. Still on a naval theme, on Trafalgar Day attention was drawn to the part the navy was playing in maintaining the safety of the nation.

The mansion in Wardown Park was used as a hospital for injured servicemen and in 1916 there were said to be 62 beds. For much of the time, the nurses were assisted by the Voluntary Aid Detachment (VADs) and, contrary to the situation found in some places, these two groups of nurses worked well together. Classes were held for the training of members of the VAD and Red Cross personnel: Miss J. Jellie taught home nursing and Dr Seymour Lloyd First Aid.

PEACE

After four troubled years, the end of the war came on 11 November 1918 and Luton people heard the good news from the Town Crier, Charlie Irons, speaking from the top of St Mary's Church tower. At Hyde School, and no doubt at all the others, the timetable was abandoned. A teacher from the Modern School, H. Hugh Watson, later recalled the moment.

> Twelve years have passed since that November day,
> When, sick of carnage, strife and clash of steel,
> Hardly believing war would ever cease,
> We heard the bells ring out a joyful peal.
> The end had come, now men had ceased to slay
> Their fellow-creatures, and at last was peace.

The Armistice was signed at Versailles on 28 June 1919 and Luton people anticipated days of joyful celebrating. Unfortunately the reality was very different and, instead of harmony, there was bitterness and discord in the town. Much of the bad feeling had been simmering during the war years but the tensions were turning in some quarters to real hostility that culminated in what has been described as 'the most outstanding event in the history of Luton in the last hundred years'. The whole sorry story has been documented, step by step, in Dave Craddock's book *Where they Burnt the Town Hall Down*.

Some of the ill feeling resulted from the food shortages. There were complaints of profiteering, butchers in particular being accused of charging too much. Then the working classes claimed that, while they were having to queue for food, the middle classes were suffering no inconvenience as deliveries were being made to their doors. A Food Control Committee was set up, according to government directives, but Luton people complained that the local Committee was not doing its job in a satisfactory manner, either in the choice of members or in actual food distribution. In January 1918 the Trades and Labour Council wrote to the town clerk listing these complaints. Then, on 29 June, nearly all the 7,000 members gathered on the Moor to protest and a deputation was sent to meet the Food Committee at the town hall. Some compromises were agreed and, later in the year, butter, meat, sugar and tea were rationed. However, bad feelings between the Town Council and the townsfolk persisted.

Another source of deep resentment concerned the treatment of ex-servicemen who had been promised homes and jobs when they returned to civilian life. What they actually found was incompetence, injustice, unemployment and lack of care and consideration for dependent families and men who had been disabled. Associations of ex-servicemen had been formed: the National Association of Discharged Sailors and Soldiers (1916); the National Federation of Discharged and Demobilised Sailors and Soldiers (1917); and Comrades of the Great War

(1917). Members of the Federation and Comrades had branches in Luton but, unfortunately, suspicion and jealousy developed between them, even though the aim of both was to improve the lives of former servicemen.

All these resentments came to the surface when the Town Council's plans for Peace Day became known. The cost of the celebrations, to be borne by the rates and by public subscription, was seen to be out of proportion while so many men were unemployed. Then, the planned official banquet was to be free to councillors but ex-servicemen would have to pay for their own meal. No women were invited and this was seen as a snub to all the women who had done so much to support the war effort. The ex-servicemen took umbrage over the arrangements and also resented the fact that the Town Council refused to allow them to hold a Drumhead Memorial Service in Wardown Park.

The Peace Procession was set to take place on Saturday 19 July, making its way from Park Street to Wardown Park. There were floats and tableaux and representatives of different groups who had been active in the war effort, together with bands and a large contingent of school children. The town's hierarchy, which had continued to be very unpopular, was met with some booing and the animosity intensified when the mayor, Henry Impey, tried to read a Royal Proclamation to the crowd. As the hostility increased, people pushed towards the town hall and the atmosphere became more dangerous. Soon the doors were broken open and angry townsfolk burst in, smashing whatever they could find and threatening to settle scores by attacking the mayor himself.

The police, together with the special constables, were able to clear the town hall and the atmosphere became calmer. Meanwhile, at Wardown Park, the people of the town were enjoying an afternoon of sports and entertainments and, in the evening, a fireworks display took place on Pope's Meadow. However, by 10 p.m., attention began to concentrate on the town hall again and that is when the disturbance turned into a full-blown riot. The town hall was set on fire and all the attempts of the local fire brigade to extinguish the flames were in vain. The building was destroyed and, famously, people in the crowd are said to have dragged out a piano from the premises of S. Farmer and Co. for a mass singsong that included the well-known war song 'Keep the Home Fires Burning'.

In the early hours of the morning of 20 July, troops from the camp at Biscot were given permission to come to the aid of the police, the crowds began to make their way home, and by 4.30 a.m. the fire had been extinguished. However, more rioting took place that evening and to a lesser extent on the following day. The forces of law and order were finally able to bring calm to the town but many buildings were left devastated. Subsequently, seven women and four men appeared at Luton Borough Court and, in October 1919, 27 men and one woman were tried at Bedford Assizes.

However, happy and peaceful celebrations did take place, largely thanks to Lady Alice Wernher, with whom the townspeople had a good relationship. Luton and District Discharged Sailors and Soldiers Association were allowed to hold their Drumhead Memorial Service at Luton Hoo Park on 27 July and, on 16 August, nearly 6,000 ex-servicemen and their partners were treated to a party there.

62 *Town hall ruins, 20 July 1919.*

On the suggestion of the king, schoolchildren were given an extra week's holiday in July to commemorate the peace. Then, on 19 September, 6,000 older children had a party at Luton Hoo Park, followed by a similar treat for 3,000 younger children the following day. Children were also presented with commemoration medals, courtesy of Alderman J.H. Staddon and Messrs Vyse and Co. Ltd.

The war was over but there was plenty to remind Luton people of the troubles they had experienced. Many families still grieved for men who had not returned or who had been disabled. The British Legion held annual outings and Christmas parties for children orphaned as a result of the war. The parties were held at the Assembly Hall in Waller Street where tables were piled high with every kind of food. There would be a concert, the highlight of which was the magician, and games. Every child went home with a 'worthwhile gift' together with fruit, nuts and sweets. In the hope that there would never be another such war, schools encouraged older children to join the League of Nations Union.

Other constant reminders of 'The War' were the old gun and tank that sat on their plinths in Wardown Park, and became a source of fascination for all the children in the town. Unfortunately these disappeared when the next conflict began; it was said at the time that they, together with gates, railings, saucepans and anything else made of metal, had gone to be recycled for the war effort. Unfortunately, most of this salvaged metalwork seems to have rusted away unused.

The Second World War

During the war, reporters at the *Luton News* collected a great deal of information about wartime events but were only able to print a limited amount of material owing to censorship regulations. However, in 1946, the newspaper published a very detailed book entitled *Luton at War* that recorded all the major events and honoured the work that was done by so many thousands of Lutonians in so many different capacities. It included a Roll of Honour and a list of Awards and Decorations.

On 3 September 1939, the second world conflict began. This time there was no frantic rush to enlist as there had been in 1914, for men, and later women, were conscripted in a more

methodical way. Compulsory registration of 20 year olds, under the Military Training Act, began on Saturday 3 June 1939. There followed the National Service Acts and, from April 1942, girls between the ages of 16 and 18 had to register and unmarried women between 20 and 30 could be conscripted into the armed forces. There were to be none of the horrors of Gallipoli or the trenches in Flanders but this war was to bring its own share of terrors for local men, especially those who were sent to Singapore and suffered for years as prisoners of the Japanese. Hostilities had affected the daily lives of people in Luton during the First World War, but after 1939 the town was to experience enemy action in a more direct and alarming way.

While the town was not faced with a need to accommodate huge numbers of troops, as had been the case in 1914, there was an influx of another kind. On 31 August notice was given that evacuation of children, pregnant women and women with young children would take place the following day and, as Luton was seen to be a safer place than London, it had been designated a 'reception area'. Since the previous January, surveys had been made of any unoccupied rooms so Luton was ready and prepared to receive the hundreds of evacuees who were expected to arrive. They were met at the station and taken to reception centres and then to the homes that had offered them hospitality. Schools were evacuated with their teachers; among these was the prestigious North London Collegiate School that came to share the premises of Luton High School.

There were plenty of unofficial arrivals as well and these were people who had been caught up with the panic of the moment and had come to Luton independently. Most of them returned home after a very short time, as did some of the schoolchildren, when the expected bombing raids on London did not immediately materialise. The number of children who did stay, however, put great pressure on the schools and contingency plans based on a shift system had to be made. Although many evacuees did return home or moved to a different area, some remained and one of the happy sides to this story is that some lifelong friendships were made.

One touching story concerns a lady from London who had lost her home. She came to Luton looking for somewhere for her family to stay and was shedding tears of desperation. A Luton lady saw her crying and asked what the trouble was and, after hearing her sad tale, said, 'You can stay at my house for tonight'. The family, five of them, stayed there until they were able to find a home of their own, and that was seven months later.

1 September was also the date marked for the beginning of the blackout. This required that every home should have some means of preventing any streak of light, however small, from escaping. Thick curtains made with blackout material helped but there were other more satisfactory methods like shutters made with wood and tarred paper that were made to fit the

63 *Evacuees to Luton in 1939.*

64 *Luton Airport, camouflaged.*

window frames. They had to be put up and taken down every day and also stored somewhere for the rest of the time. Some people stuck gauze onto their windows to hold together any glass that had been shattered in a bomb blast. There was also the problem of how to get out of the house without showing a light; the easiest way was to switch off the light first and then grope your way to the door. Torches were very precious but their beams had to be directed towards the ground, as did lights on cars. Finding one's way around in the blackout was not easy and, on the darkest nights, one had to be careful not to walk into a tree or lamp post, but struggling along with the crowds, say in George Street, did help to foster a happy community spirit.

When bombing became a very real threat, the town found another way to hide itself from enemy aircraft. It did so by installing oil-burning canisters and it was estimated that there were eventually 25,000 of them, spread out on paths all over the town. They were tended by a Smoke Company of the Pioneer Corps and, each evening, they had to decide which canisters to light according to the direction of the wind and, in the morning, it was their task to clean them. The dirty, oily mess that the smoke left on houses and gardens can only be imagined and the young men who had been up all night tending the canisters would probably have been no cleaner. They were no doubt very grateful for the cups of tea that local householders handed to them. It could well be that the smoky fog did save the town from some enemy action.

Another way of preventing enemy planes from locating the town accurately was achieved by camouflaging important buildings. Dark greens and earthy browns covered buildings so that from above the town looked like countryside. The town hall was hidden under camouflage and the roof of the Skefko building was disguised to look like a leafy road. It was commonly believed at the time that the Luftwaffe looked upon Crawley Green Road Cemetery as a distinctive landmark.

AIR RAIDS

While Luton was not bombed to the same extent as some other industrial towns, there were frequent air-raid warnings and people took to the shelters. Four tunnels were dug in the town centre: at Upper George Street, High Town, Beech Hill and Albert Road. These tunnels were used by thousands of people during raids but, when the town was having regular alarms, many used them on a nightly basis and some kind of social network evolved, especially when bunks were put in. Tunnel marshals looked after people's welfare but there were also a few undesirables who regarded them as a kind of bolthole; these were discouraged by regular visits from the police. Additional shelter for 4,000 was provided in shop and warehouse basements.

Underground shelters were dug in school fields and playgrounds. Families could have an Anderson shelter, made of corrugated iron and half-buried in the ground, and over

65   *Bomb damage, Park Street, 22 September 1940.*

66   *Bomb-damaged houses, 6 November 1944.*

10,000 of these were supplied. Householders could also choose a brick shelter for the garden or an indoor Morrison shelter, which was a kind of reinforced table. In the early days of the war these shelters were well used but, as time wore on, people often preferred to sleep in their own beds, especially as the shelters sometimes became waterlogged and damp.

The first siren sounded on 6 September 1939 but the first raid on the town came on 30 August 1940 at 4.42 p.m. Twenty enemy aircraft were involved and 194 bombs were dropped. Among the places bombed were the airport and Vauxhall Motors; the casualties numbered 59 dead, 60 seriously wounded and 81 slightly wounded. Several more raids were made in 1940, involving bombs, fire bombs, high explosives, an oil bomb and parachute mines. One of the most devastating in terms of damage came when a land mine fell in Park Street on 22 September 1940. After several more traditional bombing raids, Luton suffered casualties from a V1 flying bomb (doodlebug) on 21 June 1944 and, more seriously, a V2 rocket that fell in Biscot Road on 6 November 1944. Altogether there were 900 air-raid warnings, 107 people were killed and 500 were wounded.

The threat of invasion became very real after the fall of France and people were warned by the ringing of church bells. The Ministry of Information issued a directive explaining what should be done in the event of an invasion. It began with these words: 'If this island is invaded by sea or air everyone who is not under orders must stay where he or she is. This is not simply advice: it is an order from the Government, and you must obey it.'

MILITARY AND CIVILIAN PERSONNEL

Service personnel were frequently based at Luton and the town became an important military centre when the headquarters of Eastern Command were set up at Luton Hoo. The airport also played its part as home to an RAF Training School. Servicemen were based in Luton for all kinds of duties. One, a private in the Royal Engineers, wrote a mass-observation diary describing his posting to Luton (1941-2). He seems to have had quite a lot of free time, some of which was spent in his billet at Studley Road, reading or listening to music. He also went out to canteens, cinemas, dances, the library and local bars. He noted that he sometimes saw Ministry of Information films aimed at giving the civilian population necessary advice. One particular film described how to be safe in the blackout and one of the recommendations was to pause for a while when first going out so that eyes could become accustomed to the dark. He decided to watch people leaving the cinema to see if they had taken heed, but found that most of them ignored the advice completely.

Another group of servicemen who became familiar on the streets of Luton were the American GIs, many of whom apparently decided that Luton was the ideal place to spend their leave. No one can be sure exactly what attracted them, but come they did and eventually the American Red Cross set up a club, the Donut Club, for them in George Street and also sleeping accommodation at houses in Downs Road.

The regular emergency services were on war alert but there were also thousands of Luton people who voluntarily joined the various branches of the Civil Defence in the town. Planning began well before war was declared: enrolment of wardens, as part of Air Raid Precautions (ARP), began in 1937 and Councillor Dillingham became chief warden, a post he held until 1942. Wardens' duties would involve caring for the homeless and injured, enforcing the blackout (which is probably what they are best remembered for), firewatching and generally bringing order out of chaos. The town was divided into four groups, the number of wardens fluctuating according to the number of volunteers and also the amount of money available for manning the full-time wardens' posts.

Training 'incidents' were set up. On one occasion planes supposedly 'swooped over Marston Gardens, bombs exploded, houses were damaged and one partly demolished'. Another day a gas test was held in George Street when several people were found to be without their gas masks. Instruction was ongoing and there was a training ground at Stopsley where instructors tried to simulate the kinds of conditions the Civil Defence might face.

The Home Guard was originally known as the Local Defence Volunteers. Within minutes of the appeal for help broadcast on 14 May 1940, a queue of volunteers formed at Luton

Police Station. Sixty enrolled on the first night and by the end of the following day there were more than a thousand. Mr A.J. Mander (later Colonel Mander) was in charge and his first responsibility was to call the men to meetings at Beech Hill School to inform them of the work they would be called upon to do. Luton had to be guarded day and night. Headquarters were first set up in Dunstable Road but were then moved to the Drill Hall. Soon, it was not just a case of watching for any enemy activity, the men had to be drilled to learn to fight. The Home Guard served the town well until it was disbanded at the end of 1945.

The work of the British Red Cross Society and the St John Ambulance Brigade was vital. Before the war began, St John personnel went to London to train as instructors in air raid and anti-gas precautions and members of the Red Cross were also involved with the issuing and fitting of gas masks. Both groups regularly attended cinemas, sports activities and any public assemblies as well as manning first-aid posts. They contributed valuable service during the raids of 1940-1.

Men and women had ambulance duties and helped at the Luton and Dunstable Hospital as porters and stretcher bearers while women also helped with nursing and at the blood transfusion depots. A very special service was provided at the headquarters of the St John

67   *Wartime 'pillbox' at Stockwood Park.*

Ambulance Brigade in Barbers Lane. This was the next of kin bureau, opened in 1942, to help the families of men held by the Japanese. It is also interesting to note that Luton collected £65,000 for the Duke of Gloucester's Red Cross and St John Appeal.

The Luton and Dunstable Hospital had to keep 94 beds for air-raid casualties, which meant that the wards were crowded with extra beds. The hospital treated 500 war casualties, 271 of whom were admitted to a ward. Also among the patients were 4,754 members of the British and foreign armed forces. Doctors at the hospital were able to pioneer the making of their own penicillin.

The Luton Centre for the Women's Voluntary Services opened early in 1940 with Lady Keens as the Centre Organiser. From 1942, Mrs R.O. Andrews took over the post and Mrs Bart Milner became her deputy in 1943. The main offices were in Gordon Street but there were also offices at Leagrave and Limbury. Membership grew rapidly and reached more than six thousand. Of these, 400 were based at the Rest Centre and 4,000 belonged to the Housewives Service whose duty it was to help busy housewives and provide mobile teams during air raids. They also helped victims to clear up and restart their lives after their homes had been damaged. The responsibilities of the WVS were considerable and included clerical work, collecting salvage and savings, helping evacuees, providing transport, sheltering the homeless, and giving training in cookery, first aid and home nursing.

There was a clothing exchange depot in Melson Street organised by Mrs R. Hickman that was open for two afternoons a week, and also a wool department that functioned between May 1941 and December 1945. Altogether over 10,000 pounds of wool was issued to knitters and knitting was also done by work parties at the WVS centres. A total of over 35,000 garments were made.

An accommodation register was kept to help the billeting of evacuees, factory workers and service personnel. Then there was a canteen in Waller Street, run by Lady Keens and her volunteers, and also a British Restaurant in New Town Street. In addition, hot food from the British Restaurant was taken to men working on isolated construction work and to those without canteen facilities. The WVS also helped to run the American Red Cross Club in George Street.

From December 1941 young people were obliged to register at the age of 16, although they would not be called up for another two years. They entered into the spirit of the time and supported the junior branches of voluntary groups such as the Red Cross Society, St John Ambulance Brigade and the National Fire Service. There were also associations that trained young men in skills that would be needed when they were called up. Members of the Air Training Corps went on visits to airfields and attended classes on aircraft recognition, armaments, engines, theory of flight, and wireless operating. It is reported that between 600 and 700 youths and men from the ATC went into the services. The Sea Cadet Corps trained its young men in seamanship, signalling and squad drill. By early 1946, 44 boys had enlisted in the Royal Navy, six had joined the Fleet Air Arm and 15 had become members of the Merchant Navy. The Army Cadet Force had units at the Luton Boys' Club, the Boys' Modern School and at Leagrave and a social club was set up for them at the Drill Hall in

Old Bedford Road. A 'large percentage' of these boys went into the services, where their training stood them in good stead.

Members of the Girls' Life Brigade were taught first aid and home nursing, and also gave practical support, for example by helping on farms and looking after evacuee children. Girls at the local High School were encouraged to join a 'Company of Service' by making promises that included trying 'to find out how I may best serve the community of which I am a member' and finding out 'about the world in which I live in order to fit myself for world citizenship'. Mrs Evans, the teacher who ran the scheme, was also in charge of the Girls' Training Corps, whose members became messengers and also undertook secretarial and canteen work.

Unfortunately, not all the young people in the town were supportive. After fences and gates had been removed from the parks, gangs of hooligans took advantage of the lack of security and no doubt of the blackout. At Wardown Park concrete posts and iron seats were thrown into the lake and iron frames were smashed. Similar vandalism occurred in other local parks.

Dr Eberlie, a local GP, recalled the contribution his family made towards the war effort. He continued with his regular work but was also a member of a team that was ready to deal with bomb casualties. His wife was a night ambulance driver and the family home, Brooke House, became a sanctuary. In the early years of the war, Luton airport became the main base for the Air Ferry Service when pilots had to pick up a new plane at a factory, fly to the Luton base and then to wherever it was needed. Dr Eberlie's family offered bed and breakfast service for any ferry pilot who needed accommodation. One of these was the famous aviator, Amy Johnson. After 1942 the base was moved elsewhere and the airport was used for training.

Other guests at the Eberlie home included the Commandant Colonel Baldwin, and a young instructor, Alan Dutton, who came with his family. A group of American pilots also came for a week of rest. Sadly, one of the group was killed the day after they returned to duty which caused the doctor's family much grief. The *Luton at War* book notes that Elizabeth Eberlie became a Junior Commander in the ATS and was awarded the US Army Bronze star in 1945.

INDUSTRY

Luton's industries were called upon to redirect production towards the war effort. Vauxhall Motors Ltd was one of the major contributors and the workforce grew to 12,000 workers. About one third of the trucks supplied to the armed forces were Bedford trucks, made at the Luton plant at an average of 1,000 a week. These left the factory in convoys, some of them going along Montrose Avenue, and children from Denbigh Road School were often obliged to dodge between them on their way to school. There were no crossing patrols in those days. The Vauxhall factory also produced 'Luton's biggest war baby', the Churchill tank, 5,247 of which were made. Again, they took to the public roads and what a mess they made of them as they inched themselves slowly round the corners! Travellers on the trains to London would see these army vehicles beside the railway line outside the Vauxhall factory, and near St Albans the Handley Page bombers were lined up at the de Havilland airfield. Further south was the Hendon airfield and, for a time, there were barrage balloons in the sky over London – all signs to the passengers from Luton, often in freezing cold trains, of the battle being waged.

Other local factories went into full-time war mode and the following are just examples of the work that was done. At the Skefko Ball Bearing Co. Ltd, millions of ball, roller and thrust bearings were produced. The workers were unable to see the end product as the workers at the Vauxhall plant could, for these bearings went into all kinds of machinery, but they knew, nevertheless, that their work was vital. George Kent Ltd produced precision instruments and meters and the output of Hayward Tyler and Co. Ltd included pumps and parts for tanks.

The Davis Gas Stove Co. Ltd ceased the production of domestic cookers in favour of ammunition boxes, bombs, grenades, landmines, shells and shell cases. Electrolux Ltd also abandoned the manufacture of vacuum cleaners and refrigerators in favour of depth charges and mine charge cases. The British Gelatine Company sent 90 per cent of its output for the production of film, and most of the rest was used in medical supplies. As *Luton at War* observes, 'other things were more important than table jellies'.

Lye and Sons Ltd and R. Westly and Co. Ltd were called upon to stop the production of ribbons for hats in favour of weaving tape for parachutes and uniforms. Lye's were also able to clean and recycle thousands of metres of expensive silk for parachutes and balloons. The CWS Chocolate Factory on Dallow Road sent tins of cocoa, through the Red Cross, to prisoners of war and manufactured chocolate with vitamins to be given to children in a liberated Europe. On a much larger scale, Percival Aircraft Ltd made Oxfords and Proctors, training planes, but probably their most important product was the Mosquito bomber.

People could not choose where to work but were directed via the Labour Exchange. Once again, women were called upon to take on work that had previously been done by men, and unskilled workers took the place of skilled. Single women and those with children over 14 years of age were obliged to work, and mothers of younger children could take advantage of the Council's day nursery scheme if they wished to take up employment.

The local newspaper became involved with the production of a secret daily paper, *Nachrichten*, written by a group of propaganda experts under the *Daily Express* reporter Sefton Delmer who was based in Woburn. Hundreds of thousands of these papers were dropped to German forces in Europe with the aim of undermining their morale. Apparently the secret was so well kept that a British soldier, home on leave, was heard to compliment the Germans 'for producing such an excellent paper for their troops' and wondered 'why the British could not do the same'.

EVERYDAY LIFE

Everyday life continued in many ways much as before but against a very different backcloth. The most significant changes were probably the need to respond to air raids and the time-consuming problem of coping with shortages of just about everything. Rationing became a way of life, as did queuing. People everywhere rose to the challenge and 'Dug for Victory'. Gardens were turned over to vegetables, as was any suitable plot of land. Food scraps were put into bins that were standing in the streets and were then converted into pig food. How they stank, especially in warm weather!

Sometimes you could wander into Luton market and hear the cheeping of hundreds of beautiful little day-old chicks. People bought them for very little and took them home in a bag. There was probably a high mortality rate and such things would not be allowed today. But the chicks that did survive either laid eggs for you or supplied you with a tasty meal. Neighbours often saved their potato peelings and scraps in return for eggs. In the autumn, when harvesting was over, poultry keepers and their families were allowed to glean on the stubble in the fields around the town; it was worth the effort, even though the sharp cornstalks gouged deep scratches in uncovered legs.

As in the First World War, there was plenty of charitable work to occupy the civilian population. Money, too, was needed and there were special appeals each year. The first was for Spitfire week when enough money was raised to buy two planes. Then came War Weapons Week (1941), Warship Week (1942), Wings for Victory (1943), Salute the Soldier Week (1944) and Thanksgiving Week (1945). On top of this, people responded to the need to save and over £15m was invested in War Bonds.

Responsibilities were heavy but there was a social life too. Dances were held at the *George Hotel*, the Drill Hall, the Assembly Hall and also in church halls. There were several cinemas, some better than others, and the Grand Theatre in Waller Street. As travel was difficult and the seaside out of bounds, 'Holidays at Home' became the order of the day. The focus of much of this was Wardown Park, where an open-air theatre was built and where Thurston's Fair came for four weeks every summer. Then there was Whipsnade Zoo. At weekends and holiday times, crowded buses used to leave Luton, travelling over Dunstable Downs, to arrive just as the zoo was opening. When it was time to return home, long queues would form at the bus stop and often an extra bus would be needed to see everyone safely back to Luton.

The Music Department of the BBC moved to Bedford in 1941 and stayed for four years. Since Luton was conveniently near, the town was fortunate enough to enjoy visits from the BBC Theatre Orchestra under Stanford Robinson and the Symphony Orchestra under Sir Adrian Boult. These would be held in St Mary's Church, local cinemas or in work canteens. The Luton Choral Society and the Luton Girls' Choir also provided respite from the cares of war.

Children may not have realised how dangerous the situation was and were free to enjoy life – which they did. They were able to roam the countryside, especially those lucky enough to have bicycles. They were warned about what to do in the event of an air raid and were all drilled in the slogans of the time such as 'Careless Talk Costs Lives'. Bomb sites in the town were out of bounds but the warnings were not always heeded. One group of young boys found a pigeon by the river in New Bedford Road. It had been killed when it hit the telegraph wires but, interestingly, it had a message attached to its leg. Perhaps it was on its way to the pigeon loft behind the Drill Hall in Old Bedford Road. In retrospect, the boys should have taken the unfortunate bird to the authorities for the message to be deciphered but they did not fully realise the significance at the time. Static water tanks were certainly not erected for the benefit and entertainment of children but were there in case they were needed by the fire fighters. However, they gave the younger generation countless hours of pleasure as Robert Gurney recalls in his poem.

Water Boatmen
They were all over Luton,
those static water tanks.
There was one
in Wardown Crescent.
I used to spend hours
gazing
at the water boatmen.
They swam
with a movement
like that of a man
rowing a boat.
I loved the connection
between the word
and the action.

Another memory shared by the children of wartime Luton must surely be the day, 21 July 1943, when massed choirs of schoolchildren gathered on the steps of the cricket ground to sing patriotic songs. Also taking part were the band of the Bedfordshire and Hertfordshire Regiment, the Luton Pipe Band and the ATC Band. All the town dignitaries were present and Uncle Mac from the BBC Children's Hour gave a talk.

Victory Celebrations

Then, one day, it was all over. The town woke up on 8 May 1945 with a sense of euphoria, knowing that the dangers of the last six years were past. It would take time before the war in the Far East ended, before rationing disappeared and our servicemen returned home but the world had entered a new and more peaceful age. The country was ecstatic.

Street parties were arranged. Tables and chairs were taken out and enough food was found from somewhere. Old sheets were torn up, dyed and stitched, so that bunting and the union flag appeared on the houses. In the evening there was dancing for the older generation.

The war was truly over.

68 *Dancing in George Street on VJ Day, 15 August 1945.*

VIII

Migration

Luton has experienced movements of population throughout its existence. For example, there were the Romans, Saxons and Vikings who left their mark and, in medieval times, when Luton had become a small settled market town, life was enriched by the visits of neighbours from the surrounding areas who came to sell and buy or just to enjoy the regular markets and fairs. However, the population began to grow considerably and migration has been a very significant part of Luton life since the 19th century when the town became the centre of a flourishing hat industry. In more recent times, groups have come here from all parts of the world.

During the 'straw hat years', plait was made in the neighbouring hamlets and villages. Then, either the plaiters would bring their work into the town to be sold at the plait market or dealers would travel around the area to buy. The plait had to be sewn into fashionable shapes and, apparently, it was the ambition of girls to leave their cottage homes in order to become sewers in Luton 'which [was] considered a condition above that of a plaiter'. A *Report on Child Employment* in 1864 stated that there were many girls and women who came to Luton to make hats. 'They lodge in the town and many people let apartments for the purpose. Perhaps 500 such females will leave the town this week [early July] and 1,000 next, and will come back in August.'

Lucy Luck, who was born in Tring in 1848, wrote an autobiography and her experiences were no doubt matched by other women of the time. She was brought up in the local workhouse and, after leaving school, worked in the silk mills although she spent her evenings plaiting. After some time spent in service, she came to Luton and made an effort to learn how to sew straw hats from the plait. This meant mastering the popular styles of the season and, when a new style arrived, examining it closely to see how the work should be done. Some time later she went to a workroom where several girls worked together and then she began to earn good money.

She met a good friend and went to live, outside the town, with the family, earning money by doing outwork which had to be taken into Luton two or three times a week. After her marriage, Lucy moved to London but carried on with her straw work, sending it back to Luton every week. However, she was fortunate enough to find an employer in London who took her on for much better pay and Lucy continued to do that for the rest of her working life. Her time in Luton had stood her in good stead.

The diversity of the population in the 19th century can be appreciated by looking at figures based on the 1851 census for the sub-district of Luton.

Born in	%
Bedfordshire	65.12
Hertfordshire	19.8
Buckinghamshire	5.2
Middlesex	2.4
Northamptonshire	1.4
Essex	0.4
Cambridgeshire	0.3
Scotland	0.3 (mainly women)

Although the hat industry was focused on women, men in the town were employed to shape the hats on wooden blocks. According to Aubrey Darby, who was born in 1905, some of the skilled block makers were Italians who became the centre of a lively community in the town. Also the Vincenzi family firm made peachbloom, that is to say good quality velour, hats. Another Italian, Lorenzo Losi, visited the town from time to time and walked the streets with his 'wheezy' barrel organ on wheels. He was nicknamed 'Wet Weather' because it was said that, whenever he played, it was sure to rain. Then there was the ice-cream man who served welcome cornets from his barrow and the roast-chestnut man who yearned to make enough money to enable him to return home and buy a vineyard.

Around the turn of the century, industry moved into Luton to challenge the near monopoly of the hat trade. This created problems for the new employers as John Dony explained: 'the unorganised nature of the hat trade, its small units of production, its seasonal nature and lack of regimentation in the work place did not suit the new industries whose modern forms of production needed greater control of their workforce towards large scale organised machine production'.

The hat workers were anxious to retain their traditional freedoms and consequently the new firms tended to prefer immigrant workers who were more amenable to structured demands on their time. A notable example of this is the Davis Gas Stove Company, which opened a small branch in 1895. In 1907 the main part of the firm moved from Falkirk in Scotland, bringing workers with them; it is said that they became known locally as the 'Scotch Colony'. Also, when the Co-operative Society Cocoa and Chocolate Works came to Luton in 1902, the company brought some employees with them from London. Another example of migration into the town involved the ball-bearing firm, Skefko, which brought managers from Sweden.

The migrant population of the town grew considerably during the First World War. There was an influx of soldiers who were stationed in schools and later in large purpose-built camps in and around the town. There were other newcomers for, now that Luton had become an established industrial town, factories had redirected their output to help the war effort. Consequently large numbers of factory workers moved in, creating an accommodation problem similar to the ones the town had experienced at the height of the hat seasons. George Kent Ltd was one local factory that turned to munitions and many girls from out of town moved to work there.

BETWEEN THE WARS

Industry continued to prosper and there was a rapid growth in the population during the 1930s, most of the newcomers being from other parts of the British Isles. This account by Catherine Darlington is probably typical of many other family stories.

> People from Northern England, Scotland and Wales were desperate for work and Luton at that time had plenty to offer. My family came here in May 1935. I remember vividly arriving in Luton on that beautiful May morning in 1935, seeing flags and bunting hanging everywhere, celebrations for the silver jubilee of King George V. It was a joy to see my father and two elder brothers again. They had come to the town about two years previously, had found work and lodgings and eventually a house for the family. Unfortunately my father, a calico printer, was unable to find his trade in the town; the nearest to that being the dyeing of ribbons for the hat industry … My three older sisters were able to find employment. Another brother was, like me, still at school; he was 13 and I was nearly 10. Life did change for the better for all of us, although there was a bit of resentment from *some* local people to the newcomers, which was hurtful. But we did overcome, I think as a result of the war bringing communities closer together.

Wales was experiencing considerable labour unrest, notably the 1926 Miners' Strike. As a result there was much economic hardship and workers were being obliged to seek work elsewhere. Once again, Luton offered employment and the hope of a more settled lifestyle. It was also the case that many Welsh teachers moved to Luton schools. By 1938, there were enough 'Lutonian Welsh' for a Welsh Society to be founded.

A *Luton Guide*, published *c.*1954, looked back on the years between the wars and carried this observation:

> The worker in Luton has a long tradition of skill and independence, and pride in the town and its thriving industry are noticeable in the new generation arising from the thousands of workers who came to Luton in the thirties. Luton gave them new hope, prosperity and good living conditions, and on those foundations has been built a structure of mutual trust and respect between employer and employed.

It seems that some people were under a misapprehension concerning the number of migrants who had come to the town from other parts of the British Isles. According to a *Report of the Medical Officer of Health* (1936), only 13 per cent of Luton's population was born in those areas but it was generally assumed that there were far more because their accents were conspicuous, whereas newcomers from the South-East passed unnoticed. Another general observation was that communities kept to themselves. This may have been true in some cases, but there were certainly places that were 'mixed' and where the children played together harmoniously – until the motor car drove them from the streets that had been their playgrounds.

The Jewish Community

In the early years of the 20th century, the Jewish community began to contribute significantly to Luton life. Julius Wernher, who had made a considerable fortune from the South African diamond mines, bought Luton Hoo. Although the mansion has now been sold, his family still has strong links with the town, most notably with the plans to open up the historical walled garden on the estate.

Many Jewish families were market traders. Some, for example the Benjamin family, worked on the old open market but, in 1925, when the Plait Halls were converted into a covered market, many businesses moved there. It has been estimated that about three quarters of the market traders were Jewish. The Felson and the Harris families were two of the successful retailers and Barbara Felson can still name most of the market stalls and their respective owners. Luton market was a happy and popular place to shop.

69   *Mrs Betsy Ingham serving in her greengrocery shop in Luton's indoor market.*

There were also many families involved in the hat trade. Dr Eberlie, a well-respected local doctor, described the Jewish milliners as being 'both artistic and clever with colours and shapes'. Bermona, Marida and Edward Mann were some of the hat manufacturers. Jewish businessmen were also successful in the clothing industry, for example Ellis and Goldstein and Skirtex. Gown shops included Stones and Marie's in Barbers Lane.

Around the time of the Second World War more Jewish families came to Luton. Some were immigrants from Europe and others moved from London to live in a safer area. Michael Freedland is not sure why his family chose Luton but wonders if it was the simple fact that the first train that was about to leave St Pancras stopped at Luton station. There were about 300 Jewish families in Luton at this time and Denis Argent commented in his mass-observation diary (1941-2) that 'Luton is a rather Jewish town'. The Jewish group was very close-knit; everybody was anxious to help when others were in need and to support other good causes. Local Jewish ex-servicemen went to their own remembrance service and parade and marched side by side with others from Luton – 'a mix of British and Jewish like no other'. In 1951 the mayor, Tom Skelton, marched at the front of the Luton contingent.

Dr Eberlie remembered Rabbi Solomon in the early 1920s as an extrovert with a strong personality: 'his capacious synagogue, not far from our surgery [the surgery was at the corner of Dallow Road and Dunstable Road], was full to overflowing every Saturday morning with black-hatted Jews in their dark suits, with their smart wives and teenage children'. Another leader of the close-knit Jewish community in Luton in the 20th century was the Reverend Harry D. Ritvo (rabbi from 1938 to 1958), who is still remembered with much affection as a good man with a strong influence. The earliest meeting place was in one room in a building on Moor Path, when the congregation numbered just 30 or 40. This number increased and, during the Second World War, there were some 300 to 400 families. Jewish laws and feast days were observed and Jewish boys attended Hebrew classes.

In May 1953 came 'the materialisation of a dream', when the new Luton Synagogue and Jewish Communal Centre was opened on Bury Park Road. It was consecrated by the then Chief Rabbi, the Very Reverend Israel Brodie, in the presence of the mayor and mayoress, Members of Parliament and officials from neighbouring Jewish communities. Rabbi Brodie spoke of the importance of young people and the new synagogue was able to help them by setting up a Judean Youth Club, which is still remembered with 'great affection and gratitude'. Between 1974-6, another Chief Rabbi, Lord Sacks, came to the town to take Hebrew classes and also some services on Rosh Hashana and Yom Kippur. There is now a synagogue on Dunstable Road and the community, described as happy and thriving, is led by Rabbi Schwei. Another group, belonging to the Bedfordshire Progressive Synagogue, has been established here for over 40 years and welcomes members from Bedfordshire and from neighbouring parts of Hertfordshire. Regular services are held on Shabbat at Luton or Bedford and also on special festival days. There are currently about a hundred Jewish families in Luton.

The year 1939 brought many more new people into the town, just as the outbreak of the First World War had done. In early September trains arrived at the station with hundreds of evacuee children needing temporary homes. There was also an influx of ordinary folk who were afraid that London was about to experience heavy bombing. Most of these returned home when the expected raids did not materialise. It was not uncommon to see marching soldiers in the streets and army convoys driving along the roads. Some of the military were stationed in the town and one soldier, Denis Argent, who was billeted in Studley Road, wrote a Mass-Observation diary that recorded details of his life in Luton between 1941-2. British soldiers were not the only ones; apparently the US military found life in Luton to be very agreeable and social clubs were opened for their welfare.

Population figures quoted in a report by Grundy and Titmuss (1945) show how the population of the town had developed. Those coming from the depressed areas (Scotland, Wales and the North) totalled 13 per cent and only 46 per cent were Luton-born.

Place of origin	Number	%
Scotland	3,140	3
Wales	3,170	3
North	7,216	7
Midlands	4,901	5
East Anglia	2,611	3
South West and others	3,470	3
London	12,108	12
Remainder of South East	11,448	11
Bedfordshire	7,500	7
Luton	47,881	46
Total	103,445	100

Grundy and Titmuss were cautious about predicting the future; they expected that Luton would receive a continuous flow of immigrants but thought that the number would 'probably be lower than during peak intake before the war'. Their predictions were far from accurate; people continued to come in large numbers from the British Isles but many from much farther afield were also to make their homes in Luton.

Towards the end of the war, Luton gave refuge to another group of people; these were from a war-torn Europe, for example Poland, who were desperately in need of a new start in life. In the 1950s, trouble in Eastern Europe, resulting in the uprisings in Hungary and Czechoslovakia, saw the arrival of yet more refugees. One of these was Veronica Muzsnyai, who fled Hungary and has recently told her story to the local Voices project. She says that Luton is now her home and she is 'very grateful to Her Majesty the Queen' for allowing her to come to this country.

Also in the 1950s there was mass-emigration from Ireland. Many who came to Luton were involved in building the housing estates around the town. Others worked on the M1 motorway that came through Luton. When these workers reached Luton, the busy industrial scene attracted them and many decided to stay. By 1971, six per cent of the town's population were Irish-born. It has been said that they were called 'Brits' in Ireland and 'Pats' in England but they have kept their Irish identity and there is a strong Irish community in the town with, for example, the Irish Forum in Hitchin Road offering welfare advice. Now there is an annual St Patrick's Day Festival and, in 2009, the celebrations lasted from 13-17 March. The day itself began with a church service at Our Lady of Christians and was followed by a parade with pipe bands and dancing. There was an Irish market on Market Hill and traditional singing and dancing in the Central Square of the Mall.

The Roman Catholic Church began to grow, especially with the arrival of the Scottish and Irish communities. It seems to have been the pattern to start a mission in a particular area, followed by the establishment of a temporary church after which funds were raised for a permanent building. St Joseph in Gardenia Avenue began as a temporary church in 1937 to be followed by a new building. The Sacred Heart of Jesus is in Ashcroft Road and the Holy Ghost is in Westbourne Road. A mission was opened on Marsh Farm in 1976 and a new church, The Holy Family, in 1983. In 2002, this church joined as one parish with St John the Apostle, at Sundon Park. St Margaret of Scotland on Farley Hill was formally opened in

70   St Patrick's Day Parade.

1958 and St Martin de Porres on Leagrave High Street was consecrated in 2001. By 2004, the Roman Catholic population in Luton was over twenty-five thousand.

There are also several Catholic schools. These are: Sacred Heart Primary, St Joseph's Infant and Junior, St Margaret of Scotland Infant and Junior, St Martin de Porres Primary and Cardinal Newman Comprehensive. The local convents are the Sisters of the Sacred Heart of Jesus in Kingsdown Avenue and the Sisters of St Clare in Abigail Close. The Daughters of the Holy Spirit in Marsh Road closed in 2009 and three sisters live in the community.

To understand the changing character of immigration into Luton since the Second World War, it is necessary to consider the story from a wider perspective. Briefly, this country's status was developing from being the head of a vast empire to a member of a Commonwealth of Nations and also of a European community. Legislation opened the doors to new groups of people and helped to change the identity of Luton beyond recognition.

Until the middle of the 20th century, people who lived in the British Empire were considered to be British subjects and were permitted to settle here. Although so many people had the right of entry, the number of potential immigrants was considerably limited by the difficulties involved in acquiring travel documents and the cost of travel. However, after the Second World War, credentials were often easier to obtain, although the difficulty had by no means been overcome. Also the cost of travel from Africa, the Caribbean and the Indian subcontinent became considerably cheaper, especially with the introduction of charter flights and, in the 1950s, the increasing availability of cheap sea passages from the Caribbean. All this meant that it was easier for people, many of whom saw the 'mother country' as 'home', to come to Britain from overseas. The issues were discussed in Parliament and, indeed, the question of immigration is still under consideration.

One of the most important pieces of legislation was the Commonwealth Immigrants Act (1962) that took effect from 1 July of that year. Another significant date was 1 January 1973 when the Immigration Act (1971) came into effect and brought primary immigration to a halt. However, on the same day, Britain entered the European Economic Community, which resulted in the free movement of labour within its borders. As immigration from the Commonwealth decreased, immigration from Europe increased.

There was also emigration as people who had grown up here departed, particularly for Australia (£10 Poms), Canada, New Zealand, Rhodesia, South Africa and the United States of America. These are the thoughts of one ex-pat:

> Luton provided a good example of the best of British education, applied to the working and lower middle classes in the 50s and 60s. It resulted in many capable children getting an education that today only the wealthy can afford.
>
> From the age of 5, I took myself to school, walking at first, when primary school was close enough, then buses later, and finally bike. Society was such that no-one was overly concerned that I might be abducted, raped or murdered.

Hundreds more 'new Lutonians' appeared on the scene as a result of the London 'overspill' scheme. This was a joint venture between the London County Council (LCC), Bedfordshire

County Council and, in the case of Houghton Regis, Luton Rural District Council. The plan was that Luton companies would offer employment to Londoners, after which the LCC, which was succeeded in 1965 by the Greater London Authority, would approve the move to Luton. Families were then eligible for housing as long as they stayed in their approved employment for a certain amount of time.

The character of Luton was changing as the following figures indicate.

1981 census
The total population was 163,209. Of these,
6,591 originated from Eire (4.04%)
4,589 from Scotland (2.81%)
2,384 from Wales (1.46%)
3,302 from the Caribbean (2.02%)
2,784 from India (1.70%)
1,487 from Bangladesh (0.91%)
3,455 from Pakistan (2.11%)

PERSONAL REMINISCENCES

Below are some of the thoughts of people who have chosen to make their home in Luton. They come from various sources but several are from the Voices project based at Wardown Park Museum. A booklet, *Hello Luton, My New Home*, was produced to go with the excellent exhibition that was on display between 1 May and 6 September 2009 and the Museum holds an oral archive of all the reminiscences.

Nazia Khanum was born in East Bengal, which was at the time under British rule. When India gained independence, her home became part of East Pakistan and later Bangladesh. She received an excellent education in Bangladesh and then came to England to study, gaining a PhD at the School of Oriental and African Studies in London. Nazia came to Luton in 1983 to work in the community, breaking down discrimination and barriers and has since been employed in other areas, holding responsible posts in the field of diversity, equality and multiculturalism. As a child, she was taught that she had a duty of responsibility towards the community and has therefore been active in all kinds of voluntary work, both here and in Bangladesh. She was awarded an OBE in recognition of her work.

Nazia has continued to live in Luton and has put roots down because she appreciates the multicultural life of Luton, the fourth most diverse town in the UK with around a hundred different languages being spoken. She says Luton is friendly and people talk to each other and appreciate each other's cultures. When people mix, differences fall away for we all want the same things in life: education, employment, housing, health care and safety. There are so many hidden stories in Luton and the town has huge potential. Nazia also recognises everything that this country has contributed to the world; it may no longer be the centre of an empire but it does not have an island mentality. It still contributes justice, fairness and freedom to the world and should never be denigrated.

71   *Luton Voices Project. (Supported by the Heritage Lottery Fund, organised by Luton Museums. Project Co-ordinator Dien Luu. Logo designed by Nicolas Holzapfel.)*

Miguel Jose was born in 1954 in the Democratic Republic of the Congo. He moved to England in 1991 to 'improve his life' and came to Luton in 1998, his plan being to make some money and then return home. In England he found another world; coming here was one of the best things he has ever done and he has stayed. The English and Congolese cultures are very different. In the Congo, everybody was a friend; if people were passing by they would stop to talk, but it is not so easy to make friends here. Once keeping in touch with the family was more difficult. There were letters and the telephone but, when making a phone call, it would be necessary to plan ahead to make sure that a family member would be around to receive the call. Since mobile phones became freely available, families can keep in contact daily. Imagine – one party in Luton and the other out in the African bush!

Eva came from Slovakia. She had intended to study dentistry in her homeland but when the university introduced English into the teaching, she came to England to learn the language.

Friends told her to come to Luton because it was affordable and the people here made her very welcome. She enjoyed the local shops but also appreciated how near Luton is to London. The town offered the cinema, the library, nightclubs, sports facilities and eating out. There are all kinds of restaurants and the pubs are very attractive, especially for Sunday roasts, and also because most of them have some history attached. Eva loves the beautiful countryside around the town.

One of the biggest attractions for people from Eastern Europe is the proximity of the airport that makes it easy for them to travel home. Eva approved the modernisation which is being undertaken in the town but made this interesting observation: 'I believe that they [the Council] should leave pieces of history here as well, otherwise people will forget about it.'

Polish soldiers settled here after the war and some of their children and grandchildren are still here. Marian's father had been a prisoner of war under the Germans and was obliged to work as a coal miner. He used these skills when he came to England but later came to work at the Vauxhall factory. The Polish community in the town was very close-knit.

Bozena came when she married an Englishman and eventually settled in Luton. She looked for a Polish background for her daughter and found that there was a small Saturday school based at the Polish church in Dunstable. In 2001, this school moved to Downside School in Luton. Since 2004, when Poland became part of the European Union, many more Polish people, usually economic migrants, have made their homes in Luton. Consequently, the Saturday school has grown and there are now over 200 children enrolled. They are aware of being part of a mixed community and are helped to maintain their proficiency in the Polish language, the sixth most widely spoken in Europe. There is a Polish Centre on Market Hill where the community can socialise and learn new skills. Shops in the town sell Polish food, there are street signs and advertisements in Polish and also satellite dishes for Polish TV. The library stocks Polish books as do the local bookshops. Bozena says that there is openness, without judgement, in English life and schooling is better than in Poland.

Sarfraz Manzoor has written a book entitled *Greetings from Bury Park* in which he describes growing up in the Pakistani community in Luton. His father, Mohammed, left Pakistan in January 1963, living first in Chesham and then in Luton. In 1974, his family joined him. He worked at Vauxhall Motors and later his wife and daughter contributed to the family income by making clothes. There were strong community links among the local Pakistani families and also with the extended families back in Pakistan. The Manzoor children were taught that the whole world was open to them if they studied hard. They did so and Sarfraz Manzoor has become a successful writer and broadcaster. His believes that his father always remained Pakistani at heart and his relationship to England was always 'rooted in financial pragmatism rather than emotional attachment'. Sarfraz, however, says that he 'was born in Pakistan but made in England; it is Britain which is [his] land of hope and dreams'.

NEW FAITHS

With the arrival of immigrants from overseas, many new faiths have come to Luton. A short walk down Bury Park Road will give a flavour of the present diversity and will reveal the

Jamia Masjid Mosque, Oakdale Methodist Church, Bury Park United Reformed Church, the Restoration Revival Fellowship, the UK headquarters of the Calvary Church of God in Christ and the Sikh Temple.

Islam: In the late 1950s Muslims from the Indian subcontinent began to arrive in the town. Many of them came from Pakistan and Bangladesh, often via towns like Manchester, Birmingham and Bradford, to join friends and relatives already here. Work was easy to find at that time and many went to work in the motor industry and its suppliers. Mr Syed Rizvi explained that, when he first came to Luton in 1967, there were no mosques in the town but the Muslim population was growing and it was necessary to find somewhere to meet and to pray. In order to worship, they first hired a hall at Beech Hill School and were able to celebrate Eid in a hired hall on the corner of Oak Road and Dunstable Road, while the Roman Catholic Church of the Holy Ghost in Westbourne Road also provided them with accommodation.

The first mosque was Luton Central (Ghousia) Mosque in Westbourne Road and the second Bury Park Jamia Masjid in Bury Park Road. A house in Oak Road was purchased with the support of a London charity, the London UK Islamic Centre, which was formed in 1962 to help build bridges of understanding and mutual respect across faith communities.

Later the neighbouring house was purchased and official permission was granted for its use as a house of prayer. This is the Madinah Masjid. There are now 12 mosques, most of them having been converted from existing buildings, although the Central Mosque and another at Biscot Mill have been purpose-built. Each mosque is led by an imam with a deputy and a committee, so each is unique in its own way.

There are now around twenty thousand Muslims in the town: Arab, Bengali, Kashmiri, Pakistani, a few Iranians and a few Turkish. Most are Sunni Muslims although Shia Muslims have grown in number recently. Muslims are committed to helping the poor of this world, especially during the days of Ramadan. There are also Muslim schools: Rabia School in Portland Road and Al Hikmah School in Dunstable Road.

72 *Luton Central Mosque.*

Hinduism: Hindus, mainly from the Bengal, Gujarat and Punjab states of India, also began to arrive in Luton in the 1950s at a time when the town's industry was prospering and workers were needed. Women were able to work in the clothing business and many from the medical professions also arrived. By the end of the decade, there were about two hundred families and these were soon joined by a significant number of Hindus who came from Africa. In the 1970s, Idi Amin expelled Asian families from Uganda and many arrived here, bringing with them professional, commercial and retail skills.

Hindi and Gujarati language classes were run at Beech Hill High School. Hindus also actively participated in the formation of the Luton Community Relations Council throughout its existence. By 1967, there were around three hundred Gujarati Hindu families in Luton and, by the end of the 1970s, about a thousand Hindu families were living here. By this time, there were many second-generation Hindus, well-educated and in the professions while still retaining links with the Hindu community with its festivals and traditions. Mr M.B. Guha became the first Hindu and ethnic minority mayor of Luton (1991-2).

It became necessary to find premises for a temple and, in 1979, a former Methodist church in Hereford Road was purchased. This became a consecrated Hindu Mandir (Temple) and Community Centre. Services are held regularly, 365 days in the year. Natubhai Solanki wrote a poem about Luton, a town he has grown to appreciate. Here are some extracts:

> This town is fine, this town is mine …
> Cars, trucks and hats have long gone, replaced by wings
> Now folks our limit is the sky
> Of curries, pastas and chips, colours, costumes and
> Tongues there is a riot in the town …
> I love my town for it gave me shelter, food and wine
> Luton Town is fine, Luton Town is mine.

Sikhism: After the Second World War, a few Sikhs came from India and others came in the 1960s under the voucher system, when there was a need for workers in the town. Others came from Africa when they lost everything in the era of Idi Amin. As with other communities, people often expected to stay for a while and then return home but most eventually stayed. At first the community met in hired halls, such as those at Beech Hill and Maidenhall Schools. Although there is no particular day of worship – it is possible to 'make each day special' – Sikh families usually met on Sundays because people are not usually working on that day. There has been a Sikh temple in Luton since 1976. Initially this was one three-bedroomed house in Portland Road but later the whole row of terraced houses was bought. Now there are more than 1,000 members of the community from Luton and the surrounding areas and they meet in the former Dallow Road Junior School.

Giani (priests) are the 'learned ones'. Many come on a temporary basis but some are invited to stay longer. However, most work is done by volunteers, both male and female. The first Sikh mayor of Luton was Lakhbir Singh (2008-9). Interestingly, the title 'Singh' means 'a lion'. Females are given the title 'Kaur' which means 'princess'.

Luton is now very much a multicultural town as these figures from the 2001 census demonstrate.

Country of birth	%
England	76.8
Wales	0.9
Northern Ireland	0.7
Republic of Ireland	3.4
Other EU countries	1.3
Elsewhere	14.9

If these figures are compared with those for the East of England, it will be seen that the figure of 14.9 per cent is higher than anywhere else in the region and is also above the average for England and Wales. Also the proportion of people born in the United Kingdom is significantly below the regional and national averages while the proportion of those born in Northern Ireland and the Republic of Ireland is higher. The 2001 census also gives the figures for ethnic groupings:

White	%
British	65
Irish	4.6
Other	2.3
Other	
Mixed	2.6
Asian or Asian British	18.3
Black or Black British	6.3
Chinese or other ethnic group	0.9

Luton's main ethnic group is Asian/Asian British, with around four times the average for England and Wales. The Black/Black British ethnic group is around three times higher in Luton than nationally, and six times higher than the regional figure. It is now the fourth most diverse town in the United Kingdom with around one hundred different languages being spoken. This new identity can best be experienced at the Luton Carnival, which is focused on the African Caribbean and Latin American communities. The Carnival began in 1976 as a small Victorian street fair held to celebrate the centenary of the town as a Borough but has now become an annual event and the largest Carnival in the country after London's Notting Hill. It attracts more than 150,000 spectators and more than 2,000 participants from all parts of the world. The organisers tell us that:

> Carnival speaks the language of the street: arts and crafts, circus arts, costume-making, dance, music and theatre can increase cultural understanding and tolerance, enhance racial harmony, improve quality of life, build cultural identity and understanding, improve educational attainment and tackle social exclusion.

73-4 *Luton Carnival.*

In its early days, preparations for the Carnival were made at the Hat Factory. In spite of its name, this building is no longer a factory for making hats but is a cultural centre where over 30 creative and cultural organisations are based and where the Headstart Project offers specialist support to creative companies and individuals. Luton Carnival Arts Development Trust (LCADT) was established in 1998, and on 24 March 2009 a new state-of-the-art centre was opened in St Mary's Road at a cost of over £7m. It is officially known as the UK Centre for Carnival Arts (UKCCA) and is the country's (maybe the world's) first centre dedicated to carnival arts.

In May 2009 there was a celebratory party with a spectacular light display and a carnival procession featuring five carnival queens from across the world. The new building and its furnishings give an exciting taste of foreign lands and there is a fully equipped theatre with the stage area opening out onto the forecourt so that outdoor performances can also be enjoyed. It is already possible to study costume design, face painting, juggling, soca dance, steel pan music, stilt walking and other related skills at the centre, and from 2010 there is to be a two-year Foundation Course on Carnival Arts held in conjunction with the University of Bedfordshire.

Carnival Day is magical. There is the noise of hammering as steel pans are tuned while colourful stalls sell (or give away) all sorts of interesting items. Food from across the world is on sale: coconuts with the tops cut off (drink the milk through a straw) and spicy chicken, but local favourites such as bacon rolls are not forgotten. All the lengthy preparations come to fruition as people take their places ready for the parade to start. This begins and ends in New Bedford Road and the crowds along the route join in the excitement, while appreciating the wonderful costumes and the skills of the performers.

Wardown Park was bought over 100 years ago for the town to enjoy and has since been at the heart of much Luton life, from the 'monkey parade' through the wartime 'Holidays at Home' and happy days on the boating lake. There have been many changes but, on Carnival Day, the local population once again gathers to share a sense of community.

WHY HAVE SO MANY PEOPLE CHOSEN TO LIVE IN LUTON?

In 2004, the Luton *Herald & Post* published a list of reasons to be proud of living in Luton. They make interesting reading although some may be open to debate. For example, the status of the Luton football team, known as the Hatters, has fluctuated and the economy has shared in the international 'credit crunch'. The last point may possibly have been influenced by the fact that the list was published in the *Herald & Post*! A second list was published in the *Luton News* in October 2009 after an online poll. Some of the results are similar.

- The mix. Luton is a real melting pot that for the most part bubbles along happily rather than boiling over.
- The buzz – business enterprise created the town's prosperity and people working hard for a living are still driving us forward.

- The location – close to London but definitely not some sad southern dormitory town like many nearby.
- The links – if you need to get anywhere, Luton's the place to start with air, road and rail connections galore.
- The future – there's so much potential, both in the younger generation and the new arrivals.
- The food – we all know it's a great place to get a curry but other cuisines are making great strides thanks to creative chefs and customer demand.
- The university. Take a look because you will be impressed.
- The team – Luton Town has had their ups and downs but we're on the rise at the moment, and life with the Hatters is never dull.
- The envy – if people weren't so threatened by Luton's rough and ready vitality, they wouldn't make so many wide of the mark jokes.
- The local rag – the *Herald & Post*, now recognised as one of the best reads in the country.

> - Energy and warmth
> - Unrivalled transport links
> - London Luton Airport
> - Mainline links to London
> - The nearby M1 motorway
> - Green spaces surrounding the town
> - Comedy at the Hat Factory
> - Luton Town Football Club
> - Romantic walks and places
> - The University of Bedfordshire

Also mentioned in these reports were: the river Lea, the Carnival, the community spirit and Luton's unique diversity. It was described as a microcosm of Britain, our strengths and our challenges. There are other, similar, reasons for living in Luton that have been offered as part of the research for this book and these are described here.

Perhaps the most common reason for coming to Luton is to find work. The pattern was frequently for the main breadwinner to come to the town and, having found work and accommodation, to send for the existing family or the family-to-be. It has often been said that good wages were an attraction and it is certainly true that, for many years, Vauxhall Motors had the reputation of paying employees well. In times of labour shortages, Vauxhall Motors in particular advertised for workers. Another local project involved advertising for teachers in Gibraltar.

More than one hundred years ago, the New Industries Committee advertised 'good housing' as one of the inducements for companies to relocate to Luton. This may still be the case and property prices and rents are considered to be more affordable than they are in some nearby towns. The following example may or may not be typical: a man who was working in London said that he looked at the railway line from St Pancras. Together with his wife he studied the prices of houses in the towns along the line until they reached a place they could afford. They settled on Luton and what was intended to be a temporary move became permanent and they have never regretted their decision. The existence of cheap travel from the airport is also important, especially for newcomers from Eastern Europe.

Accessibility to London life is generally appreciated. The pleasures of the capital can be enjoyed but Luton is smaller and friendlier and certainly not pretentious. It is not crowded for in Luton 'there is space'. Some people also claim that Luton 'is fashionable'. There are opportunities for health care and education and these are especially welcomed by people from overseas. As far as education is concerned, it is said that the name of Denbigh High School is known in many parts of the world. Also the schools at Challney offer separate boys' and girls' education for families for whom this is the preferred choice.

Probably one of the best things that can be said about Luton is that it has offered a new start in life to thousands of people and for that thousands of new residents are eternally grateful. Naturally all the changes have been something of a culture shock for some older Lutonians but overall the town has continued to live harmoniously and much effort has been put into integrating the different communities. Luton has changed in many respects but it remains a friendly and down-to-earth town where people are happy to make a new home for themselves and their families.

IX

Leisure

I T IS NOT possible to say exactly how the people of Luton spent their free time over the generations but William Austin in his *History of Luton and its Hamlets* has made some interesting observations concerning the Saxon way of life. In those days, they probably enjoyed singing, improved their hunting skills and played ball games. When the weather was fine they no doubt went swimming and, in winter, practised their skating. In medieval times, as has already been noted, there were the annual fairs and these continued until recent times. When Oliver Cromwell ruled the land, pleasure-seeking was forbidden and it is recorded that, in 1528, top spinning was banned. Whatever else may or may not have been enjoyed, there was always the lovely countryside around to be explored.

This countryside supported the whole community and it was traditional for families to join in when harvests were gathered. School logbooks from the hamlet schools note that it was usual to have holidays that fitted in with the wheat harvest and there were many laments when absentees (or truants according to your point of view) were away from school to help in the gathering of other crops. These included: collecting acorns, blackberries, potatoes and strawberries in season and carting hay. Boys also took time off to assist with shooting parties. Oral evidence has added more information: a former pupil at Hyde school recalled that, while the boys helped with the heavy work, girls would sit on the carts while the horses brought the sheaves back to the farm and, until the advent of the combine harvester, families would go gleaning to collect the fallen grains of corn to take home to feed their own animals.

A schoolgirl from Leagrave wrote accounts in her school exercise book, which is now kept in the Wardown Park Museum archive. Perhaps these letters were an answer to a typical request from a teacher to write down what she had done in the holidays but they are, nevertheless, a colourful account of life in one of the hamlets 100 years ago.

July 16th 1909

Dear Maud,

I thought you would like to know how I spent our day's holiday. On Wednesday we had a day's holiday from school for Wardown Fete. On Wednesday morning my sister and I had a game at swings. Then I helped mother with the dinner. After we had had it I got my self ready and uncle took us for a nice drive to Flitwick to see some of our old friends. We went through Chalton, Fankot, Westoning, and Harlington. At last we reached Flitwick, it is a very pretty place, and nearly everybody has got a very pretty garden in front of the house. They were very pleased to see us. We could not stop very long because it had taken us longer to get there than we expected. As we were coming home we went up Harlington Hill. We all had to get out and walk because it was so steep and I picked some very pretty flowers and quakers. Then we came to Sundon and I saw a big pond and the old church. When we got home it was nearly nine o'clock so I had my supper and went to bed.
Your loving friend,

Sept. 16th 1909

As our holidays are over, I thought you would like to know how I spent them. We broke up on July 29th for five weeks holiday, but we had an extra week's holiday because of the late harvest. On August Monday it was very showery, only clearing up in the evening, when we went for a walk up the Dunstable Road. The next day was our Band of Hope Tea, when we climbed to the top of the Knoll [probably at Totternhoe]. The following Tuesday we went to Hitchin market. When we had had a good look round we had our tea and started home. On the next Wednesday it was our Horticultural Show. On the following Tuesday we went to Leighton Buzzard. The next week we went to Woburn park where we saw a lot of deer, and to Fenny Stratford. As I have no more time I will close.

Dec. 15th 1910

Mother has asked me to invite you to come and spend a few days with us at Christmas. We shall expect you on Christmas Eve by the one o'clock train. On Christmas Eve we shall decorate our house with ivy, holly and mistletoe. As Christmas day happens on Sunday we shall keep it on Monday when I hope we shall have a very pleasant and enjoyable time. On Monday we will go for a very nice walk, and have many games as Blind-man's bluff and The Postman's Knock. The following day we are going to hold our Band of Hope tea to which we hope to go. If it freezes and the ponds bear we will go sliding and skating, and if there should happen to be down-fall of snow we will go snowballing which I think we shall enjoy. We are going to have a week's holiday from school and I hope during that time we shall be able to go and visit some of our relatives that live at Luton and also visit those that live at Leagrave. During your stay with us we hope to go for many long and enjoyable walks together, and if the weather is too wet and rough to go out we will stay in and have some enjoyable games. I shall expect a letter from you telling us how long you will be able to stay and wether [sic] it will be convenient for you to stay with us for Christmas. As I have no more time and it is nearly post time I will close.
Your loving cousin.

The mention of the Band of Hope indicates that the family, like many others in Luton, was teetotal. Such groups were associated with particular churches and chapels and were the focus of much of Luton life. Sunday schools were very important and their organised anniversary treats and annual outings were eagerly anticipated. One favourite venue for outings was Scarborough's Meadow, between Ashburnham Road and Dallow Road and children taking part sometimes met in Park Square before marching to the meadow. Groups also went to Ashridge or Wheathampstead, no doubt by charabanc, or to Totternhoe Knolls, which was reached by taking the train from Bute Street to Stanbridge. Others picnicked and played games in Putteridge Park. The Adult School enjoyed Pleasant Sunday Afternoons (PSAs) and their Jubilee programme for 27 January 1912 describes how they celebrated with a visit to Sir Julius Wernher's Conservatories at Luton Hoo and also with a 'Great Jubilee Gathering' in the Plait Hall.

Church membership also put constraints on how people spent their Sundays. These reminiscences were written in the 1930s by girls at Luton High School, and help to capture that Sunday feeling.

> Sunday is a peaceful day, when even the milkman whistles hymns instead of dance tunes. After a leisurely breakfast, families might take a stroll but this was not altogether a pleasant time for children. They may not pick flowers, because they are wearing their best gloves, and the most tempting hedges and banks must be left alone for fear of scratching their Sunday shoes.

> The constant war with insects, fungi and blights, ceases for one day, the church bells ring out clearly in the morning air, best clothes, even to uncomfortable stiff collars, are worn, for it is Sunday. Down the quiet road, hymn books under their arms, a crowd of villagers file quietly into the churchyard as did their ancestors in years gone by.

While some Lutonians were happy to fill their lives with church activities, there was another side to Luton life that was not so rosy. This was based on beer houses, inns and pubs. It was thought that there were 90 licensed premises in Luton in 1846 and William Austin estimated that by 1869 there were 228, which works out at one for every 48 people in Luton over the age of 13. Lobbying by the teetotal community subsequently helped to reduce the number of licensed premises in the town.

Associated with the consumption of alcohol was the kind of 'riotous living' seen at the fairs. The 'Stattie' continued until 1929 and Anthony Darby recalled, from a young boy's point of view, some of the sights and sounds.

> Ancient bye laws decreed that showmen, quack doctors, gypsies and divers twilight characters could erect their paraphernalia in the main streets ... Outside the Corn Exchange men joyfully hurled wooden balls at coconuts artfully wedged into cup-shaped receptacles perched on sticks ... The rockmaker held court ... The 'Painless Dentist' attracted a large audience ... quack doctors [dispensed] potions guaranteed to cure every ailment, and desperately ill people [paid] out money for coloured liquids with a blind faith bordering on imbecility ... With nightfall [the Stattie] seemed like Dante's Inferno, flickering lights from kerosene flares haloed in smoke made an unearthly glow, inanimate objects came to life and the faces of the revellers appeared like the gargoyles of Notre Dame.

T.G. Hobbs, as well as supporting the teetotal movement with his Lantern Mission which 'aimed to reach people who attend no place of worship and to show, by the eye as well as the ear, the advantage of temperance, thrift and religion', was probably one of the first travel agents in the country. He organised tours that were well supported by better-off Lutonians. In the 1880s and '90s he chartered trains to take parties to Devon, the Lake District, North Wales and Scotland and then branched out by visiting Europe and hiring a steamer on the Norwegian fjords. In 1894, he claimed that the number of passengers he had 'conducted personally to English, Welsh, Scottish, Irish, Norwegian, Dutch, Belgian, German, French, Swiss and Italian scenes probably reach[ed] 10,000'.

Other ways to occupy free time, for example in clubs and societies, were listed in the many annual local almanacs and directories. Just as is the case today, these groups probably waxed and waned but looking at the lists gives a flavour of local life and it certainly seems unlikely that anyone had the need to be bored. Some of the societies, such as the Mechanics' Institute and later the Workers' Educational Association that existed for most of the 20th century, aimed to stimulate the mind. Now, in the 21st century, the highly successful University of the Third Age (U3A) is very popular and provides interest groups for hundreds of people in Luton and the surrounding areas.

All the political parties had associations and the special branches for younger members were well supported since they also provided a lively social life. Interestingly there were once members of the National Union of Women's Suffrage in the town. Professional groups like the National Union of Teachers were active and there was also, among many other similar organisations, an association for shorthand writers. Many hobby groups were formed, for example the Bedfordshire Canine Association and the Cage Bird Society, and there were also interest groups for like-minded people like model and experimental engineers and also gardeners. The Fine Art and Crafts Society held exhibitions at the Assembly Hall in Waller Street; amateur music and dramatic clubs put on concerts; dances were held at the *George* and the Winter Assembly Hall and sporting enthusiasts were probably spoilt for choice.

Caring for the less fortunate has been and still is important. Groups that worked for the good of the community included the NSPCC and the RSPCA and also the Guild of Kindness, which taught that 'you live not for yourselves alone' and supported the Bute Hospital and the Children's Home. In 1925 it was recorded that the Luton Lads' League existed to 'improve the position of the poorer lads of the town' and Girls' Aid gave 'assistance to friendless girls'. The British Legion no doubt did its best but, if a piece written by a schoolgirl in the 1930s is to be believed, there was still much to be done. She tells of a blind ex-serviceman who was singing in the street in the pouring rain. He was accompanied by his little daughter whose job it was to collect any money donated. Many Lutonians will also probably remember an ex-serviceman who regularly sold matches at a site in George Street.

In 1850 a Public Libraries Act was passed and this instigated the modern public library system. After much deliberation, a free library was set up on the corner of Williamson Street and opened in 1883. The first librarian was David Wootton. Apparently there was a good supply of periodicals and newspapers but the choice of books was somewhat limited. Indeed, at that time, there was a body of opinion that thoroughly disapproved of any kind of fiction. At first only subscribers, who paid one guinea a year, were allowed to take books home but eventually this facility became open to everyone.

A larger library was desperately needed, so the council applied to Andrew Carnegie, Scottish American philanthropist, who over his lifetime funded nearly 400 public libraries. In 1908 Carnegie promised £10,000 and a splendid new building opened in 1910, also on the corner of Williamson Street. Carnegie himself attended the opening ceremony and apparently approved of the new library that was truly a delight and has been described as an 'architectural treasure'. A new librarian, Thomas Maw, was appointed. He was progressive and well thought-of and built up the library to a higher standard. In 1925 a children's library was opened by Maud Griffiths where children in the town sought out books on Biggles, Worrals, Sue Barton or maybe *Swallows and Amazons*. Worrals is said to be based on the real-life Amy Johnson who, as a pilot, was familiar with Luton Airport. For a time a small museum was based in the library but, in 1931, that was moved to Wardown.

Frank Gardner became librarian in 1938 and, under his direction, the town's library service achieved an excellent national reputation. In 1950, Luton celebrated the centenary of the Public Libraries Act but, by this time, the Carnegie Library was much too small. In November 1962 a modern, much larger, library in Bridge Street was visited by HM the Queen. Unfortunately the beautiful Carnegie 'architectural treasure' was demolished and ugly new buildings have taken its place. The new library was upgraded in 2009 and now caters for the needs of the 21st century with computers, microfiche, microfilm and study areas. There are sections for family history and local history and the ethnic communities in the town can borrow books in their own languages. At the entrance there is a statue, donated by Vauxhall Motors Ltd, of a man and a boy, who are looking at a book together. The inscription rightly says: 'He that loves reading has everything within his reach.'

Theatrical productions have always attracted much attention. It may well be that people who lived in Luton in medieval times gathered in the churchyard to watch miracle plays and there have probably many other amateur presentations that took place in and around the town. There are certainly reports of circuses and fairs appearing from time to time; Barnum and Bailey's performed on Powdrill's grassy meadow, which was between Biscot Road and New Bedford Road; Buffalo Bill visited the town and there is a photograph of Sanger's Circus parading on Market Hill. In the 20th century, particularly during the Second World War, Thurston's Fair set up in Wardown Park during the summer.

When the Plait Halls were built, it was anticipated that the space would be used as a music or concert hall but it became a covered market instead. In 1898 a purpose-built theatre was

opened in Waller Street, opposite the Plait Halls. The opening day was a very spectacular event because the famous actress Lillie Langtry appeared. The Grand, as it was called, became a popular venue and very much a part of Luton life until it was closed in 1957. It offered a variety of shows, some professional and some amateur, and at Christmas there were pantomimes.

Lutonians who yearned to appear on the stage were able to join Luton Amateur Dramatic Society, which was formed in 1907, or the Luton Dramatic Club, opened two years later. Any profits from their shows were donated to charity. In 1962 the Library Theatre was opened on the third floor of the new library. This became known as St George's Theatre in 1985 but reverted to its old name in 1996. Many other amateur groups, such as the St Christopher Players founded in 1946, have been active and now, in the 21st century, budding thespians have a wide choice of theatrical and musical groups to join.

The first half of the 20th century was the time when the cinemas were at their most popular. There would not be enough space in a book of this size to document their history but fortunately this research has already been done by Eddie Grabham and has been published in his book *From Grand to Grove*. One of the difficulties is that cinema names were altered as they came under new ownership and also the use of the buildings changed over the years. However, in their glory days, especially during the Second World War, 'the pictures' were magical and romantic and there were frequently long queues outside the cinemas.

It is probably true to say that, at the height of their popularity, the main cinemas in the town were the Alma, the Odeon, the Palace, the Savoy and the Union. The Alma was on the corner of Alma Street and New Bedford Road. In 1955, it became the Alma ballroom and was later known as the Cresta ballroom. The Palace, in Mill Street, was opened in 1912. It subsequently became the Gaumont before taking on new lives, first as a ballroom and then as a bingo hall. The Savoy, in George Street, opened in 1938. It became the ABC in 1961 and 10 years later, when large cinemas were no longer viable, opened with a triple screen. The Union, in Gordon Street, opened in 1937, became the Ritz in 1949 and closed in 1971. The Odeon, which was in Dunstable Road, opened in 1938; it was for a time a bingo hall but is now home to an evangelical church. It is a Grade-II listed building. Cinemas also hosted pantomime and musical concerts.

There is now no market for a large cinema on this scale and entertainment in the town is concentrated on the Galaxy in Bridge Street that is home to bowling, amusement arcades,

76 *The Luton Library Players performing* Hedda Gabler.

restaurants and Cineworld, which is a 'multiplex' with 11 screens. The Hat Factory (formerly the Artezium) in Bute Street is a centre for the arts, offering a cinema, dance studio and theatre as well as an exhibition gallery and rehearsal and workshop spaces. An Arts Festival is held to celebrate art, film, literature, music, poetry and theatre.

There have been Choral Societies, at least since 1866 when the Luton Choral Society was established by William Eustace, Henry and Joseph Hawkes and Thomas Underwood. One of the conductors was Fred Gostelow, who was also a composer and organist and choirmaster at St Mary's Church. Other popular Luton Choirs that have travelled and performed extensively are the Vauxhall Male Voice Choir, founded in 1943, and the Luton Male Voice Choir, formed in 1993.

However, probably the most famous of the Luton choirs was the Luton Girls' Choir. This was the brainchild of Arthur Davies, who was also one of the conductors of the Luton Choral Society. The choir made radio and television appearances and produced over 50 recordings. After the Second World War, they began touring this country and in the 1950s travelled abroad, even as far away as Australia and New Zealand. In 1948 they performed at the Royal Palladium in a Royal Command Performance. The choir was disbanded after the death of Arthur Davies in 1977.

The Luton Mandolin Band was founded in 1886 and performed internationally under Philip Bone, who kept a most interesting music shop in Manchester Street. Luton Red Cross

77   *Luton Concert Orchestra rehearsing, conducted by Bryan Summerfield.*

Silver Band was started in 1890, possibly as an off-shoot from the Ashton Street Mission Band that had been formed in 1883. The band was to become one of the most successful in the country, much of the credit for this going to the well-respected Mortimer family who lived in Luton in the early 20th century. The name of the band was changed to Luton Town Band and it achieved national recognition, winning many awards, in particular the Thousand Guinea Trophy at Crystal Palace in 1923. Luton Symphony Orchestra has been in existence for over 50 years; it was founded in 1953 as Luton Youth Orchestra and became Luton Symphony Orchestra three years later, and exists 'to promote live orchestral music'.

The musician Stuart Goodyear has written about the plethora of bands that existed in the town and says that 'Luton was a vibrant town, which provided high class live music for dancing on a weekly basis, to suit all tastes' in halls such as the Drill Hall, Neville Hall and the Winter Assembly Hall. In the 1960s the scene began to change but the different styles of music were still catered for in private functions.

RECREATIONAL FACILITIES

In 1872, the indoor Baths were opened in Waller Street. These offered washing facilities in the days when many homes lacked them and also had two small swimming pools, one for men and one for women. They were much too small and in 1913 many improvements were made. When part of Wardown Lake was marked off for swimming, it was probably only the stout-hearted who took advantage of the opportunity, but in 1935 a large open-air pool, with a smaller paddling pool for children beside it, was opened in Bath Road. This was very popular, often with long queues outside and, on summer days, the sound of people enjoying themselves could be heard from a considerable distance. When Waller Street Baths closed in 1965, a covered pool was opened in Bath Road. Now pools are to be found in local recreational centres and there are plans for a new 50m pool at Luton Regional Sports Centre in Stopsley.

Luton Town Football Club, known as the Hatters to recall the town's closeness to the hat industry, plays a very big part in the life of the town. It was formed from two local clubs, Luton Town Wanderers and Excelsior, in April 1885 and became a member of the Southern League in 1894. Three years later it joined Division Two of the Football League and in 1914 the first division of the Southern League. The height of the club's success came in 1955 when it reached Division One of the Football League.

An early ground was in Dallow Lane but the club moved to Kenilworth Road in 1905 where it has remained ever since, in spite of several attempts to move it to a larger site. Plans were made to establish a new ground near Junction 10 of the M1 and, more recently, it was hoped to set up a large complex by Junction 12, near Toddington. The latest idea is to include a new ground as part of a proposed Bushwood development but it remains to be seen if and when the club will move. Some of the highlights in the club's history were the cup final in 1959 when the town played against Nottingham Forest and April 1988 when Luton won the Littlewood's Cup. Luton Town now plays in the Blue Square Premier League, which used to be the Vauxhall Conference and is one league below the Football Leagues.

78 *Swimming Baths, 1952.*

79 *Luton Town Football Club. Cup Team 1893-4 Season.*

Rugby was played at Luton Modern School from 1922 and an Old Lutonians Rugby Club was formed in 1930. This became Luton Rugby Club. It has had various homes but since 1988 has been based at Newlands, near Stockwood Park, and has excellent facilities. The South Beds Golf Club was founded in 1892 on common ground at the bottom of Warden Hill with wattle sheep hurdles around the green instead of bunkers. In 1903 there were 100 gentleman members, who paid an entrance fee of £3 3s. and an annual subscription of £1 1s., and 50 lady members, who paid 10s. 6d. for both. As Luton expanded, the greens had to be moved around but this is still a thriving club with good facilities. The land is owned by the Crown.

Luton offers a huge variety of opportunities for sports enthusiasts, including bowling, hockey and tennis clubs. Luton Swimming Club was started in 1887 and the Luton Wheelers Cycling Club in 1900. Vauxhall Recreation Club, at the Brache, was founded in 1931 but is now independent and open to everyone. There are other leisure centres in the town, for example the one at Stopsley, and there is a running track at Stockwood Park.

OPEN SPACES, PARKS AND RECREATION GROUNDS

Within the town there are pleasant open spaces, possibly the most popular being Wardown Park. The upper park and the mansion were opened on 8 July 1905 and the whole park on 7 May of the following year. It has been an attraction for the people of Luton for many years

81 *Mansion House, Wardown, postmarked 1908.*

and, until the middle of the 20th century, a large proportion of the populace gathered on warm Sunday afternoons to walk from the town to the park and back again. There were tennis courts and a bowling green, and paddle and rowing boats could be hired at the boathouse. Almost hidden by the bushes was a fascinating old donkey wheel (a treadmill for drawing water from

82 *The Boat House, Wardown.*

83   *The Zig-Zags performing at Wardown.*

a well). Between Wardown House and Stockingstone Road is the town cricket ground where at least one international star, Monty Panesar, a Stopsley schoolboy, practised his skills.

Another Wardown attraction was the Easter Bonnet Parade, which had its heyday in the 1950s when it would attract in the region of 40,000 people. In April 2004 it was revived as the Easter Hat Parade with more than 100 hats on display. There was a design competition with more than 1,000 hats submitted and also a charity hat auction. In the 21st century the town still gathers at Wardown, as it has done for the past 100 years, nowadays to celebrate the spectacular Carnival.

The Moor, beside New Bedford Road, is all that is left of the old Moor that once reached as far as Dunstable Road. A large proportion of it was taken over in 1868 when the Midland Railway was built but, as part of the deal, more land at People's Park, Pope's Meadow and Bell's Close was made available for the use of the townsfolk. The river Lea can still be enjoyed in this little oasis of green. There are also recreation grounds, for example Memorial Park, which was given by Lady Ludlow in memory of her younger son who was killed in the First World War. At about the same time, Dallow Downs were given to the town by Miss Joan Crawley and Stockwood Park, once home to the Crawley family, is now freely open to the public.

Bide-a-While was once a favourite spot that was much visited on summer weekends. The beautiful garden has closed but there is still the nearby Riverside Walk to be enjoyed. Bide-a-While was established by George Farr, who had an engineering works in the town. He lived in Collingdon Street but, as there was no garden, he took over three allotments in New Bedford Road, opposite Fountains Road. He grew vegetables and the garden began to grow and

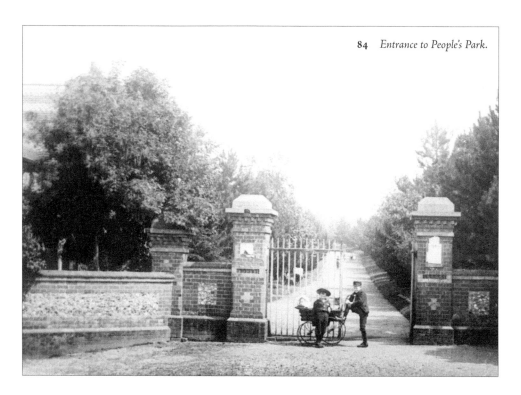

flourish, so much so that he opened it up for visitors and for social gatherings. His grandson says, 'Mount Tabor held all its garden parties there and we used to roll balls for pigs and have the Luton Band playing in the garden, and all sorts of games and high jinks and tea went on there, all funded by grandfather.' In 1951 the site was given to the Luton Borough Council.

Further afield, there is the Icknield Way Path, which is 105 miles long and links the Ridgeway Path to Peddars Way. Also, since 2009, the Luton to Hatfield Railway line has been opened up as a public footpath and forms Route 6 of the National Cycle Network. At the foot of the chalk hills, to the north of the town are the delightful Barton Springs, and to the west the bracing Dunstable Downs, both areas shaped by the glaciers. Near the Downs is Whipsnade Zoo, which was a particular favourite for the people of Luton during the Second World War when travel was restricted.

Countryside and Habitats

The environmental information here was provided by Dr Trevor Tween.

Lutonians have always been blessed with ready access to beautiful countryside. Sir Herbert Janes recalled, in words which would probably be recognised by generations of Luton children, that he knew every stretch on both sides of Cromwell Road between the railway and Wardown. 'There were places where the springs bubbled up … I have seen the flash of a kingfisher along the river, and there were little fish as beautiful as a kingfisher, and I knew not only where they were, but how to catch them.' These local delights are still there to be enjoyed and explored. Dr Trevor Tween, Environmental Manager at Luton Borough Council, has described how the river has shaped the landscape and also the natural habitats that have flourished in that landscape.

Traditionally, the Lea is said to rise in Leagrave Park, at the famous Five Springs, although it is also fed by the little Sundon Brook and the larger Lewsey and Houghton Brooks from beyond the Borough to the north-west. Enclosed by the ancient earthwork of Waulud's Bank and dividing the ancient hamlets of Leagrave and Limbury, the Lea feeds the important relic habitats of the original Leagrave Marsh and the wet woodland communities of Rotten Corner where rare trees, such as the bay and almond willows, thrive. The marsh was once extensive common land liable to regular flooding and was divided by the Midland Railway company that sensibly built a high embankment to keep the trains clear of the periodic inundations.

After the arrival of the railway in 1868, and the building of Leagrave station, the area became increasingly popular with visitors from Luton using the new service, although outings in traditional charabancs were also popular. The day out for the workers of the hat trade could have included a drink at the *Three Horseshoes* public house, paddling and catching tiddlers for the children and even the purchase of postcards crudely captioned 'Leagrave-on-Sea' to send to friends and family; the area became known as the Blockers' Seaside, reflecting its importance

85 *Flats at Five Springs from Waulud's Bank.*

86 *Leagrave Marsh.*

87 *Luton Volunteers on the Lynchets by the lime kilns, with Dexter cattle.*

for the recreation of the less affluent residents of the town. Isabella Lockett's sculpture of that name, with hats emerging from the spiky marsh vegetation, recalls the connection between this landscape and the people of the town. Although other botanists had worked there, the plant life of Leagrave Marsh became well known from the work of Dr John Dony, however he wrote in his *Flora* of 1953 that the site was already in decline.

From Leagrave Park, the Lea can be followed bubbling through traditional flood meadows and allotments at Limbury (where it is joined by the Cat's Brook) and Biscot, where it reaches its most attractive and unspoilt aspect at Fallowfield. Turning southwards, the Lea receives the additional flow from the Riddy Brook, rising a mile to the north on the old pasture land of the Riddy, now called Cowslip Meadow. Fallowfield and Cowslip Meadow have both been approved as Local Nature Reserves. The Lea now flows parallel to the old turnpike and modern A6 that is the New Bedford Road, past the oft-flooded land beyond the site of the old Mud Arch, past the ancient willow pollards, the Bide-a-While garden, the overgrown orchards and newly planted apple trees, to the site of the old ford at the foot of Stockingstone Road.

Looping back under the main road, it then passes the Bath Road pool. Adjoining the Lea nearby is a small landscaped wildlife area, once part of the grounds of the British Gelatine Works (latterly Colloids), and where once again the osiers that supplied the local basket trade can be seen growing by the river. This was the site of the first ever work party of the Luton and Dunstable Conservation Volunteers (LDCV) back in September 1984; at the present time, the group still actively manages land for conservation along the river corridor and on our local downlands.

The river re-crosses the A6, unseen below the carriageway, and enters Wardown Park, where it feeds the lake and occasionally overflows to disrupt life in the park, most notably during 2007, when the famous Carnival had to be cancelled owing to the floods that Bank Holiday weekend. Leaving the park the Lea reminds us of its importance in powering the industries of the town, as it divides into the leat, or millstream, east of the New Bedford Road, while the river itself flows to the west. The leat flowed past the site of the great Lye family dye works and fed the old North Mill, the last of Luton's working watermills which was swept away with the coming of the Midland Railway but left this reminder of its former role in grinding the corn of Luton from Domesday until Victoria.

With a final gentle meander through the ancient remnant of the Great Moor, Luton's first public space and still a common today, the Lea disappears under the railways and roads through the town centre, where evocative glimpses of open channel are still visible, hidden behind the older buildings and hinting at the role of its waters in the brewing, milling, bleaching and dyeing industries that first transformed Luton from market town to manufacturing centre. The Lea then reappears south of the town before flowing through Luton Hoo Park and then on to join the Thames. The whole river corridor in Luton is important for species such as the kingfisher, heron and water vole.

The valley that was shaped by the glacier-enhanced river can be seen by the ridges of hills to the east and west of the town. To the west are the steep chalky slopes of the Dallow Downs rising from the flood plain. Although the New Town area was developed on some of this

88   *Luton in the Lea Valley. Photograph taken from Long Croft/Winsdon Hill.*

89   *Lump of puddingstone found locally.*

land, along with the General Cemetery at Rothesay Road, much of the
hillside remained arable during the 19th century, and the steeper parts
of the hills today are a mosaic of scrub, chalk grassland and woodland,
of great importance to both the landscape character of the town and its biodiversity.

Today, this wedge of land stretches from Downs Road to the M1, and is almost all of
nature conservation value; indeed, a 2004 survey showed it easily met, together with Bradgers
Hill, the criteria of SSSI (Site of Special Scientific Interest) status for its chalk grassland, as

90   *Dray's Ditches*
      looking east.

orchids and other flowers once widespread are still common here. Meanwhile in the skies, bats, buzzards and butterflies all take flight; red kites are now seen once more; and on the ground, foxes and badgers, slow worms and lizards, and scarce spiders and beetles may all be found.

Winsdon Hill stretches from Buxton Hill in the east and curves around above Ashburnham Road to Long Croft. Here water-worn puddingstones, more familiar from Hertfordshire but known locally as 'Daller or Dollar Puddens', are sometimes found as cobbles or boulders. The grasslands to the west are of most interest to botanists, but the magnificent hedgebanks of Two Hills, topped with enormous coppiced hazels that can be traced through the scrub, are very striking.

The remainder of the Dallow Downs to the west contains large tracts of species-rich chalk grassland and scrub, but remnants of the ancient habitat of Runley Wood also survive, lending the alternative name of Runley Down to this section, although the collection of foliage here for the church celebrations at Easter led to the name of Palm Wood being used by local children. A variety of historic features add to an intriguing mosaic of natural and cultural heritage assets. Chief among these are the ancient cultivation terraces or lynchets, visible as great steps in the hillside at the western end, and the very conspicuous medieval manorial boundary hedgebank that runs the length of the hillside.

A traditional Sunday walk for the working families from the Dallow area, home to the Diamond Foundry and the CWS cocoa works, involved strolling over these hills to Bluebell Wood and on to Caddington, refreshment in the village hostelries and a stroll back, no doubt a welcome break from the toils of the working week. The building of the M1 effectively ended this tradition despite the provision of tunnels under the new motorway, although a remarkable relic of the rural Dallow Lane with thick original hedgerows still survives adjacent to the M1 at Foxdell Junior School.

On the east side of the town the chalk hills stretch from Galley Hill in the north to St Anne's Hill in the south, but are once again a continuous geographical feature. The Borough Council now owns Galley and Warden Hills, which were once part of the Waste of the Manor of Luton, although they now lie outside the Borough boundary. The common rights were held by Putteridge Bury until they were sold by the Cassel family to the Crown in the mid-1930s.

As an SSSI the area is of immense importance as chalk downland habitat, with rare plants such as purple milk-vetch, field fleawort and knapweed broomrape, but most important of all is the population of the great pignut, perhaps the largest in Britain, a species restricted to this part of the Chilterns. They have been managed from the John Dony Field Centre by Trevor Tween and colleagues since 1990; grazing was reintroduced in that year and the whole site became a Local Nature Reserve in 1993. The archaeological interest is represented by two Scheduled Ancient Monuments, Dray's Ditches and a group of Bronze-Age round barrows, and these are also associated with the ancient Icknield and Thede (Thoidweg) Way tracks that intersect here.

This gives way to the more open habitats of species-rich chalk grassland of the borough-owned part of Bradgers Hill, with a superb flight of lynchets, culminating in the old chalk working and site of a lime kiln, know to local children as Devil's Pit. This is bordered by an ancient Hollow Way where Bradgers Hill becomes Old Bedford Road, which reached its present condition through a combination of natural erosion and human traffic with livestock, creating deep and impressive sunken lanes. This whole area borders on the Chilterns Area of Outstanding Natural Beauty (AONB).

To the south of Bradgers Hill the Honeygate and Crick Hills are privately owned and very overgrown, although the habitat corridor continues to the Cowridge End slopes off Stockingstone Road and eventually to the common land of People's Park, and with relics of both lynchets and the chalk grassland floras of Hobnail Hill under the 19th-century tree plantings. Thereafter, 19th- and 20th-century developments of High Town and Hart Hill have covered most of the remaining habitats, but the creation of the church cemetery on the slopes of St Anne's Hill has inadvertently provided another area of valuable grassland habitat to the south-east of the town.

Finally, there are a few habitats that don't quite fit the general pattern; these are mostly woodlands, representative of pre-urban land use and scattered across the area. Most important

92   *Stockwood Spinney.*

of these is the ash/maple Bramingham Wood with two sections of ancient woodland, at least 400 years old, with a more recently wooded area between them. Owned by the Woodland Trust since 1985, it is managed by the Bramingham Wood Volunteers for its wildlife, but it includes the three Purley ponds within it and the Long Field to the east, forming a valuable complex of habitats.

Second in importance is the wood known as Slaughter's Wood, at Wigmore, with its interesting hornbeam coppice and a wooded green lane adjoining it. Also containing both hornbeam and hazel coppice is Bluebell Wood, more correctly Castle Croft Spring, which, with two attractive meadows, adjoins the M1 at Farley Hill. A small relic of the once large and important Spittlesea Wood still exists high on the slope above Eaton Green Road, while on Stopsley Common, LDCV have recently done much to restore the former extent of the small but historic Hayes Wood with new planting of oaks and other tree species. A small but significant strip of ancient hedgerow with some fine veteran oak trees on the county boundary at Wandon End Park has recently been added to the list of recognised habitats in the Borough.

The Twenty-First Century

It seems, then, that the people of Luton were and still are well blessed with opportunities to occupy their time. In the past, much activity was based on church membership and no doubt this is still the case among the great variety of different faiths that now exist in the town. Sports facilities are readily available and a great many interest groups have been established. There are nightclubs and the Galaxy is a popular venue for the young. Excellent hostelries still exist and many newcomers have pointed out that the town is now well supplied with restaurants offering a variety of food from across the world. Many other towns, and even villages, might envy the access that local people have to superb countryside which is still there after thousands of years, just waiting to be explored and enjoyed.

X

Luton, the Town

THERE IS NO doubt that Luton has its own special character. Words that have been used to describe it include decent, down to earth, good-humoured, hard working, independent and individualistic. It has also been noted that it has always been a town without a privileged upper class, since in Luton almost everyone worked to earn his or her own living. The spirit of independence was reflected in its long battle to control its own affairs. At the beginning of the 19th century, the county town of Bedford had a larger population than Luton, which was then a market town of about three thousand people, but by the 1860s Luton's population had overtaken that of Bedford. Consequently, the people of Luton became increasingly unhappy that administrative power was centred on Bedford.

Luton was certainly an independent little town and it kept its 'small town atmosphere' until at least the middle of the 20th century. Another indication of its special character was the particular status of its women, especially during the busy days of the hat industry. Nationally speaking, married women who worked were frowned upon, but in Luton there was usually no stigma attached to the hat workers and women were able to work and contribute to the family income for the whole of their lives.

Histories of Luton have usually included the town's hamlets. A hamlet is considered to be a small village without a church, although Luton's hamlets did in the course of time acquire their own places of worship. The hamlets were Biscot, Hyde, Leagrave, Limbury and Stopsley, but Biscot and Limbury were often linked together as Limbury-cum-Biscot. Most of them grew up near the river Lea, which rises at Leagrave, flows through Limbury and Biscot, and leaves the town beside the road to Hyde. There have been boundary changes and changes in administration over the years but one significant date is 1894 when the hamlets became known as 'Luton Rural'. Leagrave, Limbury and part of Stopsley became part of Luton Borough in 1928 and the rest of Stopsley joined Luton in 1933. Apart from the hamlets, Luton has grown to include many small settlements, often known as Ends or Greens, whose names are now familiar, for example Chaul End, Farley, Lewsey, Ramridge, Round Green, Skimpot and Sundon.

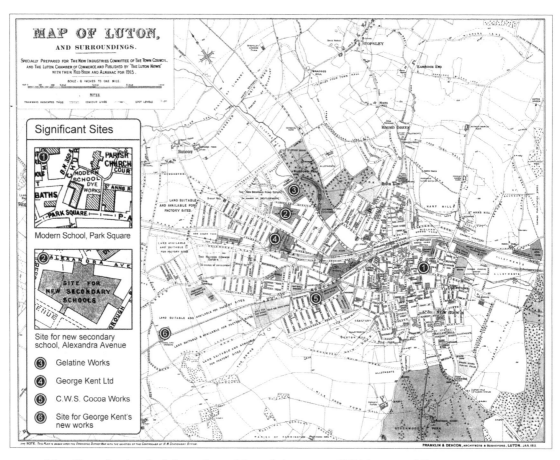

93 *Map of Luton based on the Ordnance Survey Map with the sanction of HM Stationery Office, 1915.*

The following table gives details of the population growth of Luton, the hamlets and Bedford between 1841 and 1921.

Parish	1841	1851	1861	1871	1881	1891	1901	1911	1921
Bedford	9,178	11,693	13,413	16,850	19,533	28,023	35,144	39,183	40,242
Luton civil parish	7,748	12,787	17,821	20,733	26,140	32,401			
Luton township	5,827	10,648	15,329	17,317					
Luton Borough					23,960	30,053	36,404	49,978	57,075
Hyde							557	649	671
Leagrave							801	1,270	1,643
Limbury							377	972	1,534
Stopsley							787	943	1,140

Hyde is small but very interesting. One of the mills recorded in Domesday Book, although not the original building, stands on the county boundary and there was once another at New Mill End. The water meadows can still be seen and the bridge over the river is a popular spot for bird watching. There is a church, built on land donated by the Marquess of Bute and consecrated in 1842. In the graveyard behind the church is the Wernher family vault. Hyde became a separate parish in 1895.

There are no longer any shops and the railway stations have closed, as has the *Leather Bottle*, although the sewage works, opened in 1942, still functions and is of great importance to the health of the town. The road to Someries, an interesting reminder of generations long gone, leads almost to the airport boundary; there it is possible to stand and ponder as the history of the town comes face to face with its future. Hyde, unlike the other former hamlets, retains its rural atmosphere, thanks mainly to the fact that it is cut off from Luton by the Luton Hoo Estate.

The old National School on the Wheathampstead Road has long been a private house. In 1901 a Board School was built on land donated by the Luton Hoo Estate and provided

an education for children from the surrounding area, including the estate, until 1984. The old school log books describe the difficulties experienced by staff and pupils as they travelled across the fields to school in inclement weather. One former pupil recalled that her mother used to give her a hot jacket potato to hold in her hand to keep her warm on the journey. The school is now a village hall.

Leagrave is by the source of the river Lea and stands beside the ancient earthwork known as Waulud's Bank. The marshy area around was 'common ground' with its pasture, wildfowl and watercress beds. In 1868 a railway station was opened, linking Leagrave to Luton, London and the north. This busy station has not suffered the fate of

94-6 *Hyde Church*, Leather Bottle, *Luton Hoo Station.*

many others and is now one of three that serve the town. In the early 20th century Leagrave Marsh was known as 'The Blockers' Seaside', blockers being workers who pressed hats into shape. Leagrave, with its easy access, was no doubt a pleasant place for them to spend free time with their families.

This was an attractive little community. There was the little S-bend lane that led to Lewsey Road and on to Dunstable. The Board School, with its school house, was opened in 1875 but has now been replaced by private houses. There were the local inns: the *Royal Oak*, the *Sugar Loaf* and, opposite Marsh Farm, the *Three Horseshoes*. The picturesque cottage that stood beside the *Sugar Loaf* has been moved to the Chiltern Open-Air Museum. Leagrave became a separate parish in 1895 and a part of Luton Borough from 1928.

Life in Limbury-cum-Biscot must have been interesting to say the least at the time when the river marked the boundary between Saxon and Danish territory, a far cry from the modern housing and busy roads of today. It is also no doubt difficult to equate this part of Luton with the rural paradise described by Anthony Darby, who, as a boy in the early 1900s, went to Biscot to recuperate after an illness. In later life, he recalled that Biscot was a small hamlet, four miles from the town along country lanes, and boasted two farms, the Parish Church (consecrated in 1868), a pond in the road, a nearby school and 50 cottages.

97 *Thatched cottage at Leagrave, 1961.*

Its one landmark was Biscot Mill, forever turning, looking down on the village from a hill about half a mile distant.

He stayed in a cottage with no piped water, gas or electricity and with an earth closet. But there was watercress for the picking and wild duck eggs to collect. His health soon improved because his hostess was able to make nourishing food, especially from eggs and milk in plentiful supply. Darby's paradise has gone: Biscot Mill has been replaced by an inn of the same name, the Moat House is not a farm and the school has been demolished but, for those who are interested, the river can still be explored. The hamlet became a parish in 1895 and a part of Luton Borough from 1928.

The history of Stopsley has been studied in great detail and can be read in James Dyer's book, aptly named *The Stopsley Book*. There are people living in Stopsley who still share a sense of community with its village spirit and individuality even though it has been administered as part of Luton since 1933. The civil parish covers a large area, from Someries Castle in the south to Galley Hill and the Icknield Way in the north. Stopsley retained the feel of a village until well into the 20th century. At its heart was the village green

98   *Windmill at Biscot.*

where villagers congregated on Bonfire Night. There was the police box and, beside the green, the maroon Corporation buses waited before their return journey to Luton. The centre of the village has been destroyed by development, although the *Sportsman* (*c.*1820) has survived, but Stopsley Common and the lynchets on Bradgers Hill are reminders of the past where country lovers can still explore and find typical downland flora.

ADMINISTRATION

Luton had been a municipal borough since it received a Charter of Incorporation in February 1876. George Bailey, formerly secretary of the Board of Health, was the first town clerk, Edward Woakes continued as the Medical Officer of Health and William Bigg, a Quaker and retired bank manager, became the first mayor. However, the town continued to be run by the same 'small-town hierarchy' although in different official capacities. This seemed to work well for many years and a report by Grundy and Titmuss in 1945 described a similar state of affairs.

> There is a richness of informal social intercourse, a diversity of small groups pursuing their interests unobtrusively, ample opportunity for discussing the affairs of the town and many an exchange of ideas by chance meetings; for those who are interested in the future of the town still know each other by sight and know where to find each other at most times of the day.

Stephen Bunker, writing about the links between local commerce and the religious outlook, described a town that old Lutonians can still remember, a town with 'good stewardship, hard work, honesty, self-discipline, sobriety, punctuality, plainness, [that] all suited a town the commercial nature of which precisely required these standards of personal conduct'. Luton continued to be a prosperous town, even when most of the country was suffering acute economic depression. Vauxhall Motors, for example, was still advertising for workers when other parts of the country experienced high unemployment.

On 30 June 1926 Luton celebrated the Golden Jubilee of the granting of Municipal Borough status. The celebrations included a Swimming Gala at Wardown Lake and children from all the schools in Luton went to Pope's Meadow for tea and enjoyed bread and butter, buns and cakes and tea to drink.

Although with borough status Luton had achieved a measure of independence, administration was still shared with Bedfordshire County Council, which had been set up under the terms of the 1888 Local Government Act. Luton had very little in common with Bedford, which unlike Luton had a 'leisured class'. Many residents in the county town had been in the army or the colonial service and had chosen to move there in order to enjoy a relaxing retirement. Another major difference was the existence of the Harpur Trust, which provided, among other things, funding for the well-known and respected schools of Bedford. However, over the years, Luton became not only larger but also richer. It was not surprising then that the town aspired to a higher level of control, namely county borough status. The fight began in 1914 and continued for 50 years with much lobbying at Westminster by local Members of Parliament until the aim was achieved. Not long before county borough status was finally granted, an official town guide (c.1954) painted a picture of Luton. It stated that the town had a clean and clear atmosphere 'due to the large-scale use of electricity and the town's isolation from other industrial areas'. The council also claimed that it had worked hard to provide housing and, as a consequence, Luton was ahead of all other municipal boroughs in achieving its housing targets. It was a busy industrial town: manufactured goods included aircraft, cars and clothing while brewing, the chemical industry, precision engineering and printing were thriving. Although the hat industry was no longer the staple trade, there were still many hat factories, especially near the town centre.

In 1961, there were 84 county boroughs in the country, many of them with a smaller population than Luton. Luton therefore considered that it had a right to the same status. There were costs to be considered for the council would have to pay compensation to Bedfordshire County Council since Luton would no longer be making a large contribution to the county exchequer. There would also be some boundary changes. All the difficulties were overcome and, in February 1964, the House of Lords approved the granting of county borough status to Luton to take effect from 1 April. Many administrative departments were transferred to Luton and employees of the County Council who were working in the town became employees of Luton Corporation. The mayor, Alderman Leslie G. Bowles, said:

> It ought to make local government more efficient, since many services will then have control on the spot, instead of some miles away; but the real satisfaction is very much the same satisfaction that a man derives from attaining his majority in that, however much freedom he has had before, he is now solely responsible for his own affairs. Independence is a natural characteristic of all human beings.
>
> We can now build up our local pride and tradition in a town of some importance. For, let us make no mistake about it, Luton has come a long way since its incorporation as a borough in 1876.

The Corporation allocated a sum of £12,000 to be spent on festivities. They also were in receipt of gifts for, on the celebration day, the leading industrial organisations in the town presented the Council with pieces of silver at a special ceremony in the Council Chamber. The mayor, town clerk, aldermen, councillors, magistrates and officers of the Council went in procession from the town hall to the Parish Church where a civic thanksgiving service was held. A new avenue of trees was planted in Wardown Park to commemorate the event and, in the afternoon, there was a parade from Manor Road to Wardown and over 80 local firms and organisations took part in the celebrations. Later there were high wire and trapeze demonstrations followed by dancing near the bandstand. At 9 p.m. came a firework display. Also the Museum put on an exhibition on the history of Luton and every schoolchild in the town was presented with a specially written book on the town's history entitled *The Story of Luton*.

A souvenir issue of the *Luton News* provided some interesting statistics concerning the town's history. Gibbs and Dandy, builders' merchants, had served the town since 1849. Blundell's, the department store on Market Hill, had been retailing since 1852 and Mares, the gentlemen's outfitters, since 1865. Luton Industrial Co-operative Society had been established in 1883 and old Lutonians will remember this beautiful shop, with the magnificent staircase, on New Bedford Road where money was sent to a central payment area by overhead wires. Anyone who grew up in Luton will almost certainly be able to tell you their old family dividend number.

Vauxhall Motors had come to Luton '3,251,052 cars and trucks ago' and, at the airport, Derby Airways were offering flights to Belfast, Guernsey and Jersey, some of them in a 75-seater Argonaut aircraft. People were buying their own houses and the estate agents, Ronald Mayne & Co. in Bute Street, were offering mortgages with monthly repayments on a £1,000 loan at £8 11s. 8d. per calendar month over a period of 15 years. Luton Building Society in King Street had assets exceeding £3,500,000.

Luton enjoyed its comparative freedom for just 10 years. Then, under the terms of the 1972 Local Government Act, county boroughs were abolished and, in April 1974, Luton lost its independence. However, all was not lost for, in 1997, the government changed former county boroughs large enough to function independently into unitary authorities. Luton became a unitary authority on 1 April 1997, thus becoming a single-tier authority responsible for all local functions. The *Luton News* reported that there were nine departments in the new council and the number of employees had risen from 1,600 to 7,000, including the number of staff working in local schools. All the money from the local council tax would now be spent exclusively in the town and the annual budget for 1997-8 was set at £158m. By 2010 the number of employees of Luton Town Council had increased to ten thousand.

For political purposes, the town is now split into 19 wards: Barnfield, Biscot, Bramingham, Challney, Crawley, Dallow, Farley, High Town, Icknield, Leagrave, Lewsey, Limbury, Northwell, Round Green, Saints, South, Stopsley, Sundon Park and Wigmore. Luton has broken free from County Council control, so what will be the next step? Some dream of city status.

99 *Cecil Harmsworth at the 1911 by-election. The policemen are wearing straw helmets.*

Luton has had some interesting Members of Parliament, all of whom are listed in Appendix II. It would not be possible to write about each one in a book of this size but it is worth remembering a few. Cecil Harmsworth (1869-1948) was elected as Member of Parliament for Luton in 1911 and continued to represent the town until 1922, years that included the duration of the First World War. After being created 1st Baron Harmsworth, he became a member of the House of Lords. He was also a director of the Amalgamated Press and chairman of Associated Newspapers, which was founded by his brother, Lord Northcliffe. Luton's Member of Parliament between 1929 and 1945, again covering years when the country was at war, was Leslie Burgin (1887-1945). He held several government posts and was the first Luton MP to become a member of the Cabinet when, in 1939, Neville Chamberlain made him Minister of Supply.

However, probably the most colourful of Luton's Members of Parliament was Charles Hill (1904-89), who represented the town between 1950 and 1963. Charles Hill became famous during the Second World War as the 'Radio Doctor' with a Friday morning slot on the Home Service, during which he gave practical advice to the nation on how to stay healthy. Lord Hill of Luton, as he became in 1963, was appointed chairman of the Independent Television Authority and, later, chairman of the BBC. Michael Freedland, who was then a reporter on the *Luton News*, has written a description of him.

100   *Dr Charles Hill voting in 1950.*

He was a character who was, I since realise, about the best constituency member I have ever met … Hill looked like an overgrown Just William … he was an extraordinary man, who had been brought up in a London slum by a widowed mother, had worked his way through medical school and yet had become a confirmed Tory … Of course he was brilliant – which was why he almost immediately got office, first as a parliamentary private secretary, then as Postmaster-General … and finally as Chancellor of the Duchy of Lancaster, in charge of the government's information services.

There are also other layers of administration that affect the town. For some years the East of England Regional Assembly had councillors elected from the region's 52 councils and representatives from the private, voluntary and community sectors that advised the government on regional planning, housing and transport and was responsible for promoting the economic, environmental and social well-being of the East of England. Luton is also represented at the European Parliament as part of the Eastern region. Members of the European Parliament are elected every five years by proportional representation. They do not sit in national delegations but according to their political affinities.

HOUSING AND TRANSPORT

At the end of the 19th century, when the New Industries Committee was advertising for manufacturers to move to Luton, the town was described as having a good standard of housing. As in most towns, there were some poor areas but most of Luton's slums had been demolished by the 1930s. Since Luton continued to be a boom town, good housing had to be provided.

Much of the housing in Luton was built by small builders, frequently for renting, and many roads of terraced houses were built in the 19th century. In the 20th century larger companies, such as the Luton Land Company, bought up land for development. Middle-class areas, with sturdy houses, were to be found in George Street West, Hart Hill and New Bedford Road.

The town spread outwards with both private building and council housing. The lane to Dunstable became a road with unattractive ribbon development and, as no 'Green Wedge' was retained, it was soon impossible to tell where one town ended and the other began. In fact, the boundary is at the top of Poynters Road, where the *Halfway House* stands. By the outbreak of the Second World War, more than one thousand council houses had been built. At that time, there had been 1,200 unoccupied houses but soon these were all taken and, by the end of the war, there was a housing shortage and a waiting list of more than five thousand. There was a need for more builders, partly because prisoners of war, who had supplied a labouring force, had returned home, and many of the vacancies were filled by workers coming to Luton from Ireland. Supposedly as a temporary measure, prefabricated houses (prefabs) were erected, for example at Leagrave. At Ramridge End, the remarkable 'tin town' appeared, the work of immigrant Irish labourers.

Between 1945 and 1964, 15,000 houses were built, some of them private and others built by the Corporation. H.C. Janes was a well-known and successful builder who produced hundreds of affordable homes. Before 1939 he sold more than 8,000 houses, mainly to investors and,

101   *Prefabricated housing estate at Leagrave, 1947.*

after the war, another 8,500 mainly to owner/occupiers. Other private builders appeared as more people could afford to buy.

To be allocated a council house, families had to go on a waiting list based on a points system. Council house estates grew up at Farley Hill, Marsh Farm, Runfold and between Wigmore and Ramridge End. Another housing scheme was the 'London Overspill'. People on Luton council house waiting lists might have thought that Londoners were jumping the queue but this was a separate scheme, agreed in 1958, that was run jointly by the London County Council (later Greater London Authority), and Bedfordshire County Council. Overspill estates were built at Lewsey Farm and at nearby Houghton Regis.

Over the years, with full employment, rooms in larger houses were filled with people paying rent and multiple occupation became very much the norm when thousands of newcomers arrived from overseas. A more recent change in the housing scene has been the erection of blocks of flats to accommodate students at the local university.

The 'Green Belt' scheme was intended to protect areas of undeveloped land around towns to preserve the natural environment, improve air quality and provide educational and recreational opportunities. However, as the town continues to grow, the 'green' fields are being threatened and there is pressure on local councils to allow more building to ease the national housing shortage. A scheme to build 1,000 homes in Hertfordshire, to the east of Luton, has been shelved but plans to build more than 5,000 houses to the south of the town for the Bushwood Green scheme threaten Aley Green, Pepperstock and Woodside as well as depriving Caddington of its village atmosphere. It remains to be seen how much of the beautiful countryside around Luton will disappear.

In the early 20th century, it became fashionable for towns to have a tramway system and Luton was no exception. The Luton tramways came into service on 21 February 1908, the opening ceremony being performed by the local MP, T. Gair Ashton. The trams served the town for 24 years, not without a few minor mishaps. There was one major accident when, in December 1916, a tramcar coming down Midland Road failed to negotiate the left-hand turning into Old Bedford Road and hit a wall on the opposite side of the road. The last tram ran in April 1932.

The tram depot was at Bailey Street (by Park Street). Apparently slight changes were made to the routes from time to time but the main ones are thought to have been: Park Square, via Upper George Street to Dunstable Road, near Kingsway; the town hall to Round Green via High Town; and London Road, through George Street, to Wardown.

The town had two railway lines: one, which still exists, went from the Midland Road station to St Pancras and, in the other direction, as far as Scotland. The other station was at Bute Street, where trains from King's Cross continued, via Dunstable, to Leighton Buzzard and linked up with the Euston line. This train was fondly known as the 'Dunstable Dasher' or 'Flyer' but the line was closed in 1965 under the Beeching axe. A third-class return ticket

102   *Farley Hill Estate, 1951.*

to St Pancras in 1903 cost 2s. 6d. and 50 years later 9s. 2d., but much cheaper workmen's tickets could be bought for early morning travel from both Bute Street and Midland Road. These tickets were not restricted to workers and there are many still living in the town who will remember taking advantage of these convenient workmen's trains. In 1953 students from the Modern Schools could purchase tickets to London plus seats at the Old Vic theatre for 13s. 6d. It was also possible to get to London and beyond on the London Transport Green Line coaches from Park Square.

In those atmospheric days of steam, trains travelling south from Luton terminated at King's Cross or St Pancras. Then came Thameslink and it became possible to travel from Luton, through London, to Kent in the east or south to Brighton via Gatwick. The Midlands and Yorkshire can still be reached by a direct line from Luton. In 2008 a spectacular upgraded station, now known as St Pancras International, was opened and this is becoming the hub for various lines from around the country. Trains, like Eurostar, which use the new high-speed link to the Channel Tunnel, run into St Pancras so now travellers can leave from one of the Luton stations and, with just one change, arrive at Brussels, Lille or Paris, the journey time between Paris and Luton being around three hours.

In 1959, the M1 Motorway was opened. Since then connecting motorways have been built and Luton has easy access to many different parts of the country, as well as to the Continent via the M1, the M25 and the Channel Tunnel. All these transport routes are advantageous to local commerce. London Luton Airport is a base for several low-cost airlines that offer direct

103　*The cooling towers near St Mary's Church. These were an outstanding landmark.*

104   *Building the M1, 1958.*

flights to many parts of the United Kingdom, Europe, the Far East, the Middle East and Scandinavia. The modern Luton Parkway station connects to the airport with a shuttle bus. The airport has become very important to Luton, especially as it provides employment for many thousands of people.

FAITH IN THE TWENTY-FIRST CENTURY

The religious dimension has been, and still is, important to Luton but the scene has now changed almost beyond recognition. Historically, most groups shared a Christian outlook but, whereas denominations would once have felt a need to point out differences in interpretation, the emphasis now is on shared faith. Many groups have united, sometimes because of size and sometimes because of a mutual commitment. The three town centre Baptist churches, Park Street, Union Chapel and Wellington Street, amalgamated in 1975 and are now known as the Central Baptist Church and meet in a fine new building in Park Street. The former chapel in Wellington Street now houses offices while the building in the old Union Chapel has been made into Housing Association flats. The Congregational Church at the top of King Street, once a notable local landmark, is there no longer, nor is the Central Mission on Midland

Road with its fine hall, although the Congregational Church in Bury Park still stands as it has done since 1903. However, in 1972 Congregationalists and Presbyterians joined to become the United Reformed Church and now work together, sharing ministries with other churches.

Methodism played a very important part in the life of the town and one of the most significant buildings was their chapel in Waller Street which opened in 1863. Another, in Chapel Street, was opened about the same time and in the 20th century this became the base for Luton's Industrial Mission, which was opened in 1957 and run by an inspirational industrial chaplain, the Reverend William Gowland. He believed in taking Christianity into the work place 'where people work and play, sweat and swear', and as Luton was an industrial town this type of mission was very appropriate. Another industrial chaplain was Ivor Clemitson, born in Harlington and educated in Luton, who in 1964 became industrial chaplain to the Diocese of St Albans. Between 1974 and 1979, he became the Member of Parliament for Luton East. Another important Methodist church was the Railway Mission, beside the station in Midland Road. The different groups of Methodists all united in 1932 when a Deed of Union was introduced. In 2003 an Anglican-Methodist Covenant was signed and it is possible that Anglicans and Methodists will soon unite.

The Salvation Army is not only a focus for Christian worship but also claims to be the biggest provider, apart from the government, of social, community and welfare services. They will assist in finding missing relatives, provide for the homeless and give support at major incidents and natural disasters. The Salvation Army in Luton supports two places of worship and also has a branch of the Salvation Army Trading Company Ltd in George Street. This is a national company, founded in 1991, that is the United Kingdom's leading textile and clothes recycling company.

The Quakers, or Society of Friends, have also played an important part in the history of Luton with many prominent residents, for example the Brown family, contributing to the town's success. In 1963 the Friends moved from their Meeting House in Castle Street to premises in Crawley Green Road and take an active part in the ecumenical life of the town.

During the 20th and 21st centuries, the move towards unity has been demonstrated by some notable initiatives. For example, there were the Luton and District Free Church Council and the Council of Churches. Churches have opened their doors and looked for shared interests. An example of this is the combined work of the Bury Park and Beech Hill Council of Churches, Anglican, Catholic and Methodist, which reaches out to the local community. A recent survey indicated that 65 per cent of the local population would not consider going to church, so the rector of St Mary's, together with volunteers from other churches, has initiated a town centre chaplaincy to care for the spiritual needs of local people. Pastors are on the streets at certain times and the project has received positive support from churches, council leaders and from the business, commercial and retail sectors of the town. It is likely that a chaplain will be appointed and a regular base opened.

During the last century, members of other faiths arrived in the town, many of them from overseas, and have set up their own places of worship. The 2001 census gives the following figures to indicate the proportions of religious belief in Luton.

	%	
Christian	59.6	
Buddhist	0.2	
Hindu	2.7	highest in the East of England
Jewish	0.3	
Muslim	14.6	very much the highest in the East of England
Sikh	0.8	highest with Bedfordshire
All other religions	0.3	
No religion	14.1	lowest in the East of England
Religion not stated	7.2	

Many representatives of these different groups have joined together to form the town's Council of Faiths (LCOF). The members, together with Grassroots, an ecumenical group, work together to strengthen the relationships between their faiths. Special occasions are celebrated together, for example Fairtrade Fortnight, Global Exchange, Holocaust Memorial Day, Inter Faith Week and World Religions Day and invitations are extended to festivals such as Christmas, Diwali, Eid and Hanukkah. A recent project has been the production of an excellent Faith Map that shows the location of the different places of worship in the town. Another shared activity is the annual Faith Walk. The chairman of the Luton Council of Mosques, Dr Fiaz Hussain, commenting on the 2009 walk, said:

> We are all human beings and at the end of the day we all have the same values. We might wear different dress, eat different things and pray in a different way, but we are all human, and we all want what is best for ourselves and for others. The Faith Walk brings out those similarities …
>
> The walk depicts unity and togetherness and that people want to live together peacefully. It is a chance for people to celebrate and share their beliefs and practices with people of other faiths and of no faith. The more people join the more we can demonstrate that Luton is a peaceful town where people get on with each other.

LUTON COUNCIL OF FAITHS

105 *The Luton Council of Faiths.*

Luton has altered and there will surely be more changes in the future. People still have their own opinions and beliefs but it has to be agreed that friendship is better than friction and harmony than disharmony.

GLIMPSES OF THE PAST

It is a matter of great regret that many historical sites have disappeared, although glimpses of the past are still to be found. Probably the saddest tale concerns the 'disappearance' of the river that gave the town its name. In fact, it is still there although town planners have more or less buried it beneath tons of concrete but, with the eye of imagination, it is possible to see what might have been: a clean little river with grassy banks where local people could sit on warm days and find a breathing space away from the noise and bustle of the town. The unfortunate reality is that there are probably people in Luton who do not know that the town even has a river.

The most important building from an historical point of view is the Parish Church, which is dedicated to St Mary. It is still an imposing sight in the centre of the town although it no longer stands in open ground; instead it is crowded around by modern buildings such as the Mall and the university. The church has been the focus of Christian life in the town for hundreds of years and it is still so today. It is the largest in the county and has a 98-foot-high tower. Both the tower and the walls are built of knapped flint and Totternhoe stone in a chequer-board pattern. It is now a Grade-I listed building and consequently any changes have to conform with regulations set out by English Heritage. For many years, during the earlier part of her reign, Queen Elizabeth II came with His Royal Highness Prince Philip to the Sunday morning service nearest to their wedding anniversary, as they regularly spent that weekend at nearby Luton Hoo.

There are many reminders of the past. For example, the north transept has a window, named after the Reverend James O'Neill, who was vicar between 1862 and 1897. This window depicts King Athelstan, the first king of all England, who reigned from 925 to 939; Robert, Earl of Gloucester, who established this church in A.D. 1121; John de St Albans, the first perpetual vicar of Luton (1219), and Lord Wenlock.

The old and the new meet in the south porch. The heavy old wooden doors were given to St Mary's by Cardinal Wolsey, who was patron of the church during the reign of Henry VIII. Now there are new untreated oak doors on the other side of the porch, courtesy of the Friends of Luton Parish Church. Also, in 2002, glass doors were added to both the north and south porches. The Reverend Canon Nicholas Bell, the present vicar, envisaged that light would be able to 'flood in to the west end of the building allowing the church to show a welcome'. He also hoped that the designs of the doors would 'reflect an ecumenical and multicultural appeal and be linked with the town and university'.

Funding for the glass doors came from the Friends of the Church and the artist was Tracey Sheppard. The designs on the north doors include the lily and the rose, symbols of the Virgin Mary. The south doors have a watery background, reminiscent of the river Lea, with handprints

106 *Pulpit in the parish church.*

from members of the church, some clear and some engraved, to give a multicultural feeling. There are ears of wheat, the bread of life, and cedar, oak and olive leaves 'for the healing of the nations'. On the handles are engravings of a lion and a lamb. The rose, bee and wheat can also be seen on Luton's coat of arms while the lion is on the arms of the university.

The Bell Chamber is in the west tower. In 1430 there were four bells. In 1948 a new ring of 10 bells was cast by John Taylor & Co. of Loughborough; these were rung for the first time in 1949, and in 1984 two new bells were added to complete the ring of twelve. The clock had been silent for 28 years but has now been restored, courtesy of the university, and began to chime again at midday on 11 November 1999. The university uses the church each year for the ceremony of conferring degrees.

Throughout the history of the church the focus has been on the Christian faith but nowadays, as part of a multicultural town, St Mary's has chosen to work with Churches Together in Luton and Luton Council of Faiths. In June 2009 a joint statement was issued: 'Together with others working for good interfaith relations in the town, we will do all we can to support the building up of common ground between us … we seek to respond to those challenges in friendship and cooperation rather than through prejudice, hatred, racism and religious intolerance.'

Market Hill, outside Debenhams, is a useful place to stand and ponder the past. Once the Corn Exchange, built in 1869 to replace the old Market Hall, stood in the middle of this space. and before it the Ames memorial drinking fountain, known as the Pepperpot. On the far

107　*Charlie Irons, the Town Crier, on the corner of Chapel Street and Stuart Street.*

108　The Heights, *formerly* The Crown.

109   *The Crown Court, Market Hill.*

110   *The Cattle Market,*
postmarked 1907.

side of the road is the *Red Lion Hotel*, one of most ancient in the town. It was a coaching inn and was built on the site of the Brotherhood House where members of the Luton Fraternity enjoyed sumptuous feasts in medieval times.

The *Crown Inn* existed from at least the early 16th century and has also been known over the years as the *Rat and Carrot* and the *Nickel Bag*. This inn is said to have been used by Baptist ministers who stabled their horses there while they preached at the Park Street Baptist Church. It is now known as *The Heights*. Nearby is the relatively new Crown Court where serious offences are tried by a jury and appeals from magistrates' courts are heard. This is in contrast to the system that existed in Luton in the Middle Ages whereby many crimes were judged at the court leet, which met on a regular basis, probably in the churchyard just a few minutes walk from Market Hill.

Park Square was the heart of medieval Luton and, over the years Park Street has been home to brewing companies and also the Monday cattle market. Visiting this market was a treat for children although the all-pervading smell of the brewery rather spoiled the atmosphere. In 1908, the *White House*, built around 1780 and the home of the Burr brewing family, was demolished to make way for the new Luton Modern School building. Since then, this part of Luton has been the focus of further education in the town and the University of Bedfordshire now stands on the site.

Other interesting inns are to be found in Park Street. The *Brewery Tap* is a timber-framed building and dates from the 17th century. During the 19th century, together with the neighbouring house, it served as the local workhouse. The *Cock Inn* also dates from at least the 17th century. This was an old coaching inn and it is said that the proprietor, William Clarke, won a competition by making the return journey to London in one day. In the mid-19th century it was the meeting place for Luton's Board of Health.

George Street, running in the opposite direction from Market Hill, was once the site of the plait market and home to busy hat factories. Then, until the building of the Arndale (now the Mall), George Street became the shopping centre and was home to Buttons, Gibbs and Dandy, Marks and Spencer, Woolworth's and many more well-known stores. The *George Hotel* was a centre for much of the town's social life but that has completely disappeared. The *Bell Hotel*, another coaching inn, also stood in George Street, but is not entirely forgotten for its name can still be seen over the building that is now Waterstone's. Wellington Street was laid out in the 1840s with homes for the middle classes: doctors, merchants and solicitors. It was also, around the turn of the century, a busy shopping centre.

The town hall is a very distinctive building and impossible to miss. This is the 'new' town hall that was opened in 1936 to replace an earlier one burnt down in the riots on the night of 19 July 1919 on what has been described as the worst day in the history of Luton. It is a sorry tale and well documented in Dave Craddock's book, *Where they Burnt the Town Hall Down*. Unsurprisingly, the new building was designed to be fireproof. It is faced in Portland stone and has a tower 141 feet high. The design has Art-Deco features, a style that was popular at the time. Many of the symbols on the town's coat of arms have been used, including a sheaf of wheat to recall the days of the straw hat industry. The bee is the symbol of industry and the rose and thistle may refer to the town's connection with the Marquis of Bute. Each face of the

111 *Clearing the site for the new town hall, early 1930s. The Carnegie Library and the War Memorial can be clearly seen.*

clock, which strikes every quarter hour, is nine feet eight inches in diameter. The town hall was opened by His Royal Highness the Duke of Kent in October 1936. In front of it stands the War Memorial, which was unveiled in December 1922 by Lady Ludlow.

St George's Square is set out where once Bridge Street, Manchester Street and Williamson Street provided the town with busy thoroughfares. The beautiful old Carnegie Library, which stood opposite the town hall, has regretfully been destroyed. Now St George's Square is an open-air space with seating around and is used for arts events, concerts and festivals. In 2009 a water feature with multiple jets was installed. The centre of the town, between St Mary's Church and St George's Square, has been taken over by the Mall, formerly the Arndale Centre. When it was built, much of the buried history of the town was lost and it is to be hoped that, if and when the proposed extensions to the Mall and the Northern Gateway are built, any artefacts that are uncovered will be saved and carefully recorded.

Most of medieval Luton will probably never be reclaimed but fortunately, memories and photographs can tell us about the Victorian and Edwardian part of Luton that now also lies buried under the Mall. This was Waller Street, a road that followed approximately the same

112   *George Street, Easter 1946.*

113   *Manchester Street.*

114　*The Corner of Manchester Street and Collingdon Street.*

115　*Manchester Street, 1965.*

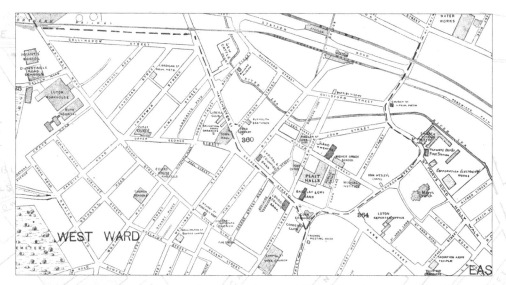

116 *Map of Luton presented as a supplement to the* Luton and District Year Book and Almanack, *1904.*

line as the Mall does today. Waller Street was laid out in 1859 on gardens belonging to John Waller, who came from a well-established Luton family. His nine-acre estate was sold and the fields that had led down to the river Lea were built over. Bob Norman, who worked in Waller Street for nearly 30 years, has taken a 'nostalgic walk' along that road so that Lutonians who have come to the town since the Mall was built can get a glimpse of life in the days when Waller Street was a busy and thriving part of Luton. In fact, some of these roads still exist as service roads beneath the Mall.

117 *Entrance to the covered market from Cheapside, c.1960.*

118 *The Herts and Beds Bacon Factory, formerly the old Post Office in Cheapside. Cheapside to the right; Barbers Lane to the left, c.1960.*

One narrow little road that ran from Cheapside to Waller Street was Barbers Lane; this dated from medieval times and was named after an important local family from the 15th century, the Barbars or Barbours. The Plait Halls had an entrance in Waller Street and the indoor market was a very popular shopping area, with a variety of stalls from antiques to clothing, fish stalls to greengrocers. Nearby were the indoor Baths that became the Assembly Hall in the winter.

On the opposite side of the road, on the site of Henry Brown's former timber yard, stood the Grand Theatre which was opened 1898. Waller Street Boys' School, nearby, was the only Higher Grade School Luton ever had. It was well respected and not a few notable Lutonians were educated there in the

119 *Corner of Waller Street and Bute Street, c.1960.*

120   *Waller Street Methodist Church, established 1863.*

days before the Modern School opened in 1904. There was also a Pupil Teacher Centre and, for some years before the Second World War, the School Clinic and School Dentist were based at the back of the Waller Street School.

Other buildings that were important to the life of Luton people were the Masonic Hall, built in 1923, Waller Street Methodist Church, opened in 1863, and the Central Youth Headquarters. Incidentally, it was then completely safe for young people to come and go as they pleased, even if they were alone. In the spirit of self help, the Friendly Societies Medical Institute was welcomed in 1892; there, for a small weekly payment, the poor could access medical care. There were hat manufacturers and the Amalgamated Tobacco Corporation, which produced Mills Special 'England's Luxury Cigarette', and also a well-known DIY company, Wenham and Fay. A ladies' hairdressing salon specialised in bobbing and shingling, while a pet shop called 'Bleak Hall Pet Farm' and a beauty parlour that went by the name of 'Dandy Dog House' catered for the grooming of animals.

In Luton, inns were never difficult to find. The *George Tap*, which was trading by 1895, had a blue-tiled outer wall and occupied the site of the first building in Waller Street, a cottage occupied by the ostler who worked at the *George Hotel*. The *Panama Lounge* stood near the entrance to the Plait Halls.

Waller Street was a busy little shopping centre. Blundell's had a small shop crammed with toys, prams and bicycles. Robert Lacey, at No. 39, ran a saddler's business for many years. He was a harness maker, an important person in the days before motorised transport. He would have horse collars, saddles and leather straps hanging outside his shop. Brooks Typewriters existed in the days before computers ruled our lives, and newsagents, like Mr Young, sold the

Hotspur, the *Rover* and the *Wizard*. However, Waller Street had entered the 20th century before its demise for Tesco opened its first store there. All these memories now lie buried but, hopefully, are not forgotten.

Probably one of the most important buildings, away from the town centre, is the Luton and Dunstable Hospital. This, too, can tell a story since it represents the culmination of health care over the centuries. In medieval times, the Church took responsibility for the care of the old and the sick in small religious houses and some provision was made in Luton, as earlier chapters have explained. Later it became the responsibility of the parish to provide care for anyone born within its boundaries. Two years after the passing of the 1834 Poor Law Amendment Act, a new workhouse on the corner of Dunstable Road and Dallow Road was opened by the Board of Guardians. In 1913 it was replaced by a new building which, in 1929, became known as St Mary's.

There was also a cottage hospital in High Town which moved to a site given by the trustees of the Marquess of Bute on the corner of Grove Road and Dunstable Road. It was funded by endowments, legacies and subscriptions and local people entered whole-heartedly into

121   *The George Tap, Waller Street, c.1960. Barbers Lane is to the left.*

122 *Waller Street, c.1960.*

fundraising. The new hospital was opened in 1882 and by 1896 it had become known as the Bute. Medical care was in the hands of the nurses and also local doctors who, according to Dr F. Eberlie, gave their time freely. He said, 'None of us thought it strange. It had always been so … It was a duty and an honour for all dedicated doctors to help without pay the poor and the desolate.' The doctors did, however, treat private patients as well. It was not at all uncommon at that time for doctors to perform operations in private houses.

The Bute Hospital was no longer large enough to serve the town so fundraising in the form of dances, fêtes and weekly contributions began. Donations were received, for example from Lady Ludlow. The new hospital, now the Luton and Dunstable Hospital, was built on green fields at the junction of Dunstable Road and Lewsey Road and was opened by Queen Mary on 14 February 1939. It is difficult to equate the airy and spacious hospital as it was then with the crowded and busy one we see today. The L&D, as it is generally known, was the last hospital to be built in the country before the introduction of the National Health Service in 1948. There have been many extensions over the years and the hospital continues to grow with several specialist departments. Medical care for the people of Luton has grown beyond imagination since the days when French monks set up a hospital for the poor at Farley.

Another of Luton's architectural gems was the Modern School in Bradgers Hill Road, now the Sixth Form College. This was designed by Marshall and Tweedy and built in 1938 by

A.C. Janes. It was the winner of an international competition for the most outstanding pre-war school design in Britain. Sadly, like so many of the town's finest buildings. (Unfortunately, the demolition workers moved onto the site in August 2010, in spite of many protests from former scholars.)

There is much to see in Luton to remind us of the past but, in open land not too far from the vast new hospital, the river Lea still springs to life. This is where people first settled, long before anyone even dreamed of a town called Luton. It would be appropriate therefore for anyone interested in the history of the town to wander down there and take a look. Waulud's Bank still exists and perhaps, with the mind's eye, images of Luton as it was thousands of years ago can still be seen.

LUTON'S FUTURE

Luton has come a long way from the small settlement in the valley of the Lea. It has had many different focuses during its life: agriculture, brewing, hat making and industry. Lately the employment scene has diversified and its future is still being defined. One very important element that has helped to create the completely new Luton we see today is the arrival of many people from overseas. Lutonians have accepted that this is now a multicultural town and hands of friendship have been freely extended.

Luton Forum 2000 was formed to challenge the image that the town is 'fractured or ill at ease with itself'. All kinds of groups in the town including business and commerce, education, environment, health and social departments have become partners with official organisations such as the National Health Service to work together to achieve this aim. In January 2010 a campaign by Luton Borough Council and Luton Forum, to be called Luton in Harmony, was launched with the aim of uniting the town and celebrating its ethnic diversity.

If the characteristics used to describe the town at the beginning of the 20th century, decent, down to earth, good-humoured, hard working, independent and individualistic, survive then Luton is sure to have a happy future.

APPENDIX I

Population Figures

Census	Population	
1821	2,986	township
1831	3,961	"
1841	5,827	"
1851	10,648	"
1861	15,329	"
1871	17,317	"
1881	23,960	borough
1891	30,053	
1901	36,404	
1911	49,978	
1921	61,342	
1931	70,486	
1951	110,381	
1961	131,505	
1971	161,178	
1981	163,209	
1991	171,671	
2001	184,371 (92119 m. and 92252 f.)	

The figures for the civil parish to 1891 include the township of Luton and the hamlets of East and West Hyde, Leagrave, Limbury and Stopsley.

The Office of National Statistics (ONS) estimated the population of Luton in 2007 to be 188,800 and 191,800 in 2008, although Luton Borough Council believes the figure to be higher.

APPENDIX II

Mayors and Members of Parliament

MAYORS

May 1876	William Bigg	November 1904	George Ordish
November 1877	John Cumberland	November 1905	Asher J. Hucklesby
November 1878	Arthur T. Webster	November 1906	Edwin Oakley
November 1879	Hugh Gunn	November 1907	Harry Arnold
November 1880	John Cotchin	November 1909	Albert Wilkinson
November 1881	John Webdale	November 1911	Herbert O. Williams
November 1882	John Dawson	November 1913	Walter James Primett
November 1883	Henry Wright	November 1915	John Henry Staddon
November 1884	George W. Gilder	November 1917	Charles Dillingham
November 1885	William Mayles	November 1918	Henry Impey
November 1886	William Blundell	November 1919	Arthur B. Attwood
November 1887	Samuel Weatherhead	November 1920	Harry Arnold
November 1888	Peter Alexander	November 1921	Murry Barford
November 1890	Alfred Toyer	November 1923	Arthur B. Attwood
November 1891	Edwin Oakley	November 1925	Albert Wilkinson
November 1892	Asher J. Hucklesby	January 1929	Herbert O. Williams
November 1894	Edwin Oakley	November 1929	Murry Barford
November 1895	Samuel Bird	November 1930	Charles H. Osborne
November 1896	Asher J. Hucklesby	November 1931	Murry Barford
November 1897	George Warren	November 1932	George W. Walker
November 1899	Asher J. Hucklesby	November 1934	John T. Harrison
November 1900	Low Giddings	November 1935	Cyril C. Dillingham
November 1902	Charles H. Osborne	November 1937	John T. Harrison
November 1903	Albert Arthur Oakley	November 1938	Sir John Burgoyne

November 1944	Lady Keens	1978-80	William Harry Copland
November 1945	Walter G. Roberts	1980-1	Marjorie Elisabeth
November 1946	George F. Seaward		(Betty) Dodd
November 1947	William J. Edwards	1981-2	Leonard Chantler
May 1949	Claude A. Sinfield	1982-3	Michael John Garrett
May 1950	Robert Colin Large	1983-4	Frank Stanley Lester
May 1951	Richard C. Oakley	1984-5	Marion McCarroll
May 1952	Thomas Skelton	1985-6	Audrey Lilian Bush
May 1953	Sir Herbert C. Janes	1986	Alfred Henry Scott
May 1954	Hedley C. Lawrence	1986-7	Marion McCarroll
May 1955	Ernest K. Hickman	1987-8	Pauline Wolsey
May 1956	Frederick W. Bates	1988-9	Audrey Lilian Bush
May 1957	Sidney Charles Hayne	1989-90	Frank Stanley Lester
May 1958	Florence M. Brash	1990-1	Henry Goldsmith
May 1959	Barbara Andrews	1991-2	Mukunda (Mick) Guha
May 1960	Jack Couldwell	1992-3	Ray Sills
May 1961	George L. Matthews	1993-4	Jose Fensome
May 1962	Hugh M. Drummond	1994-5	Desline Steward
May 1963	Leslie George Bowles	1995-6	Mohammed Ashraf
May 1964	Frank Beckett	1996-7	Mick Hand
May 1965	Francis Goodyear	1997-8	Masood Ashtar
May 1966	Samuel Gonshor	1998-9	Derrick Patten
May 1967	Frank Stanley Lester	1999-2000	Raja Mohammed Saleem
May 1968	Cyril Jephson	2000-1	Waheed Akbar
May 1969	John Ian Macdonald	2001-2	Brian Devenish
May 1970	John Hillier	2002-3	Raja Mohammed Saleem
May 1971	James Cussen	2003-4	Michael Dolling
May 1972	James McGrath	2004-5	Doris Hinkley
May 1973	Herbert C. King	2005-6	Haji Abid
April 1974	Walter G. Roberts	2006-7	Julian Wates
May 1974-5	Hedley Cyril Lawrence	2007-8	Norris Bullock
1975-6	Desmond Charles Fuller	2008-9	Lakhbir Singh
1976-7	Frank Stanley Lester	2009-10	Mohammed Riaz
1977-8	Kenneth John Furlong	2010-11	Tom Shaw

1885   Cyril Flower – Liberal

1892   Samuel Howard Whitbread

1895   Thomas Gair Ashton – Liberal

1911   Cecil Bisshopp Harmsworth
       – Liberal

1922   Sir John Prescott Hewett – Tory

1923   Geoffrey William Algernon
       Howard – Liberal

1924   Terence James O'Connor –
       Unionist

1929   Edward Leslie Burgin – Liberal

1931   Edward Leslie Burgin – National
       Liberal

1945   William Warbey – Labour

1950   Charles Hill – Conservative

1963   William Howie – Labour

1970   Charles Simeons – Conservative

Luton East – constituency created 1974,
       abolished 1983

1974   Ivor Clemitson – Labour

1979   Graham Bright – Conservative

Luton West – constituency created 1974,
       abolished 1983

1974   Brian Sedgemore – Labour

1979   John Russell Carlisle –
       Conservative

Luton North – constituency created 1983

1983   John Russell Carlisle –
       Conservative

1987   John Russell Carlisle –
       Conservative

1992   John Russell Carlisle –
       Conservative

1997   Kelvin Hopkins – Labour

2001   Kelvin Hopkins – Labour

2005   Kelvin Hopkins – Labour

2010   Kelvin Hopkins – Labour

Luton South – constituency created 1983

1983   Graham Bright – Conservative

1987   Graham Bright – Conservative

1992   Graham Bright – Conservative

1997   Margaret Moran – Labour

2001   Margaret Moran – Labour

2005   Margaret Moran – Labour

2010   Gavin Shuker – Labour

Bibliography

Articles

Boutwood, J.A., 'Luton Hoo', *Bedfordshire Magazine*, Vol. IV, pp.328-34

Freeman, C.E., *A Luton Baptist Minute Book 1707-1806* (Bedfordshire Historical Records Society, hereafter BHRS), Vol. 25 (1947)

Godber, J., 'Old-Time Luton', *Bedfordshire Magazine*, Vol. 9, No. 68, Spring 1964, pp.135-8

Lea, V.W., 'John Green, Master Brewer', *Bedfordshire Magazine*, Vol. VII, pp.155-8

Tibbutt, H.G., 'Some Bedfordshire Links with Unitarians and Liberal Christians', *Transactions of the Unitarian Historical Society*, Vol. XIV, No. 3, October 1969

Woodcock, P., 'The Taverns in the Town, Part I', *Bedfordshire Magazine*, Vol. II, pp.90-6

Woodcock, P., 'The Taverns in the Town, Part II', *Bedfordshire Magazine*, Vol. II, pp.129-35

Books

Allsopp, A., *Crimson and Gold, Luton Modern School, Luton High School for Girls and Luton Technical School* (Book Castle, 2004)

Allsopp, A., *The Education and Employment of Girls in Luton 1874-1924*, BHRS, Vol. 84 (The Boydell Press, 2005)

Antrobus, S., *We Wouldn't Have Missed it for the World: The Women's Land Army in Bedfordshire 1939-1950* (Book Castle, 2008)

Arnold, J., *Shell Book of Country Crafts* (Shell Marketing, 1974)

Ashen, J., Gudgin, V.A., Jakins, E. and Walker, R.G., *Vox Angelicus* (A Premier Fois Publication, 2001)

Austin, W., *History of Luton and Its Hamlets*, Vols I and II (County Press, 1928)

Baker, L., *The Story of Luton and Its Public Libraries* (Bedfordshire County Library and Luton Museum and Art Gallery, 1983)

Bell, P., *Belief in Bedfordshire* (Belfry Press, 1986)

Benson, B.M., *The Story of Round Green* (published privately)

BHRS, Vol II, 'Luton's Markets and Fairs', pp.170-81

Bunker, S., *Strawopolis* (BHRS, Vol. 78, 1999)

Bunker, S., Holgate, R. and Nicholls, M., *The Changing Face of Luton* (Book Castle, 1993)

Cobbe, H., *History of Luton Church* (George Bell and Sons, 1899)

Collett-White, J., *How Bedfordshire Voted*, Vols I and II, BHRS, Vols 85 and 87 (The Boydell Press, 2006, 2008)

Cook, C.R., *The Story of Limbury cum Biscot* (Colin R. Cook in association with Book Castle, 2007)

Craddock, D., *Where they Burnt the Town Hall Down* (Book Castle, 1999)

Currie, M.R., *Hospitals in Luton and Dunstable: An Illustrated History* (Advance Offset, 1982)

Darby, A.S., *A View From the Alley* (Luton Museum and Art Gallery, 1974)

Davis, F., *Luton, Past and Present* (W. Stalker, 1874)

Dony, J.G., *A History of Education in Luton* (The County Borough of Luton Museum and Art Gallery, 1970)

Dony, J.G. (on behalf of the WEA), *The Story of High Town* (Bedfordshire County Council, 1984)

Dyer, J., *Rhubarb and Custard: Luton Modern School & Luton Grammar School for Boys* (Book Castle, 2004)

Dyer, J., *The Stopsley Book* (Book Castle, 1998)

Dyer, J., *The Story of the Stopsley Schools* (Luton Museum and Art Gallery, 1989)

Dyer, J. and Dony, J., *The Story of Luton* (White Crescent Press, 1975)

Farr, G., *The History of a Family Firm* (Select Publishing, 2008)

Eckett, M., *Signals, A Railway Miscellany* (Book Castle, 2008)

Escott, B.E., *Twentieth-Century Women of Courage* (Sutton Publishing Ltd, 1999)

Field, C.D. (ed.), *Luton Odyssey: Reminiscences of Lily Field for 1915-52* (York Publishing Services Ltd, 2008)

Freeman, C., *Luton and the Hat Industry* (Borough of Luton Museum and Art Gallery, 1976)

Godber, J., *History of Bedfordshire 1066-1888* (Bedfordshire County Council, 1969)

Goodyear, S.A., *A Hatful of Music: The Dance Band Days in Luton, Dunstable and District* (Book Castle, 2003)

Grabham, E., *From Grand to Grove: Entertaining South Bedfordshire* (Book Castle, 2007)

Grundy, F. and Titmuss, R., *Report on Luton* (Gibbs, Bamforth & Co. Ltd, 1945)

Gurney, R., *Luton Poems* (Verulamium Press, 2005)

Hardisty, O., *Blitzing Vauxhall: A Dogsbody's War Diary* (Book Castle, 2005)

Hey, D., *The Oxford Companion to Local and Family History* (Oxford University Press, 1996)

Hinde, T. (ed.), *Domesday Book* (Guild Publishing, 1985)

Houfe, S. (ed.), *Through Visitors' Eyes* (Book Castle, 1990)

Luton in the 1930s (Luton Borough Council, 2001)

Luton News, Luton at War (White Crescent Press, 1982)

Madigan, J.T., *The Men who wore Straw Helmets: Policing Luton 1840-1974* (Book Castle, 1993)

Malcolmson, R. and P. (eds), *A Soldier in Bedfordshire 1941-2: The Diary of Private Denis Argent Royal Engineers*, BHRS, Vol. 88 (The Boydell Press, 2009)

Manzoor, S., *Greetings from Bury Park* (Bloomsbury Publishing, 2008)

Meadows, E. and Foster, N., *Saint Mary's Luton 1896-1976* (White Crescent Press Ltd, n.d. but after 1968)

Norcott, K.T., *Chalk on my Shoes: Memoirs of a Chiltern Childhood* (Book Castle, 2006)

Morris, J. (ed.), *Domesday Book Bedfordshire* (Phillimore, 1977)

Peaple, C.J., *The Blockers' Seaside: A Selective History of Leagrave* (Challney Community College, 1980)

Public Health Act (W. Clownes & Sons, 1850)

Richardson, J., *The Local Historian's Encyclopaedia* (Historical Publications Ltd, 1977)

Richer, A.F., *Bedfordshire Police 1840-1990* (Hooley, 1990)

Rogers, K., *The Stories and Secrets of Luton's Medieval Jewel* (St Mary's Parochial Church Council, 2000)

Schneider, J., *Exploring Past Times* (Manshead Archaeological Society of Dunstable, 1995)

Smith, S., *Pubs and Pints: The Story of Luton's Public Houses and Breweries* (Book Castle, 1995)

Smith, W., *Dunstable, Its History and Surroundings* (Bedfordshire County Council, 1980)

Spencer, R.G., *British Immigration Policy since 1939. The making of multi-racial Britain* (Routledge, 1997)

Thompson, J.S. (ed.), *Hundreds, Manors, Parishes and the Church* (BHRS, Vol. 69, 1990)

Victoria County History Bedfordshire (A. Constable & Co. Ltd, 1904)

Vigor, P.C., *Memories are Made of This* (Luton Museum and Art Gallery, 1983)

Vowles, G.A., *Century of Achievement: A History of Local Education Authorities in Bedfordshire 1903-2003* (Bedfordshire County Council, 2003)

Ward, A.J., *Strike Up the Band* (Book Castle, 2003)

Wash, R., *An Illustrated History of Luton Town* (Desert Island Books, 2004)

Wiltshire FHS, *The Book of Trades or Library of Useful Arts*, Vols I, II, III (reprinted 1977)

Wood, T. and Bunker, S., *A Hatful of Talent: The Founding of the University of Luton* (University of Luton Press, 1994)

EDUCATIONAL MATERIAL

Luton Museum Education Service, *Keep Smiling Through*, a Second World War Information Pack

Luton Museum Education Service, *Luton in the 1750s*, Luton Museum Learning Pack

Kilby, K., 'A Town and Its Trades, Luton, 1850', Bedfordshire Education Service (1983)

Town Directories and Year Books

Upstairs Downstairs Wardown House, an Information Pack from Luton Museum Education Service

WEA, *Blockers, Boaters and Boots: 50 Years of High Town* (Bedfordshire Leisure Services, 1984)

UNPUBLISHED

Kennett, D., *Luton: A Centenary History*

Moore, V., *Browns and Greens* (Putteridge, 1970)

Wing, M., *Murder in the Family*

NEWSPAPERS

Luton News and Souvenir Editions, available on microfilm

MAPS

Luton in 1815 from the 1904 *Year Book*

Map of Luton, 1855

Luton in 1876 (year of inauguration), E.A. Cumberland (Wardown Park Museum)

Luton and the hamlets, May 1891. Ordnance Survey 1-inch Bedfordshire (Dr James Dyer)

Map of Luton presented as a supplement to the *Luton District Year Book and Almanack*, 1904 (Wardown Park Museum)

Map of Luton based on the Ordnance Survey Map with sanction of HM Stationery Office, 1915 (Wardown Park Museum)

Index

Note: Numbers in **bold** refer to illustrations.

roads, 4, 6, 7, 33-40, **34-7**, 51, 178-9
Robert, Earl of Gloucester, 15, 21
Robert de Waudari, 15
Roman Catholic Church, 33, 131-2
Romans, 6-9
Rotherham family, 21, 24, 57
Round Green, 7, 2

St Albans, 7; St Albans Abbey, 20-1, 25
St George's Square, 187
Salt Way, 10
Salvation Army, 180
Saxons, 9-12; Saxon cemetery, 9
Scargill family, 67-8
Scottish community, 126-7
Second World War: air raids, **66**, **115**, **116**,
    115-17; blackout, 113-14; camouflage, 114,
    115; Civil Defence, 117-20; conscription,
    104, 112-13, 119-20; Eastern Command,
    117; evacuees, **112**, 113, 130; GIs (American
    servicemen), 117; Home Guard, 117-18;
    rationing, 109, 122; victory celebrations, 123,
    124
secondary education, 81-2, **82**
Sharpenhoe, 5
Sikhism, 137
Simon de Montfort, 16
Sixth Form College, 195
Skefko (SKF), 97, 121, 126
slave trade, 28
Someries, 24, **62-3**, 63-4, 89
de Someries family, 23, 63
Someries Farm, 24, 64
Sowerby family, 66
Station Gateway, 102
Stockwood Park, 24, 64-7, 104, **162**, **163**;
    Stockwood Park Discovery Centre, 2, 8, 10,
    17-18, 24, 65, 67, 69
Stone Age, 2-4, **4**
Stopsley, 2, **4**, 6, 10, 66, 89,170,
Sunday schools, 74-6, **75**, 145
swimming, 69, 151, **152**, 171
Sworder, T., 87-8

Tallebosc (Talibosc), 13
Tasciovanus, 7
technical education, 81, 84-5
temperance, 45, 144-5

theatres, 147-9, **149**
Thoidweg Way, 6
tithes, 20
Town Crier, 20, 109, **184**
town halls, **54**, 56, 110, **111**, 186-7, **187**
trades, 47-9
transportation, 28-9

UK Centre for Carnival Arts, 86
unitary authority, 173
University of Bedfordshire, 67, 85-6, 100-1,
    140

Vauxhall Motors, 95, 96-7, **96**, 106, 120-1, 141,
    171, 172
vestry, 50, 52
Vikings, 9-10
Voices Project, 133-5, **134**
Vyse & Sons, 92, 94, 111

Waller family, 56, 92
Waller Street, 187-93, **191-5**
Walter Wright Ltd, **94**, 95
Warden Hill, 1, 2, 4, 10
Wardown, 67-70, **68**, 108-9, 110, 111, 120, 122,
    140, 144, 153, **154**, **155**, 159, 171, 172
water supply and sanitation, 51
Watling Street, 7, 10
Waulud's Bank, 3, **3**, 4, 10, 195
Wellington Street, **39**
Welsh community, 127
Wenlock family, 23-4
Wenlok Jug, 24, **24**, 65
Wernher family, 20, 60-3, 104, 110-1, 187
Wessex, 10
Westly & Co. Ltd, 93, 121
Whipsnade Zoo, 122
Whitbread's Brewery, 88
Whiteley Hat Co., 94
William the Chamberlain, 13, 14
William the Conqueror, 13
William, Earl of Gloucester, 20
workhouse, 50, 51, 193
WVS, 119
Wycliffe, John, 25

York House School, 73